The Correlates of War: II

The Correlates of War: II

Testing Some Realpolitik Models

Edited by J. David Singer

THE FREE PRESS
A Division of Macmillan Publishing Co., Inc.
NEW YORK

Collier Macmillan Publishers
LONDON

To Stuart Bremer,

colleague nonpareil

Copyright © 1980 by The Free Press
A Division of Macmillan Publishing Co., Inc.

All rights reserved. No part of this book may be reproduced or transmitted in any form or by any means, electronic or mechanical, including photocopying, recording, or by any information storage and retrieval system, without permission in writing from the Publisher.

The Free Press
A Division of Macmillan Publishing Co., Inc.
866 Third Avenue, New York, N.Y. 10022

Collier Macmillan Canada, Ltd.

Library of Congress Catalog Card Number: 79-1956

Printed in the United States of America

printing number

1 2 3 4 5 6 7 8 9 10

Library of Congress Cataloging in Publication Data

Main entry under title:

The Correlates of war.

    Includes bibliographical references.
    CONTENTS: v. 1. Research origins and rationale.
v. 2. Testing some realpolitik models.
    1. War. 2. International relations. I. Singer,
Joel David
U21.2.C67   327'.11   79-1956
ISBN 0-02-929010-4

Contents

Acknowledgments   vii
About the Contributors   ix
Introduction   xiii

I. METHODOLOGICAL PERSPECTIVES

1. The Trials of Nations: An Improbable Application
   of Probability Theory *Stuart A. Bremer*   3
2. The Measurement of System Structure *James Lee Ray*   36

II. ACCOUNTING FOR THE ONSET OF WAR

3. National Capabilities and War Proneness *Stuart A. Bremer*   57
4. Status, Capabilities, and Major Power Conflict
   Charles S. Gochman   83
5. Influence Strategies and Interstate Conflict
   Russell J. Leng   124

III. ACCOUNTING FOR THE EXPANSION OF WAR

6. Interstate Alliances: Their Reliability and the Expansion
   of War *Alan Ned Sabrosky*   161
7. Wider Wars and Restless Nights: Major Power
   Intervention in Ongoing War *Yoshinobu Yamamoto
   and Stuart A. Bremer*   199

IV. ACCOUNTING FOR THE OUTCOMES OF WAR

8. The Costs of Combat: Death, Duration, and Defeat
   Cynthia A. Cannizzo   233
9. Postwar Industrial Growth *Hugh Wheeler*   258

V. THE FINDINGS AND THEIR IMPLICATIONS

10. An Interim Summary and Evaluation *Karl W. Deutsch*   287

    Notes   297

    Combined References   305

    Correlates of War Project Bibliography   323

Acknowledgments

Because all the contributors to this volume are associated with the *Correlates of War* project and have conducted most of their research while studying, visiting, or teaching at Michigan, there will be an inevitable overlap in our debts. First and foremost, we are indebted to one another; we have learned from and interacted with one another in a myriad of ways and contexts in recent years. And, even as many of us have moved away to other centers in America, Europe, and Asia, we have remained something of an "invisible college," exchanging ideas, data, findings, interpretations, and manuscripts and, in a few cases, continuing or initiating research collaboration.

Among those who have contributed to these papers, in addition to those who appear as our ten authors or co-authors, are Melvin Small, Michael Wallace, Richard Stoll, Michael Champion, John Stuckey, Bruce Bueno de Mesquita, Urs Luterbacher, Richard Eichenberg, Steven Meyer, Lutz Erbring, Thomas Kselman, Robert Rood, Michael Brecher, Alan Levy, and Fred Klein. In addition, most of the research reported here was conducted during the period when the project was supported by the U.S. National Science Foundation, under grants 010058 and 33120, and the University Consortium for World Order Studies.

About the Contributors

Stuart A. Bremer received his Ph.D. in Political Science from Michigan State University (1970) and has taught at the University of Michigan. Currently a Research Fellow at the International Institute for Comparative Social Research, Science Center Berlin, where he leads a research group concerned with global models, he is the author of *Simulated Worlds* (1977), as well as of a number of articles.

Cynthia Cannizzo received her Ph.D. in Political Science from the University of Michigan (1976) and is now an Assistant Professor of Political Science and a Research Associate of the Mershon Center at Ohio State University. Her current research focuses on problems and effects of conventional arms transfers. Her publications include "Capability Distribution and Major Power War Experience, 1816-1965" (1978), and (as editor) *The Gun-Merchants: Politics and Policy of the Major Arms Suppliers* (1979).

Karl W. Deutsch received his J.U. Dr. from Charles University in Prague (1938) and his Ph.D. from Harvard (1951) and is now Professor of Political Science at Harvard. He has taught at Massachusetts Institute of Technology and Yale, and served on visiting appointments at several universities in Europe and America. His current research, in collaboration with Stuart Bremer in Berlin, focuses on the development of a computer model of the global system. Among his many publications are *Nationalism and Social Communication* (1953 and 1966); *The Nerves of Government* (1963); *The Analysis of International Relations* (1968); *Politics and Government* (1974);

and the forthcoming handbook *Methods of Political Behavior Research.*

Charles S. Gochman received his Ph.D. in Political Science from the University of Michigan (1975) and is currently an Assistant Professor in the Department of Political Science and a faculty member of the Center for Arms Control and International Security Studies at the University of Pittsburgh. In collaboration with historian Thomas Kselman of the University of Michigan he is currently completing a book on interstate conflict since the Napoleonic Wars.

Russell J. Leng is Professor Political Science and Dean of Sciences at Middlebury College. He received his Ph.D. from American University (1967) and has held visiting appointments at American University and the University of Michigan. He is currently collaborating with Hugh Wheeler on an investigation of influence strategies and serious disputes. His published papers include "Behavioral Indicators of War Proneness in Bilateral Conflicts" (1974) and "Toward a Multi-Theoretical Typology of International Behavior" (1977).

James Lee Ray received his Ph.D. in World Politics from the University of Michigan (1974), taught at the State University College in Fredonia, New York, and is now Assistant Professor of Political Science at the University of New Mexico. He is currently engaged in empirical analyses of hypotheses based on dependency theory. His publications include "Status Inconsistency and War Involvement in Europe, 1816-1970" (1974), and *Global Politics* (1978).

Alan Ned Sabrosky received his Ph.D. in World Politics from the University of Michigan (1976). He has been affiliated with Middlebury College, the Foreign Policy Research Institute, and the U.S. Military Academy, and is now teaching at Catholic University. He is currently investigating the problem of war expansion. His publications include *Blue-Collar Soldiers? Unionization and the U.S. Military* (1977); *Defense Manpower Policy: A Critical Reappraisal* (1978); and *The Eagle's Brood: American Civil-Military Relations in the 1980s* (1979).

J. David Singer received his Ph.D. from New York University (1956) and is a Professor of Political Science at the University of Michigan. He has taught world politics at Vassar, Oslo, Geneva, and Mannheim, and has consulted for such agencies as the U.S. Arms Control and Disarmament Agency, the Department of the Navy, and the Office of the Secretary of Defense. Among his earlier books are: *Financing*

International Organization (1961); *Deterrence, Arms Control, and Disarmament* (1962); *Human Behavior and International Politics* (1965); *Quantitative International Politics: Insights and Evidence* (1968); *The Wages of War, 1816-1965: A Statistical Handbook* (with Melvin Small, 1972); *Beyond Conjecture in International Politics: Abstracts of Data-Based Research* (with Susan Jones, 1972); *The Study of International Politics: A Guide to Sources for the Student, Teacher and Researcher* (with Dorothy LaBarr, 1976); and *The Correlates of War: I—Research Origins and Rationale* (1979).

Hugh Wheeler received his Ph.D. in World Politics from the University of Michigan (1975), taught at the University of British Columbia, and is now Assistant Professor of Political Science at Middlebury College. In collaboration with Russell Leng, he is currently investigating the relationship between influence strategies and serious dispute. His published papers include "The Effects of War on Industrial Growth," *Society* (1975).

Yoshinobu Yamamoto received his B.A. (1966) and M.A. (1968) in International Relations from Tokyo University, and his Ph.D. in World Politics from the University of Michigan (1974). Now an Associate Professor of Political Science at Saitama University, Japan, he is studying the relationship between politics and economics at the international level. He has published, in Japanese academic journals, several articles on international conflict.

Introduction

This volume of the *Correlates of War* series differs from the first one in several significant ways. Most evident is the fact that the editor figures prominently in each of the papers in Volume I but is barely visible in those found in this volume. As their authors will tell you, I was not exactly passive here, but the work in each of these is decidedly that of the young scholar whose name appears on it. Many of these papers are, not surprisingly, derived from research originally undertaken for the doctoral dissertation. And, whereas Volume I was so arranged as to reveal a logical (and essentially chronological) evolution of one scholar's thinking, the organization of Volume II reflects the examination of separate but related questions by several minds at approximately the same time. In the former volume, a great deal of intellectual history had to be covered, but, with most of that behind us, we concentrate here on matters less preliminary and more substantive.

Another of the easily discernible differences is that all of the papers in Volume I had already been published elsewhere, whereas none of those found here had yet been set in print. We include here only a modest fraction of the analyses done within (and at the fringes of) the project to date. First, a fair number of analyses that we have conducted are not yet written up in any publishable form and serve rather as internal working papers from which we try to build. Second, there are those papers that were completed long enough ago that it would have made little sense to hold them until this collection was ready for publication. In addition to the three analyses that were reprinted in Volume I, a good many others have already appeared elsewhere, and their full citations will be found in the Project Bibliography. Then, third, when a good paper is completed, it is difficult to defer its publication, especially after it has been presented and well received at a professional meeting. Thus, despite the possibility of eventual inclusion in this volume, a number of our more recent papers "got away" but several now appear in *Explaining War* (1979).

Turning to more substantive differences, one on which we dwell here, as well as in quite a few of the papers that follow, is the extent to which the earlier volume reflects not only a heavy involvement in immediate policy issues, but an overly optimistic sense of how much is known about the dynamics of international conflict. Whereas that first volume only *ends* with papers reflecting our effort to explain the incidence of war, this second volume *begins and ends* with work reflecting that goal. The policy analyst and peace activist who thought that we might already know enough about the problem to begin pressing a given set of solutions in the 1950s is now, in the 1970s, working with a research team whose dominant mark is that of agnosticism.

That agnosticism, though it leads us in a clear research direction, reflects two different considerations. First, it reflects our scientific belief that not nearly enough evidence is in to support *any* theoretical model that purports to explain the occurrence and incidence of international war. Second, it reflects our political belief that, even if we and other researchers *were* sold on a given model, its effect on the policy makers of the world would be negligible. That is, such a model would almost inevitably be more complex than, and probably quite different from, the kind of models—implicitly as well as explicitly— used by most decision makers. Thus, a substantial amount of *empirical evidence* would be necessary to weaken the hold of the several conventional wisdoms that guide foreign policy elites and counterelites as they try to cope with the war/peace problem, now and in the future. As intimated, then, we are driven in the direction of systematic empirical investigation not only because it seems the most promising strategy for unraveling the theoretical question of "why war?," but also because it seems the most likely way of weaning the influentials and their critics away from those inconsistent, often self-serving, and probably incorrect "theories" that have led nations to such grief in the past.

Some Metatheoretical Preliminaries

This volume, like its predecessor, is intended not only to bring the research community up to date on a major project, but to serve as a textbook in the broadest sense of the word. All too many students (as well as teachers, journalists, and practitioners) have little understanding of the ways in which knowledge is generated and codified, and all too many of us in the world politics field have the notion that "truths" in the form of theoretical propositions are generated by good thinking or flashes of intuition, not to mention long experience. Although all these may be necessary, none is sufficient, and I would be pleased if these volumes not only help to advance our knowledge about international conflict, but also illuminate some of the problems that are encountered in the search for knowledge about any macrosocial phenomena.

Returning, then, to the matter of agnosticism, and the danger of believing too readily in one or another explanatory model, the problem is equally serious for the theorist and the practitioner. Having addressed the latter's role and the *applicability* of knowledge to the policy process in Volume I, let us focus here on the theoretical side of the question and concentrate more on the acquisition and codification of knowledge.

Once the researcher has decided on the general phenomena to be explained and has developed indicators of the outcome variable(s), the difficult issue of explanatory variables must be addressed. This is, of course, another way of saying that alternative theoretical models must be considered and/or constructed, on the basis of available evidence as well as speculation. In some of the more advanced sectors of social science (perhaps microeconomics or electoral behavior), there may be appreciable evidence behind a widely accepted framework, merely requiring the researcher to select among slightly varying versions of the accepted model, make certain refinements, and get on with the investigation.

But in a research area characterized by considerable speculation, widely disparate models, and little evidence—much of it inconsistent—this is no easy task. Worse yet, because so much is at stake, and many researchers care so much, students of international conflict are often too willing to seize on the most intellectually plausible or cognitively comfortable model available. For centuries, scholars and practitioners have written, spoken, and—alas—acted with great conviction about the causes of war and the conditions of peace. As we might surmise, these putative explanations have varied not only from generation to generation and decade to decade—usually in a cyclical and noncumulative fashion, but also from nation to nation, ideology to ideology, and class to class (Howard, 1978). My colleagues and I hope that the approach taken here will help to put an end to faddism, and that the kind of modeling and analysis we use will encourage a steady and cumulative movement toward increasingly powerful and accurate explanatory models.

Before laying out the variables, the theoretical assumptions, and the framework, let me refer briefly to a few of the more critical metatheoretical assumptions that shape our research strategy. Throughout, it should be stressed that, on a project such as this, the director can hardly claim to speak for all of his colleagues and students. Though we continue to share a good many epistemological and theoretical—as well as normative—predispositions, some important differences nevertheless remain. In my judgment, this is as it should be, not only because diversity can be stimulating and mutually educational, but also because it is inappropriate for a scholar to impose his views on his students. Further, as anyone who knows my associates can attest, any such effort would almost certainly come to nought.

Exploration and Verification

Turning, then, to the more important of our assumptions regarding research strategy, and bearing in mind that not all of the contributors to this volume will share my views, let me first mention the familiar inductive-deductive issue. My position is spelled out in more detail elsewhere (Hoole and Zinnes, 1976) so we can be brief here. Few scientists would challenge the proposition that theory building, in the sense of acquiring and codifying knowledge, requires a healthy mix of formal modeling and empirical observation, but the consensus evaporates when it comes to the proportions in the mix and the order in which they are used.

My earlier comment regarding the need for theoretical agnosticism is particularly germane here, given the contemporarily available mix of theoretical formulations and empirical evidence. Although few of the former satisfy the criteria of internal consistency or disconfirmability, most of them have, for one observer or another, a certain plausibility. But this just is not good enough, and, even if they were to be translated into clear, formal, elegant statements from which nontrivial deductions can be made, the task is only begun. Quite essential is the decomposition of such models into manageable and parsimonious language, operationalization of the variables and parameters and then construction of their indicators, followed by acquisition of the relevant data and the appropriate analyses thereof.

One difficulty with this strategy, however, is that we are in no position to select or formulate a given model with much confidence. Not only is there little evidence in support or refutation of most of the putative explanations, but there is little more evidence of either the purely descriptive or the correlational sort; the basic existential mapping has barely begun. As Northrop (1971) and others have noted, every science must go through the "natural history" stage prior to the conjecture and refutation stage (Popper, 1962). In other words, there is the logic and science of exploration, discovery, and heuristics (Lakatos, 1976), and there is also the logic and science of disconfirmation, and, in the international conflict field, we seem to be unambiguously in the early stages of the first. It follows, then, that we need, if anything, to put more of our resources into these inductive activities at the moment.

None of this is to either deny the advantages of more formal theorizing or the disadvantages of empirical work that is not informed by a well-articulated model. One thinks, for instance, of the more solid basis for "causal" inferences that are possible when one's empirical findings are interpreted in the context of a formal model. Similarly, one thinks of all the pitfalls that await the researcher who is carried away by "goodness of fit." Just as we dare make no claim to success on the basis of a model's elegance, popularity, or logical coherence, we dare not forget that goodness of fit may be necessary, but hardly sufficient. In any event, one finds in this volume a rather clear reflection of these considerations. Two of the papers (Bremer's "Trials of Nations" and the Yamomoto-Bremer paper on intervention into ongoing war) are heavily oriented toward the formal side, although each rests equally on a solid empirical base. Similarly, even the most inductive of the papers take, as their point of departure, a well-articulated, if merely verbal, theoretical model.

A General Systems Taxonomy

Closely related, given the difficulty of comparing and integrating the results of separate empirical analyses, is a second major component in our research strategy: the development of a taxonomy that might maximize such comparability and then go on to enhance the integration and codification of the empirical findings. The language of the general systems approach (Miller, 1978; Singer, 1971)—which is appreciably different from the approaches of Parsons or Easton in sociology and political science, as well as from the systems analysis approach of operations research—seems quite appropriate to this task, in as much as we hope to integrate not only the work of diverse researchers within this project, but that of others with an even greater diversity of concepts and explanatory models.

Because of its atheoretical and essentially content-free attributes, the general systems taxonomy offers a limited set of moderately abstract variables (or, more precisely, classes of variables) that fall together nicely in a framework that has little tendency to push the results into any given theoretical direction and is equally hospitable to radically different—and hence allegedly incommensurate—theoretical perspectives. Whereas all too many frameworks include categories that virtually foreclose all but the intended interpretation, this one is remarkably multitheoretical, if not downright agnostic. To illustrate, if one were working from a geopolitical orientation (such as Spykman, 1944; Mackinder, 1942; or Choucri and North, 1975), there would be little difficulty in incorporating such material variables as national resource limits and distance to foreign supplies or such relational ones as industrial interdependence or intersecting spheres of influence. Similarly, a Marxian orientation (Lenin, 1939; Hobson, 1938) might be pursued by incorporating such structural attributes of the nations as surplus profit rates or such cultural ones as the extent and depth of class consciousness in the urban proletariat.

In addition to its hospitality to contending explanatory models and its ability to ease the cumulative comparison and integration of results from many types of investigation, the movement of world politics and other social science scholars toward this sort of framework could appreciably enhance our ability—and hence our incentive—to communicate with one another. Finally, if one believes, as I certainly do, that virtually all the models now in circulation are woefully incomplete and that anything approximating a coherent theory will have to embrace such explanatory variables as those of an economic, strategic, psychological, and geographic sort, again the general systems orientation should offer one possible framework for bringing these factors together in an integrated fashion.

Levels of Aggregation

Yet a third metatheoretical consideration concerns the level of aggregation at which to look for our explanatory variables. We begin with the premise that any ultimately acceptable theory must be reductionist, in the sense that decisions linking certain causal factors and the war/no-war outcomes are taken by human groups whose individual and collective beliefs and behaviors must therefore be included in the explanatory process. But at the same time we suspect that it is prudent to "black box" the microlevel decision processes until we have a much more complete picture of the relationships between certain macrolevel phenomena and our outcomes. The better our understanding of those patterns, the more decisively we can sort out the painfully large number of decision-making models; if, for example, we can find no regular association between foreign investment or trade and the incidence of war, we would be more justified in excluding inputs from economic interest groups from our decision-making model.

There is, of course, a second—and less evident—reason for leaving the conflict decision process unobserved for the moment. This is the strong suspicion that there is rather little variation in that process and its decision rules as we look across types of nations and across periods of time. Although I suspect this to be true for a wide range of routine decisions, from diplomatic to economic, I suspect that it is particularly true for those decisions that are made in the midst of conflict and confrontation. And, as every researcher knows, if there is little or no variation across cases in one's explanatory variables, they can hardly be expected to account for variation in so radically fluctuating an outcome as war.

In any event, this is merely a working assumption and, like others that are outlined in the following paragraphs, is open to empirical challenge; although there is already some evidence on these questions, it seems sufficiently inconclusive to justify the tentative positions we take here.

Deterministic and Stochastic Elements

Another major assumption is that our search for regularities implies neither deterministic laws nor constant ones. Not only do we expect our ultimate explanations for different types of war to have a strong—and, if such fields as metallurgy or physical mechanics offer any guidance, not necessarily diminishing—probabilistic component. We also expect the relationships amongst our variables to show discernible change across time; as certain basic attributes of the global system change, the relative potency of our explanatory variables can also be expected to change, and one of our tasks is to account for the changes in what it is that accounts for the incidence of war. Given the frequency with which critics tell us that there can be no scientific theory *because* these relationships undergo change in magnitude and/or direction, this latter point needs particular emphasis.

One way of illuminating these notions is to draw an analogy with genetics and procreation. At any given point in the evolution of a species, its genetic pool has a certain distribution of genes and chromosomes, and that distribution is itself a product of both deterministic and stochastic "laws." Thus, if a given pair of creatures mate at that point, there are two sets of probabilities: (1) that of any progeny resulting at all, and (2) that of the particular characteristics of such progeny. If fertilization occurs, the probability of issue is a virtual certainty, and, if live birth occurs, the gender is fully determined, if not fully predictable. However, whereas such attributes as the weight and strength of the offspring are likewise skewed in one direction or another, neither of these is fully determined. Finally, the next time these same two parents procreate, the second offspring's gender and other attributes can easily be quite different from those of the first.

Now, if we think of the attributes of the global system as analogous to those of the genetic pool, of the attributes of the interacting states as analogous to those of the interacting mates, the probability of war or no war as analogous to that of a boy or girl, and the probability of its expansion or extended duration as analogous to the weight and strength of the offspring, the point should be clear. In international conflict, as in procreation, there is a mix of deterministic and stochastic laws at work, but, whereas geneticists have a reasonably solid command of these laws and the way in which they operate, political scientists are still searching for those that affect the unfolding of international conflict. Thus, genetic counseling is today a respectable and useful sector of the medical profession, whereas security policy counseling remains somewhere between fortune telling and advice to the lovelorn!

The Theoretical Framework and Its Assumptions

Whereas the focus so far in this section has been on certain metatheoretical issues of a fairly general applicability, the discussions that follow are more closely related to the theoretical framework within which our research has begun and to the more important assumptions that inform the model. Bearing in mind that we use the word model to convey something more than a taxonomy but considerably less than a theory, let me summarize the general class of variables around which the model is being constructed.

Classes of Explanatory Variables and Their Relative Potency

There are two ways in which to arrange a verbal summary of our theoretical framework. One is in the order of the postulated potency of the classes of variables, and the other is in the temporal order in which these variables fall along the road to the war/no-war denouement. But, because the order is approximately the same in each, there is no awkward trade-off, and a rather direct and clear overview is easily obtained.

"In the beginning," there is the global system and its regional subsystems, manifesting a variety of structural, cultural, and material attributes; of these attributes, some remain relatively constant for the entire time period, others change slowly in a trendlike, cyclical, or random fashion, and yet others change more rapidly in one of the above patterns. The *structural* attributes of the global system or any of its regional subsystems may be thought of in terms of horizontal and vertical dimensions. Among the horizontal ones are diplomatic, alliance, trade, and IGO (intergovernmental organization) membership configurations, as well as the isomorphism of those separate configurations, plus the direction or rate of change in any or all of them. Among the vertical ones are the rank configurations of the system's members in terms of military capability, industrial strength, diplomatic importance, and so forth; again, there is the isomorphism among these rankings and the direction or rate of change.

By *cultural* attributes, we mean the distribution patterns of perceptions, preferences, and predictions held by elites, counterelites, and publics on matters germane to international conflict. Given the stance that we take on national attributes in general and on the decision process in particular, it should not be surprising that we have payed little attention so far to the cultural variables. This is not because they are not important; with some modest changes in outlook on the part of a fairly modest fraction of the world's population, war *might* disappear from the face of the earth. But the evidence, such as it is, strongly suggests that these perceptions and predictions (more than preferences, in our judgment) that are so necessary to war are (1) too invariant across time and space and (2) too heavily dependent on the structural attributes of the system and its national components. I have dwelled on this problem in the system transformation context (Singer, 1977) as well as the deterrence (1962) and the diplomatic influence (1963) contexts and need not pursue the subject any further here. Suffice it to say that, in my view, the psychocultural variables are the ones that will need to be changed first if the incidence of war is to be reduced but that these are unlikely to change until much more evidence in support of specific *structural* changes is in, disseminated, and evaluated. But, as I have suggested (1973), this process will require not only a great deal more knowledge about the structural and behavioral factors that make for conflict, its escalation, and war, but an epistemological revolution that will permit more human beings to seek, understand, evaluate, and respond to that knowledge. Given the performance of the social sciences, as well as their treatment by political elites and others, the prospects are not very encouraging.

Turning next to the third set of attribute variables—*material* or physical attributes of the system, its subsystems, and its components—we find that class of phenomena whose explanatory popularity has been all too similar to a roller coaster. Geography, demography, topography, natural resources, and technology have waxed and waned as the allegedly key variables in understanding international conflict. Several times during the nineteenth century, especially when European colonialism was at its apogee, territory and bodies and minerals and foodstuffs loomed large in the scholarly literature as well as in partisan tracts and governmental memoranda.

This emphasis then reappeared in the 1930s, was largely obliterated by the emphasis on ideology and military strategy in the Cold War period, and has now come back as the lodestone variable in an appreciable fraction of the scholarly and official literature in many parts of the world (Choucri and North, 1975; Meadows et al., 1972; Mesarovich and Pestel, 1974). Although any cumulatively oriented researcher would take a dim view of this cyclical preoccupation, one would nevertheless agree that these are far from negligible in their objective importance. Thus, we give considerable attention to the material capabilities of the states and coalitions thereof. This class of variables is an integral part of the explanatory model in five of the eight theoretical analyses in this volume, and it plays an equally important role throughout the project.

Once we have considered attributes of these three basic types applied to system, subsystem, and components, the second major class of variables is that of *relationships*. We mean here, of course, not the statistical or causal relationships amongst variables, but the bonds, links, and associations between and among the states that comprise the system. These, as already suggested in our discussion of structural variables, are diplomatic, military, and economic, as well as geographic. That is, states may be bound, for example, via the presence of diplomatic missions, membership in intergovernmental organizations, and economic interdependence, along with geographic proximity, location of seas and mountains, and so forth.

Well worth noting next is that the *relational* dimension is quite distinct from the *similarity* dimension. Both conceptually and empirically, there is little reason to treat the bonds and links between states as identical to the similarities and differences of states; to a limited extent, one finds that differences are associated with distance and similarities with closeness, but the distinction must never be blurred. Similarly, the structural attributes of any system (such as its polarity) may often be inferred from, and measured by, the relationships (such as alliances) among its components. But, again, they are not the same thing.

The final class of explanatory variables in the model is the *behavioral:* those external actions and interactions manifested by the national governments as the conflict process unfolds. These are seen not only as flowing from the systemic conditions and dyadic relationships of the contending states and, then, in turn modifying those two sets of phenomena in subsequent iterations. They are also—and primarily—seen as the connecting link between the ecological context and the result of the conflict sequence in the form of a war or no-war outcome. These, then, are the major sets of variables in our basic interstate conflict model, and, when combined with the theoretical assumptions articulated below, we should begin to see more clearly how they might be expected to impinge on one another and on the incidence of international war.

One of the first steps to take in moving from vague hunch to testable model is that of winnowing out one's list of explanatory variables. It is well known that if we incorporate enough variables in a model, we can get closer and closer to accounting for all of the variance in the outcome. We do so, however, at the cost not only of parsimony and elegance, but, more importantly, the ability to make theoretical sense of the results. As the taxonomy outlined above reminds us, there is no end to the number and variety of variables and indicators that might plausibly be incorporated into the explanatory scheme. As a matter of fact, one of the more important differences between the ideographic approach of many historians and traditional political analysts and the nomothetic approach of the behavioral scientist is that the former try to "explain" a *single* case with a plethora of variables, whereas the latter try to account (in either the statistical or causal sense) for the outcomes in *many* cases on the basis of a minimal number of variables.

In any event, we have here the equivalent of a matrix of variables to choose from, with the rows representing the several levels of aggregation (individual, group, organization, state, region, globe, etc.) and the columns representing the classes of variables (attributes, relationships, and behaviors). What theoretical assumptions do we operate from as we select from such a matrix? The first is that international conflict is best understood in terms of an unfolding escalatory process, from which there are not only many exits, but also some choice points at which, if exit is *not* selected, the probability of war can rise appreciably. A corollary is that different classes of variables will exercise differing effects on that probability, depending upon the stage of the escalatory process. Let us, then, outline those stages.

Temporal Stages in the Conflict Framework

At the earliest point and the lowest level is mere rivalry, a relationship characterized by mutual salience and in which the ratio of competitive to cooperative interactions crosses, and remains above, some discernible threshold for several years. We have, for the present, no interest in this phenomenon of rivalry because (1) there is so much of it, (2) it barely rises above the "noise" level in the system, (3) it often fades away as readily as it appears, (4) it stems from a bewildering array of sources, (5) it is not particularly dangerous, and (6) even if it were, it will be a long, long time before we have the knowledge and the will to modify all those attributes of the global system and its national components that make such rivalry an inexorable by-product of membership in the contemporary system.

But, if there is little that can be done to ameliorate rivalry and there is no great incentive to search for those solutions, the picture is quite different when we move on in time and up the conflict ladder from the relationship of rivalry to that of disputatiousness. This more conflictful relationship is marked by behavior that is explicitly designed to thwart or to punish the other protagonist and implies a significant allocation of attention and resources to that objective. Highly valued interests (however defined and by whomever) are now threatened and defended, with disputes falling into the category of either mild or serious. In a *mild dispute*, the governments select from among the entire range of diplomatic, political, and economic instrumentalities, but, no matter how intensively or effectively they are utilized, the interaction remains nonmilitary. In a *serious dispute*, however, one or more of the protagonists invokes military instrumentalities explicitly for the first time, and these can be of three distinct sorts: (1) an explicit *threat* to use military force under certain contingencies, (2) the *display* of military force in the context of the dispute, and (3) the actual *use* of military force, short of war.

Although we have no idea of the number of mild disputes (not to mention the far more ubiquitous rivalries) that have occurred since the Congress of Vienna, we now know that there have been about 300 serious disputes involving one or more major powers in the 1816-1975 period. Our estimate is that this number would be perhaps 700-800 if all sovereign states were included, even though the *possible* number of disputatious dyads would lead us to expect a much larger figure. Major powers not only get into war much more frequently than other states, as Bremer's paper on national war proneness shows, but they also get into many more of those military confrontations that mark the boundary between mild and serious disputes. More interesting than this speculation (and much of the data, as well as synopses of each major power dispute, will be in a forthcoming handbook by Gochman and Kselman) is the fact that only about 10% of these serious disputes go all the way to war. War—defined as sustained combat involving regular armed forces of two or more sovereign states and leading to at least 1,000 battle fatalities among combatant personnel—is the most dramatic stage in our model; *The Wages of War* (Singer and Small, 1972) present the coding rules, rationales, and resulting data sets. But the onset of war is not the final stage in the escalation model.

International war not only occurs (with an almost clockwork regularity of six times per decade, if we include colonial and imperial, as well as interstate wars), but continues for periods ranging from a few days to a few years. Furthermore, although most international wars begin as dyadic wars, additional states intervene with appreciable frequency. Thus, the next stage is that of war expansion. And, as Iklé (1971) and others remind us, *Every War Must End*, bringing us to the termination stage. Finally—because the consequences of war are likely to affect the probability of successive war—we treat war outcome, measured here in terms of military victory and defeat, plus demographic and industrial costs, as our final stage before closing the feedback loop.

The Decision Process

Having laid out the several stages in the conflict process and having examined some of their implications, we can now take a closer look at the assumptions we make regarding the decisions that mark the several stages in that process. And, because we insist on black-boxing these phenomena, leaving unobserved for the present what goes on in the black box, it is incumbent on us to make explicit our notions—stated rather baldly for lack of space—as to what happens, and why. Turning first to the general decision rules that govern most states in most conflictful interactions, we begin with the assumption that governmental decision makers are highly responsive to, but considerably adept at moulding, the articulated and aggregated interests of the various sectors and strata in their societies. Thus, every national security decision will reflect, directly or indirectly, the pluralistic distribution of power within that society, be it near the autocratic or democratic end of the spectrum. From this, it follows that a central and continuing preoccupation of the decisional elite is to remain in office, despite the dramatic range in size, type, ethnicity, level of industrialization, and so forth.

With that objective reasonably secured, their next preoccupation is with minimizing foreign intervention into their state's domestic affairs, and thus with minimizing the influence of others on their foreign and military behavior. Put differently, the second preoccupation is to maximize national autonomy. This is, of course, convergent with the classical realpolitik view (e.g., Morgenthau, 1951), but it treats the acquisition of national "power" as an objective that is both limited in scope and *instrumental* in character, rather than suggesting that power is pursued as an *intrinsically* desirable asset, of which there can never be enough.

Another way to look at these assumptions is to think of the decision process in terms of the choices confronting the decision makers. When the options are relatively numerous, as they are in most normal interstate interactions that occur under a roughly equal mix of competition and cooperation, things are far from determined. Domestic opinion is usually diffuse and far from crystallized, and the possible range of the other government's responses to a given move is quite broad. Further, the secondary and tertiary consequences of a given move are not only difficult to predict, but they are also not likely to be dramatically desirable or undesirable; regardless of the move selected, life will go on pretty much as it has.

However, as the relationship takes on increasing salience as well as increasing competitiveness, and the protagonists have moved into the mild dispute stage, the predictability of the others' response may not become much better, but its consequences certainly become more serious. Now, more is at stake, domestic interests are more clearly and vigorously articulated, and thus more discernibly aggregated, less diffuse, and more crystallized. As a result, the range of options tends to be appreciably diminished. And, if the protagonists escalate the conflict further, and find themselves in a military confrontation—thus marking the onset of a serious dispute—those conditions become even more pronounced. Domestic pressures are stronger and more dichotomized, the choice is in some approximate sense reduced to war or no war, with the range of no-war actions similarly truncated, and the consequences of either move are likely to be dramatic.

Further, to carry one's state to the brink and then back off is not only difficult to achieve, but can be costly in its consequences. Domestically, one's popularity and support must almost inevitably suffer, and, abroad, one's credibility is seriously eroded. Thus, the more constant internal attributes of the state itself are likely to diminish in their potency, whereas the attributes of the system (global and regional) in terms of alignments and of capability distributions are likely to take on greater force, as are, of course, the relative capabilities of the protagonists.

Throughout the entire escalatory process, certain choices become less and less probable and others become more and more probable. If the die are not yet finally cast, they have increasingly been replaced by a single coin with only two faces. Of course, the *objectively* available options, even at the brink of war, remain relatively numerous, but many of them require behavior that "just isn't done," and this seems to hold not only for the lengthy time span under consideration, but also for the allegedly very diverse range of cultures, modal personalities, and the like. To paraphrase Gertrude Stein, in conflict "a state is a state is a state," and, if this premise is correct, we should be quite justified in deferring any thorough investigation into the black box of governmental decision making until we have more carefully sorted out which behaviors occur under which particular conditions.

In sum, we remain—at this juncture in our overall investigation—satisfied that our working assumptions and the research strategy they imply are appropriate to the tasks at hand. But, given their obvious vulnerability to empirical—or perhaps even logical—challenge, it should come as no surprise that we hold to them in a relatively tentative manner. As with all researchers, we recognize the necessity to make, and to articulate, a number of simplifying assumptions in order to get on with the job, and as with most prudent researchers, we try to remember that they are *only* assumptions.

From Framework to Model

As already suggested, we use the word "theory" in this project in a more reverent fashion than is customary. We do not use it interchangeably with assumption, hunch, suspicion, or correlation, taxonomy, typology, framework, paradigm, or model, and do use it only to mean a body of codified knowledge that purports to explain the distribution of a given set of outcomes. Similarly, it seems to me that the word "model" should also be used more carefully, and we thus treat it as the bare bones of a theory: the specification of variables and the hypothesized direction (if not the strength) of the relationships among them. As a model is tested against the empirical evidence, revised, and tested again, it gradually looks more like a theory. It may be modest in scope or limited in empirical domain and generality, but if it (1) contains an explanatory mechanism that is credible to a fair number of other specialists and (2) is consonant with the observed phenomena in the referent world, it qualifies as a theory in our lexicon. Thus, the line between model and theory need not be too sharp, and the same holds for the lines among framework, taxonomy, and model. The key difference is in the specification of the direction of the relationships among the variables, or more precisely, the *indicators* of these variables. Whereas a taxonomy identifies the variables and a model specifies the "nature" of their connection, a framework merely tells us, however imprecisely, which variables are thought to be connected.

Having thus identified the classes of variables (but not specified those falling in each class, given the variety of queries examined in this volume) and having spelled out a number of our metatheoretical and theoretical assumptions, the next step would be to articulate our theoretical framework and then convert it into a model. But, as should be all too evident, that last step is just not possible. We are—in this volume—at too early a stage in our model building, index constructing, data generating, and hypothesis testing to propose a model that is sufficiently precise and sufficiently general to be of much use. Too many of our submodels (or multivariate hypotheses) have yet to be put to the empirical test, and these are not only quite diverse, but not yet fully compatible. The latter confession may seem inconsistent with my claims for the general systems taxonomy, but as I indicate in the paragraphs that follow, a variety of scientific and pedagogical considerations would make full integratability of these submodels premature. And a reading of the papers that constitute this volume will, I think, demonstrate the wisdom of "deferring gratification"; there is still too much brush-clearing to be done, simply in the sense of ascertaining what goes with what. Hence our distinction between research of an exploratory sort and that of a confirmatory sort, to which we point in the near future.

Here, then, we merely reiterate that we view international conflicts as passing through stages: (1) rivalry, marked by an ongoing imbalance between competitive and cooperative interactions; (2) mild dispute, marked by one or both parties' resort to nonmilitary measures to thwart, resist, or damage the other; (3) serious dispute, marked by one or both parties' resort to military threats, displays, or actual use of force short of war; (4) onset of war, marked by reciprocal and sustained military combat by regular armed forces; (5) expansion of war, marked by sustained military intervention by regular armed forces of third parties; and (6) war termination, marked by a return to conditions 3, 2, or 1. At the threshold that separates each stage from the next, all five classes of variables are seen as potentially capable—alone, additively, or multiplicatively—of keeping the conflict at the given stage, leading it back down to a lower stage, or pushing it up to a higher stage of conflict. Which of these, in which combinations and in which sequences, best explain the movements along the conflict continuum, is, in the general systems tradition, of course, the concern of our investigation. And, finally, it is understood that the objective and perceived conditions and events at each stage can affect the joint governmental decisions to escalate, deescalate, or remain at the same stage for a given series of moves and countermoves.

One other factor that precludes any detailed or thorough integration here is the fact, oft-alluded to but not yet made explicit, that this set of papers addresses a rather wide range of outcome variables, of which the incidence of war is but one, but even this variable takes several forms and is measured in several ways. Given the frequency with which we have made this point elsewhere, explained the reasoning, and presented the indicators and the data (Singer and Small, 1972; Hoole and Zinnes, 1976), there is no need to go into the question again here.

The Findings and Methods

If this volume is to serve its dual purpose, a brief discussion of our methods is definitely called for. While a fair amount of our methodological orientation is implicit in the theoretical and metatheoretical discussions that have preceded this section, some of these points are best illuminated in the context of our findings and what we and others might make of them. As I see it, methodological problems are of two basic sorts, depending on the research objective at hand. One sort of problem is that associated with *generating* the data—specifying the spatial and temporal domain, delineating the cases, and observing and measuring the phenomena of interest. The other is that of *analyzing* the data and *interpreting* the results. Having made a minor career of writing on the first of these, and having seen to it that our procedures, rationale, and results are incorporated in our analytic papers or reported separately (see the Project Bibliography), I see no need to dwell on these problems of the first sort here. Also, each of the theoretical papers in the volume deals with this problem in appropriate detail, as does the Ray paper on measurement of the system's structural attributes.

Turning to the data analysis side, most of the papers found here do an appropriate job of describing and defending the specific methods that were used by each investigator, but some of the more general issues might be addressed in our discussion of the findings problem. Despite the efforts of Karl Deutsch in this volume, as well as those of Wallace (forthcoming) and Starr (1976), it is premature to seek a highly integrated and nicely cumulative set of results.

Partly, as mentioned, it is because neither here nor in the project as a whole do we yet converge on a single query. International war is manifested and measured in several ways. At the system level, there is the frequency of war over a given period of time in the global system or regional subsystems or the severity of such wars as measured in battle fatalities or the magnitude in nation-months. At the dyadic level, for any given pair or aggregation of pairs, the same concepts of frequency, severity, and magnitude may be used. And, at the nation level, for a single state or class of states (such as members of the "central," "peripheral," or "major power" subsystem), we again may be interested in accounting for the mere frequency, or the severity, or the magnitude. Further, for any of these we may use indicators that reflect war entry, war onset, war underway, or war termination.

Finally, as in the Gochman chapter, and in many of the studies that are now under way, we use the simple war/no-war outcome, but only in the context of a prior serious dispute, marked by a military confrontation. This reflects, of course, the notion that we can go only a small part of the way toward a theory that explains the incidence of war if we merely ask under what conditions it does occur; a research design that pays no attention to the *no*-war outcomes is all too incomplete. Thus, we have invested heavily in identifying and describing all military confrontations (so far, only for the major powers) so that we can address what has been, from the beginning, one of our central queries: What is it that differentiates those serious disputes that end up in war from those that do not?

A second factor that temporarily precludes complete integratability of our findings is the use of alternative indicators for our explanatory variables. Thus, a concept as important as national capabilities—variously known as power, strength, potential, influence in the literature—is not one whose measurement we would settle on quickly. It has, as the Bremer, Gochman, Sabrosky, and Wheeler papers make evident, a range of reasonable interpretations and, therefore, a range of plausible indicators. As our work progresses, and the predictive as well as the correlational validity of the alternatives become more evident, we will want to settle on a few versions of the capabilities concept and on specific indicators of each. Given the absence of a valid indicator—despite the suggestive efforts of Knorr (1970), Morgenthau (1972), German (1960), Fucks (1965), and even Cline (1975), to mention a few—it would be premature of us to settle on any one of our own constructions at this juncture. The same holds for several other of our key variables.

A third and related source of imperfect compatability is that of differing spatial and temporal domains. Even though the project as a whole is working toward a theory that will embrace the entire global system from the Congress of Vienna up to the present, it seems quite reasonable to conduct preliminary studies on smaller segments of space or time. This is partly a function of incomplete data sets, the limits of time that should be devoted to a doctoral thesis, and shortages of funds and computer availability. But it can also be a function of two more positive considerations, of which one is theoretical and the other is methodological. For example, given the empirical fact that an extraordinarily large fraction of these international wars is accounted for by fewer than 20 of the nearly 200 states that have trod the international stage since Waterloo, it would hardly make theoretical sense to include all of the nonwarring states in such investigations as Bremer's "National Capabilities and War Proneness" or Wheeler's "Postwar Industrial Growth." On the methodological side, it is often desirable to explore the applicability of a model vis-à-vis one subpopulation of states or regions and then try to confirm it vis-à-vis a different subpopulation.

Then there is the all too familiar problem of different analytic procedures. Despite occasional claims to the contrary, the field of social science statistics is in an infuriatingly backward and confused state, particularly when it comes to macrosocial phenomena that are examined in the longitudinal mode. Methodologists and researchers vary considerably in their notions as to how best approach a given design and analysis problem, but worse than that, some of them tend to be dogmatic in their assertions and intolerant of alternatives. Further, we have occasional cases in which a given school will insist on a certain approach or procedure for years, as if it were almost a matter of salvation versus damnation, and then will blithely shift its position with only the barest genuflection to its hitherto sanctified principles.

It is little wonder that social scientists, then, develop a certain skepticism toward members of the "method of the month club" and tend to rely more on their own statistical intuitions and research experience. This certainly describes my response to methodology, and it finds its expression in a very catholic approach to modeling and data analysis. Hence, our investigations will often, at this stage of the game, utilize methods whose diversity does indeed make for less than perfect comparability among the results.

But the final and most serious reason for the lack of integratability at this stage is that our results are, in fact, frequently inconsistent. These inconsistencies may well stem from any or all of these considerations, along with such problems as measurement error. But the inescapable fact, borne out by Deutsch's paper here and Wallace's paper in our early-warning indicators volume (Singer and Wallace, *To Augur Well*, 1979) is that sometimes our findings just do not converge in the theoretical sense.

Why is it, for example, that several indicators of "structural clarity" are positively associated with the onset of war in the nineteenth century and negatively in the twentieth, whereas other putative indicators of the same concept point in just the opposite direction (Singer and Bouxsein, 1975; Singer, 1977)? Or, to take another interesting case, why is it that Wallace (1973) finds a positive association between status inconsistency and the incidence of war at the system level, whereas neither Ray (1974) nor Gochman (1975) find any clear pattern when they disaggregate and focus on the individual states themselves? Several possibilities come to mind. One is that the presence of status inconsistent states, especially if they are high on capabilities but low on prestige, can create enough problems of predictability to increase the error rate of *other* states in the system; just as certain personality types *give* heart attacks rather than *get* them, certain national types help to *generate* war, but somehow remain aloof from them.

These and other anomalies and inconsistencies are not, of course, grounds for despair. Rather, they remind us that, when an area of scientific inquiry is as close to infancy as ours and is still very much in the "natural history" stage, (Northrop, 1971), it would be surprising if everything *did* fall into place. Thus, we have a number of ideas, theoretical and methodological, that might explain these apparent anomolies, and some of them are currently being pursued. But, if we followed the advice of some of our critics and went in hot pursuit of every inconsistency that turned up, the likelihood of cumulative progress would be severely reduced. That is, once the obvious problems, already summarized, have been considered and found *not* to explain a given anomoly, the next step would be to introduce a new explanatory or control variable and ascertain whether things then fall into place. Given the number of scholar-years that go into the construction of each indicator and the generation of each data set, such instantaneous pursuit would lead us all over the theoretical map and slow down even further a research and discovery pace that is already painfully slow. Thus, we will attend to these in due course, counting on the strong likelihood that many of these inconsistencies will be cleared up as we conduct those studies that are scheduled to be done anyway.

What Happens Next?

The ultimate objective of the *Correlates of War* project, scientifically speaking, is to produce a compelling and relatively complete theory of the causes of different types of international war. That we are, more than a decade after launching the enterprise, painfully short of that goal, is all too manifest. I have already suggested some reasons why the process should be so time consuming (others are quite self-evident), and any further embellishment seems unnecessary.

Let me, rather, say a few words about our current foci and where we expect those to lead. In the period since this set of hypotheses and model testing papers was finished, two dominant lines of investigation have been continued. One of these is the examination of the effects of system structure on the incidence of war at the global level. The basic hypothesis here is that the greater the clarity of the system's structure, the greater the predicability of state behavior and of crisis outcomes, and therefore the less the likelihood of war (Midlarsky, 1975; McClelland, 1968). More specifically, if we think of the vertical dimensions in system structure as reflecting the "pecking order" for diplomatic importance, industrial might, military capability, and so on, the greater the clarity of these rankings at a given moment and the greater their isomorphism to one another, the easier it is for decision makers to predict who will dominate whom in a confrontation or crisis.

But, because states are always showing some degree of alignment with one another, and the outcome of a confrontation rests on the estimated capabilities of *all* the protagonists, decision makers also need to know who will coalesce with whom, and with what probability. A close look at the alliance, diplomatic representation, international organization, and trade configurations should help predict such coalescence, as should the extent to which those configurations are isomorphic to one another across each of the several relational dimensions. And, of course, the greater the predictability of who will be on which side and which side will dominate, the lower the danger of governments stumbling into war.

This simple proposition, readily derived from the realpolitik literature, turns out, however, to have two problems for the researcher. The first, as any careful balance-of-power analyst would note, is that high predictability of the results of a confrontation need *not* make for a low likelihood of war at all. To the contrary, it is *ambiguity* in the structure of the global or regional system that leads to caution and prudence and, therefore, to a decreased danger of war. I put it this baldly to illustrate a more general observation: there is virtually no generalization found in the literature of international conflict that does not have its countergeneralization, often in the same piece of work, and occasionally only a few pages apart. That we find competing hypotheses should cause us no alarm, but that our colleagues should express no awareness of these incompatible assertions and should make them with such confidence—*that* is a cause for alarm. Of course, one rarely finds such assertions in this precise a form, and the very ambiguity and imprecision of much of the realpolitik language may itself be a major source of these inconsistencies.

The other problem is one of valid measurement. As I noted earlier, we have encountered several anomalies in our results on the relationship between system structure and war, and the explanation may well rest with our indicators. To take one of the more likely candidates, we may well be making an invalid inference when we interpret a high concentration of capabilities in the hands of a very few powers as a situation of high clarity and low ambiguity. As we noted at the time (Singer and Bouxsein, 1975) this particular indicator as well as others may be open to alternative interpretations. In any event, this is one of the theoretical lines that we are now pursuing, but not because it could lead directly to the confirmation of an explanatory model. As suggested earlier, goodness-of-fit when the model is predicting from systemic attributes to systemic war would not confirm any explanatory hypothesis. But it would (1) suggest which types of decision-making models to attend to first and (2) provide an important set of control variables when examining, inter alia, the dyadic conflict process. Thus, a number of other system level models and hypotheses continue to hold our attention.

Another current focus, as might be expected, is the formulation and testing of several escalation models. Responding to our recurrent query (what distinguishes serious disputes that *do* go to war from those that do not?), we continue to examine a range of theoretically plausible approaches with a heavy emphasis on such explanatory variables as capabilities, alliances, preparedness levels, prior war experiences and outcomes, industrial growth, foreign investment, economic interdependence, and so forth, while controlling for a variety of global and regional conditions. While the data acquisition, index construction, and analyses go on, we are in the process of constructing a computer simulation of the escalation (and deescalation) process.

Needless to say, we think that we will find (and already are finding) a few classes or types of serious dispute, each characterized by a slightly different war-inducing configuration. As these findings take on greater clarity, we will introduce more detailed data on the specific moves and countermoves of the protagonists, and, as those more complete models improve in their postdictive power, we will be able to shift back and forth more readily between our statistical analyses and our simulation runs. In a crude sense, they should eventually become indistinguishable, one from the other.

A number of other investigations, some as doctoral dissertation projects and others of a more collaborative sort are also under way. But it cannot be stressed too often that we continue to invest heavily in index construction and data acquisition, and, if our judgments turn out to be correct, and we have indeed identified the really critical variables, as well as the ways in which they interact with one another, that investment will have been fully justified. If not, we will move on to other models, other variables, other data sets and hope that eventually we or others will discover the "right" combination.

Thus, no data set is forgotten and no analysis is a waste of time, if we keep our eye on the queries that continue to preoccupy us and on the analyses that led us to inconclusive results.

This volume, then, is another interim report from a project that was envisaged from the beginning as an effort to pick up where Lewis Richardson and Quincy Wright left off. Despite the diverse epistemologies and theoretical emphases that we bring to the problem, all of us hope that our work to date has moved humanity a bit closer to the understanding and eventual elimination of war and has been a credit to those two pioneers of the peace research movement.

The Organization of This Volume

There are five sets of papers here, beginning with the Bremer and Ray treatments of two rather different methodological problems in Part I. Using the hypothetical case of nation X in the docket for alleged crimes against the peace of the world, Bremer treats us to a lively dialogue on the ways in which frequency distributions of war experience might be interpreted. In the Ray essay, we find a discussion of the role of system structure in accounting for the incidence of war, along with ways in which these characteristics of the international system might be measured and interpreted. Although neither of these papers should be thought of as *essential* to the understanding of the balance of the volume, and are included as much to illustrate the diversity of the methodological problems encountered in a search for the causes or correlates of war, they nevertheless each shed considerable light on several of the papers that follow.

In the more substantive parts of the volume, we assign our seven analyses to three separate parts. In Part II, Bremer turns to the matter of accounting for the simple occurrence of war at the nation level—the extent to which the war proneness of nations is associated with their material capabilities during our standard post-Napoleonic period. Then Gochman employs a slightly more complex model in examining a more diverse outcome phenomenon—the extent to which the interaction between such capabilities and the nations' diplomatic status levels might account for varying levels of conflict proneness among the major powers. Finally in this part, Leng addresses the larger question of which influence strategies are most and least effective in producing compliance in interstate conflicts, with the onset of war one of the more costly manifestations of noncompliance.

Given our assumption that different processes may be at work not only at the different stages of conflict up to and across the threshold of war, but also in the expansion or extension of war, we shift in Part III to two papers that address the latter problem. First, in the context of measuring the war-time reliability of alliances, Sabrosky examines the conditions under which alliance commitments are honored, and ongoing wars thus expanded. Second, Yamamoto and Bremer articulate a number of probability models of war expansion, in which each major power's intervention in ongoing war is a function of how many of the *other* major powers have already intervened.

Then, in Part IV, we shift from the expansion of war to the outcomes of international war during the same post-Napoleonic era. In the first of these two analyses, Cannizzo examines the effect of relative capabilities, inter alia, on the outcome of war, in terms of the fatalities produced, the wars' durations, and which side emerges victorious. In the second, Wheeler offers a systematic examination of the ways in which the duration, intensity, location, and military result of these wars affects the level and industrial growth rates of the participants in the years following.

In the final part, Karl Deutsch attempts to summarize and then interpret the findings from the nine papers just described, along with those emerging from several other of the project's studies. These, as well as all other of our published reports are listed in the Combined References list for all works cited anywhere in this volume, which is followed by the Project Bibliography.

The Correlates of War: II

I

Methodological Perspectives

1

The Trials of Nations: An Improbable Application of Probability Theory

Stuart A. Bremer
Science Center, Berlin

[Translator's Note: While engaged in a search for data concerning the size of the Swiss navy in 1852, I uncovered the following in a remote region of the library. It appears to be a verbatim—but incomplete—transcript of a judicial proceeding against a prominent nation-state accused of a serious crime against humanity. I have translated and edited this work because I thought it would be of interest to my colleagues. All references to the identity of the nation involved have been deleted for obvious reasons.]

The People of the World Versus Nation X

BAILIFF: Hear ye, hear ye, the Court of the World is now in session. Judge Crater presiding. All rise.
JUDGE: Bailiff, please read the charges and specifications.
BAILIFF: The sovereign nation-state of [X] is accused of excessive

---

Notes to this book appear in the section starting on p. 297.

war involvement thereby constituting a public menace and endangering the peace of the world.

JUDGE: How does the accused plead?

DEFENSE ATTORNEY: [Nation X] pleads not guilty, your Honor.

JUDGE: A plea of not guilty has been entered for the defendant. The court may be seated. Is the prosecution ready to proceed?

PROSECUTING ATTORNEY: Yes, your Honor.

JUDGE: Is the defense ready to proceed?

DEFENSE ATTORNEY: Yes, your Honor.

JUDGE: Does the prosecution wish to make an opening statement?

PROSECUTING ATTORNEY: Yes, your Honor. I intend to show beyond a reasonable doubt that the defendant [Nation X], is guilty of excessive war involvement and should be barred from the family of nations. The facts speak for themselves. The career of this nation-state is full of violence and death. In the period of January 1, 1816 to December 31, 1965, a mere 150 years, this nation has managed to become involved in 14 wars, which resulted in millions of deaths for all participants. This defendant has become involved in a war about once every 11 years, on the average, and has sacrificed over a million of its own people in this madness. Surely, the world must be protected against such nations; they are a menace to mankind. If behavior such as this on the part of a nation-state were to go unpunished, a terrible injustice would be done to humanity. I intend to show that a verdict of guilty is justified.

JUDGE: Thank you. The defense may proceed with its opening statement.

DEFENSE ATTORNEY: Thank you, your Honor. The "facts" that the prosecution has presented in its opening statement are irrelevant to the case at hand. At best, they constitute only circumstantial evidence, and the defense intends to show that all of the evidence offered by the prosecution is of the same nature. Indeed, the prosecution neglected to mention any intention of establishing motive and, instead, merely implied that my client's motives are aggressive and expansionistic, when, in fact, my client is the most peace-loving of nations. It is true that my client became involved in some wars in the period under consideration, yet these involvements stemmed from concerns for the well-being of other, weaker nations that were being threatened by nations not so generously motivated, or my client's wars resulted from vicious and scurrilous attacks upon [Nation X] itself. The right of a nation-state to act in self-defense is sacred and recognized under law.

I intend to show that my client is not guilty and that a verdict of innocent is warranted. To decide otherwise would be a grave injustice to my client and all other nations so falsely accused.

JUDGE: Thank you, gentlemen, for your brief and concise statements. The prosecution may call its first witness.

PROSECUTING ATTORNEY: Your Honor, the prosecution intends to call only one witness, the renowned authority on probability theory, Dr. Zed. Dr. Zed, will you please take the stand?

[The witness is sworn.]

PROSECUTING ATTORNEY: Dr. Zed, would you please give us the benefit of your expertise in the area of probability theory as it pertains to this case?

ZED: I'll do what I can. As I see it, the problem we are confronting here today is one example of a large class of problems we call decision-making under uncertainty, with which probability theory was designed to deal. The question is whether or not this nation is excessively war-prone.

DEFENSE ATTORNEY: Your Honor, I object to the witness' use of the word war-prone and his assumption that there are such things as war-prone nations. Since no supportive evidence has been offered, I move that this testimony be striken from the record.

JUDGE: Dr. Zed, are you prepared to clarify and support your statements?

ZED: Yes, your Honor.

JUDGE: I will delay ruling on the defense counsel's motion. Proceed, Dr. Zed.

ZED: Thank you, your Honor. I purposely used the term war-prone in order to minimize pejorative connotations. Obviously a nation-state can become involved in wars for a variety of reasons—some noble, some not. As I see it, it is not a matter of condemning nations that have excessive war involvements, but, if we want to eliminate or reduce war, we need to recognize that it is not something that all nations are equally likely to engage in. Once we have ascertained who these nations are, the international community can decide on what steps are necessary to deal with the situation. Let me use an example. Suppose we had a factory that employed many men, and we discovered that a few of these employees were involved in many, many more on-the-job accidents than the average employee. This might be because they are careless individuals, or it might be because they work in hazardous environments. Either way, if we wanted to improve the plant's safety record, we would want to take note of the unevenness of the distribution of these accidents in formulating a plan. I see the involvement in wars by nations in the same way. That is why I use the term war-prone.

As to the second point, I think that I can show beyond a reasonable doubt that some nations are more likely to become involved in war than others, and therefore are what I call war-prone.

I will proceed in the following way. First, I will posit for the sake of discussion that all nations are equally war-prone, and then, with the aid of a few simple assumptions, we will examine the empirical evidence and see how likely it is that the original proposition is true. In this way we can measure the credibility of a particular hypothesis. I think this will become clearer as I go along.

The first thing we need to do is establish some notation. In what follows, R will stand for the rate of war involvement per year for a nation. It is analogous to the probability that a nation will become involved in a war in any given year. The hypothesis that all nations are equally war-prone becomes a mathematical statement when we recast it to say that the value of R for each nation is the same as that for every other nation. All R's are equal, if you will.

Now, in order to test this hypothesis, we need to make some additional assumptions. First, we need to assume that the probability of more than one war involvement during a given period of time is small. This is not a critical assumption since, by making our time intervals sufficiently short, we can pretty much guarantee that this assumption will not be violated. As a matter of fact, there are only three instances of a nation's becoming involved in two wars in a single year in the data compiled by Professors Singer and Small, and this covers 144 nations and 150 years of time, so I will use the year as my unit of time.[1]

The two remaining assumptions that we need to make are more critical, however. The first of these is that nations don't change their rates of war involvement over time; or in technical terms, we assume that war involvement is a stationary process. The second assumption is that the likelihood of a war involvement in a particular year is neither increased nor decreased by the occurrence of war in some previous year. This is often referred to as the assumption of independence. In this specific case, this assumption means that the decision as to whether to go to war or not is unaffected by whether or not a nation has become involved in a war in an earlier time period.

DEFENSE ATTORNEY: I object, your Honor. These are clearly false and unwarranted assumptions.

JUDGE: I think it would be more proper for you to raise these points in cross-examination. Objection overruled. Please continue, Doctor.

ZED: Thank you, your Honor. Perhaps an analogy would be useful at this point. Suppose the war determination process was as follows: each nation has an urn containing red and white balls, and each year it draws a ball from its urn. If it is a white ball the nation avoids war, but if it is red it becomes involved. Regardless of the outcome, they replace the ball so that the chances of becoming involved in a war don't change from year to year. In addition, they don't change urns, which is implied by the stationarity assumption. The question is, do all the nations' urns have the same proportion of red and white balls?

DEFENSE ATTORNEY: Objection, your Honor. Surely the witness is not seriously trying to persuade this Court that nations decide matters as important as war involvement by drawing balls from urns?

JUDGE: Dr. Zed?

ZED: I am not saying that this model is an accurate representation of the decision process preceding a war involvement, but rather I am saying that the decision process may be such that it is *as if* it were as I have described. One way of looking at the problem is to view the ultimate outcome of involvement in war as a phenomenon determined by a large number of factors, each of which is relatively unlikely to occur and, by itself, harmless. But, when these factors happen to be present at the same time, war involvement becomes highly likely. And since decision makers, per se, control only a small fraction of these factors, the result is, for all intents and purposes, generated by what we call a stochastic process.

It may be that, when I am finished, you will not find what I have to say all that helpful; yet in my own mind I think it is highly relevant to the problem at hand.

JUDGE: Objection overruled. Proceed, Dr. Zed.

ZED: Well, as I was saying, these assumptions allow us to use what is referred to as the Poisson probability model, named after the great

French mathematician Simeon D. Poisson, who lived from 1781 to 1840. It has been profitably applied to the study of the number of Prussian cavalry officers dying from horse kicks, the number of bomb hits in various areas of London, the number. . . .

JUDGE: Dr. Zed, will you please come to the point?

ZED: Forgive me, your Honor. Stated simply, we can use the Poisson distribution to tell us the likelihood that a nation will become involved in a specific number of wars within a specified period of time, under the assumptions outlined above. More specifically, we know that the probability that a particular nation will experience k wars in t years, given a rate of war involvement R, is equal to

$$\frac{e^{-Rt}(Rt)^k}{k!}$$

To take a simple example, if we assume the rate of war involvement to be 1/10, or an average of one war every ten years, we can compute the probabilities of different numbers of war involvements during a decade.

Number Of War Involvements	Probability
0	.37
1	.37
2	.18
3	.06
4	.02
5	.003
6	.0005
7 or more	.0001

As we can see, our hypothetical nation could expect to avoid war altogether in 37% of its decades of existence and have only one war involvement in an additional 37% of its decades of existence. The probabilities of more war involvements decreases as the number of involvements increases. Notice that the last entry in the first column is *7 or more* war involvements. This represents the cumulative probability of 7 or 8 or 9 or 10, and so on, war involvements. As you can see, it is extremely unlikely, although not impossible, that a nation with this rate of war involvement would become involved in five or more wars in a given decade, as the odds of this happening are about 270.3 to 1. If we actually observed a nation with five war involvements, we might be inclined to decide that the true rate of war involvement for this nation is higher than 1/10. Am I making myself clear?

JUDGE: I think so, but I do wish you would get on with substantiating your argument that war-prone nations exist.

ZED: I'm just coming to that, your Honor. Singer and Small list 144 nations that have existed at one time or another during the period 1816 to 1965; altogether these nations make up 7,115 nation-years of existence.

JUDGE: I'm not sure I follow that.

ZED: Well, let's take an example. The United Kingdom remained a sovereign state for the full 150 years that separate January 1, 1816 and December 31, 1965, whereas Poland, which existed as a sovereign national entity during the same period for the years 1919-1939 and 1945-1965, had a "lifespan" of 41 years. Together, these two nation-states represent 191 nation-years of existence. For example, the 47 nations that Singer and Small designate as European collectively represent 3,274 years of existence. When we add in the nation-year figures for the other regions of the world, the final total is 7,115.

If we count war involvements by these same states using the Singer and Small definition, we find that there are 239 war involvements during this period.[2] The typical rate of war involvement then would be 239 war involvements per 7,115 years, or about .0333. That is, on the average, a nation can be expected to become involved in a war once every 30 years.

What I have done is to take this typical rate of war involvement—.0333—as the value of R in the earlier formula and have examined the war experience of each of the 144 nations in order to discover which of those nations were significantly *more* war-prone and which were significantly *less* war-prone than the "typical" nation.

Let's take the case of [Nation Y], for example. In 150 years of existence the average nation-state would experience .0333 × 150 = 5 wars. During this period, however, [Nation Y] was not involved in any wars. The question is, if [Nation Y] were a typical nation, how likely is it that it could have avoided war altogether during the 150-year period? A table of the Poisson distribution reveals that the probability of such an occurrence is .0067. Because this probability is very small, we might be inclined to conclude that [Nation Y] is a less war-prone state.

On the other hand, some nations have been involved in far more wars than one would expect if they were average states. [Nation Z], for example, experienced 19 war involvements in 150 years. How likely is this if [Nation Z] is typical? As it turns out, the probability of this is quite a bit less than 1 in 10,000, and, in fact, it's probably closer to 1 in 1 million.

It can be easily shown that there are at least half-a-dozen other nations that deviate markedly from what we would expect if they were typical nation-states. This suggests to me that the population of nation-states is not homogenous with respect to war involvement, and it seems reasonable to posit that we are dealing with at least two kinds of nation-states, the more war-prone and the less war-prone, rather than one type of nation-state. Your Honor, does this clear up what I mean by war-prone and why I believe that there are more and less war-prone states?

JUDGE: Dr. Zed, may I see the list you have compiled?

ZED: Of course, your Honor.

JUDGE: This is indeed interesting. Bailiff, would you mark this Exhibit 1 for the prosecution?* I find your argument persuasive, Dr. Zed, and therefore I will overrule the objection raised by the defense. You may proceed.

ZED: Thank you, your Honor. I would like to return to the general question of how probability theory may be useful in deciding whether [Nation X] is guilty of excessive war involvement.

In this case, you have two hypotheses: the defendant is innocent, or the defendant is guilty, and obviously if we accept one, we reject the other. May I use the blackboard, your Honor?

JUDGE: Certainly.

ZED: I see the problem this way.

		Decision	
		Innocent	Guilty
Truth	Innocent	1	3
	Guilty	4	2

There are four possible outcomes.

1. Innocent-Innocent: The defendant is innocent and the verdict is innocent.
2. Guilty-Guilty: The defendant is guilty and the verdict is guilty.
3. Innocent-Guilty: The defendant is innocent and the verdict is guilty.

*Exhibit 1 follows these notes.

4. Guilty-Innocent: The defendant is guilty and the verdict is innocent.

The first two of these four possible outcomes are correct decisions, as together they comprise what we, in a moral sense, consider justice, and this is what we strive for. The last two, however, are errors that we want to avoid, or failing that, try to minimize. Because a defendant is presumed innocent, we want to give that hypothesis the benefit of the doubt. We commonly refer to this as the null hypothesis or H_o. The other hypothesis is understandably referred to as the alternative hypothesis or H_1. Hence, our two hypotheses are

H_o: The defendant is innocent.
H_1: The defendant is guilty.

In the third outcome we listed—the defendant is innocent but the verdict is guilty—we have committed the error of rejecting the null hypothesis when it is really true. This is called *type I* error in my business, and in this case it would mean punishing an innocent party—an injustice against the accused nation-state, if you will. The fourth outcome—the defendant is guilty but the verdict is innocent—involves accepting the null hypothesis when, in truth, it is false. This is referred to as *type II* error, and here it would entail letting a guilty party off scot-free, an injustice to the global society.

DEFENSE ATTORNEY: I object, your Honor. This testimony is irrelevant and immaterial.

JUDGE: I am inclined to agree. However, the prosecution should be given sufficient time to demonstrate relevance. Objection overruled. You may continue, Dr. Zed.

ZED: Thank you, your Honor. I think the relevance will become clear shortly.

In order to handle this decision problem, we need to make some assumptions. Because it is highly unlikely that nations are equally war-prone, let us assume instead that there are two types of nation-states: those that have a low rate of war involvement and those that, for whatever reason, have a higher rate of war involvement. The question before us then becomes is [Nation X] one of the former, or one of the latter? If we designate the rate of war involvement of a nation as R_x and the war propensities of the two classes of states listed earlier R_{LWP} and R_{MWP}, respectively, our null and alternative hypotheses become

$H_o: R_X = R_{LWP}$
$H_1: R_X = R_{MWP}$

PROSECUTING ATTORNEY: You mean that the verdict of innocent is equivalent to saying that [Nation X] is one of these less war-prone states, whereas a guilty verdict says it's one of the more war-prone states?

ZED: Exactly. Now, in order to determine which of these hypotheses is more likely to be true we need to make some additional assumptions. First, we need to once again assume that the probability of a nation's becoming involved in more than one war during one unit of time, which, in this case is the year, is small. As I have already indicated, this assumption seems reasonable given the relative rarity of this event in the Singer and Small data.

The remaining two assumptions are more critical and controversial. Once again we need to assume that we are dealing with a stationary process. This means that [Nation X] is not one of the war-prone nations some years and one of the less war-prone nations other years. In other words, a nation maintains its basic propensity to war involvement over the period that it is observed. The third assumption is the same independence assumption which we talked about earlier; that is, a war involvement in one year makes a subsequent war involvement neither more nor less likely.

Now, let's recall our rival hypotheses:

H_o: The defendant is innocent of excessive war involvement, or

$$R_X = R_{LWP}$$

H_1: The defendant is guilty of excessive war involvement, or

$$R_X = R_{MWP}$$

If we know at this point the values of R_{LWP} and R_{MWP}, we could, using the Poisson distribution I described earlier, compute the probability that we will correctly label the nation under consideration as one of the more war-prone or one of the less war-prone states. We found earlier that the typical rate of war involvement for all nations was 239/7115, or about .0333 wars per year. That is, on the average, a nation can be expected to become involved in a war once every 30 years. This is, of course, not a good estimate of R_{LWP} as we have included the war experiences of those nations that are more war-prone as well as those that are less war-prone. For the sake of discussion, let's say that the rate of war involvement for a less war-prone nation is an average of one war involvement per 50 years. Thus, R_{LWP} would have a value of .02.

The rate of war involvement for the more war-prone nations, R_{MWP}, is not so easily estimated. Clearly this is more of a normative question than an empirical one, and, because there is no body of law to fall back on, we need to appeal to reason with the hopes of formulating an ethical consensus as to what constitutes unacceptable behavior on the part of a nation. My thinking along these lines is as follows. Our typical nation, on the average, became involved in a war every 30 years. Now it seems to me that a nation that averages one war per decade is clearly different from, and a far less desirable neighbor than, the nation that has only one-third of that frequency. Ultimately, of course, each of us must decide whether or not an average of one war involvement per decade is unacceptable behavior. And, if one believes that this standard is either too stringent or too lenient, one can replicate my calculations with whatever standard one chooses and then see what the implications are.

For the moment, then, I will assign R_{MWP} the value of .10. Given these estimates of the relevant rates of war involvement, the hypotheses that we discussed above are

H_o: $R_X = R_{LWP} = 1/50$
H_1: $R_X = R_{MWP} = 1/10$

That is, either [Nation X] is one of those less war-prone nations that have a low rate—1/50—of war involvement, or else it is one of those nations that are more war-prone, with a rate of war involvement equal to 1/10.

Now let's examine each of the two hypotheses as they pertain to the case at hand. Let us assume first that the nation-state being judged is really one of the less war-prone states that has, nevertheless, had the misfortune of being inadvertantly dragged into a large number of wars. Using the Poisson distribution and assuming that R_X is 1/50, that is, assuming that [Nation X] is a less war-prone state, we can ascertain the probability that, by chance alone, [Nation X] would be involved in a given number of wars in 150 years. Rounded off to the nearest three decimal places these probabilities are

Number Of War Involvements	Likelihood By Chance Alone
0	.050
1	.149
2	.224
3	.224
4	.168
5	.101
6	.050
7	.022
8	.008
9	.003
10 or more	.001

Please note that the last value in the left-hand column says that *10 or more* war involvements have an approximate probability of .001. This is a cumulative probability, as it is the sum of the probabilities of exactly 10 or 11 or 12 or 13, and so on, war involvements. We can see that there is about one chance in a 1,000 that a less war-prone state would have 10 or more war involvements in 150 years.

JUDGE: This is all very interesting and educational, but I'm not sure of its relevance.

ZED: What I have talked about thus far concerns the fundamental principles that we now are in a position to apply to this case.

JUDGE: Proceed.

ZED: Thank you, your Honor. Suppose we were to establish a decision rule, which I think you refer to as a precedent, that any nation shall be judged guilty of excessive war involvement if involved in 14 or more wars in 150 years, which is the defendant's record, but innocent if it is involved in 13 or less wars. That is, we assume that 14 or more war involvements in 150 years is considered to be evidence of guilt beyond a reasonable doubt.

Now we know that our decisions would not be perfect, but if we are willing to make the assumptions that I outlined earlier, we can considerably clarify the situation as to the probability of making mistakes. Let me put the little drawing I used earlier back on the board, slightly modified.

			Decision	
			Innocent	Guilty
Truth	$H_0: P_X = P_{LWP}$	Innocent	1	3
	$H_1: P_X = P_{MWP}$	Guilty	4	2

Let's assume, for the moment, that the defendant in this case is innocent, that is, that the true rate of war involvement for [Nation X] is 1/50. Using the decision rule of 14 or more war involvements in 150 years as sufficient evidence for conviction, how likely are we to wrongly convict an innocent nation. Or, to put it another way, what proportion of truly innocent nations would we wrongly convict in the long run using this rule?

From our probability tables, we find out that the probability of 14 or more war involvements in 150 years by a less war-prone state, $R_X = 1/50$, is less than .0001. As a matter of fact, it's about three chances in a million. The probability that we would *correctly* judge a nation innocent using this rule is one minus the probability of incorrectly judging a nation guilty, or, in this case, greater than .9999. Remember that these probabilities were derived by assuming that the defendant is truly innocent. Let us now assume that the nation is guilty. Now assuming that [Nation X] is *guilty* is equivalent to saying that $R_X = R_{MWP} = 1/10$, that is, that the true rate of war involvement for this nation is 1/10. How likely is it that we would correctly judge a nation such as this guilty using our decision rule?

Once again our probability tables provide the answer, and we find that the probability of 14 or more war involvements in 150 years, given a rate of war involvement of 1/10, is about .64. In other words, 64% of the truly guilty nations would be correctly judged guilty if we used the decision rule invoking 14 or more war involvements. What about the probability of making the mistake of letting guilty nations go free? Well, this is simply one minus the probability of correctly judging a guilty nation guilty, or in this case, .36.

We have all the information we need now to put your decision in context. If we put the probabilities I have calculated in the diagram, the result looks like this:

		Decision	
		Innocent	Guilty
Truth	Innocent	> .9999	< .0001
	Guilty	.36	.64

If we look at this table, we see that the principle advantage of the decision rule we are considering, in terms of setting a precedent, is that very few innocent nations will be judged guilty. In other words, the probability of committing what we call a type I error is very small. The defect of this rule is that over one-third of the truly guilty nations would go unpunished. In probability terms, our type II error is quite large. In fact, it is over a hundred thousand times greater than our type I error.

The defense attorney earlier urged the Court to be especially careful about convicting an innocent nation, or, in our terms, he was arguing that we should guard against a type I error. The prosecution, on the other hand, urged the Court to make all efforts to avoid letting the guilty go free; that is, keep the probability of committing a type II error small.

JUDGE: Is there anything more you would like to add, Dr. Zed?

ZED: Yes, your Honor. I have taken the liberty of examining the war involvement records of all 144 nations in Singer and Small's *The Wages of War*. The analytical method that I have outlined cannot be applied to all of these nations. In particular, I have had to exclude those 77 nations that had no war involvements during the observation period. One can easily see that a decision rule specifying zero or more war involvements as evidence of guilt would results in 100% of the guilty being convicted, yielding a zero type II error rate, but such a rule would also wrongly convict all of the truly innocent; thus, the probability of committing a type I error would be 1.00. So, as you can see, it doesn't really make sense to consider these states within this logic of analysis. I should hasten to point out that about two-thirds of these states existed for less than two decades during the century and a half we are concerned with, and it is therefore not surprising that they would not have any war involvements, as even a more war-prone nation stands a good chance of not having a war involvement in such a short period of time.

In preparing this list, I have taken into consideration the number of war involvements and years of existence for the remaining 67 nations and have computed the relevant probabilities that, under the assumptions discussed above, we would commit the error of wrongly judging each nation to be guilty of excessive war involvement, or the error of deciding that a truly guilty nation is not guilty. These probabilities are based on each nation's historical experience, and, as I think you'll see, they suggest that there are several other nations which merit special attention.

JUDGE: May I see that, Dr. Zed?

ZED: Certainly, your Honor.

JUDGE: This is an interesting document, Dr. Zed. I share your conclusion that there are other cases worth investigating. Bailiff, please see that a copy of this list is forwarded to the Office of the Special Prosecutor for Global Affairs.*

PROSECUTING ATTORNEY: Your Honor, I have no further questions for this witness.

JUDGE: Does the defense wish to cross-examine the witness at this time?

DEFENSE ATTORNEY: It does, your Honor.

Dr. Zed, your testimony has been interesting and educational but irrelevant to the case at hand. In your testimony you made a special point of telling us that the probabilities you were reporting pertained to the likelihood of committing errors of one sort or another. Is that correct?

ZED: Yes.

DEFENSE ATTORNEY: And is it also correct that your calculations concerning these errors are based on the "long run," whatever that might mean, rather than the specific facts of this case?

ZED: No, that is not quite correct.

DEFENSE ATTORNEY: Let me rephrase the question. The crux of your argument seems to be that, given your assumptions, a verdict of guilty in this, and all similar cases, would result in only a few erroneous convictions. Is that a substantially correct restatement of your opinion?

ZED: That is not my opinion, that is my deduction.

DEFENSE ATTORNEY: Very well, Dr. Zed. Can you tell me whether my client, if found guilty, would be one of those nations that properly deserves condemnation or one of those that receives a "bum rap," as it's known in the vernacular?

ZED: I have never stated that such nations should be condemned, I merely opined that they should receive special attention. But to come to your question . . . the answer is no. I can. . . .

DEFENSE ATTORNEY: You really can't tell us anything about the guilt or innocence of my client, can you Dr. Zed?

PROSECUTING ATTORNEY: I object, your Honor. . . .

JUDGE: Sustained. The defense counsel will please allow the witness sufficient time to respond to the question. Continue, Dr. Zed.

* Apparently, no copy of Zed's list was included in the transcript of the trial. After considerable investigatory work, I discovered a copy of the elusive list in Judge Crater's collected papers, and it is reprinted as Exhibit 2.

ZED: What I wanted to say is that, if I may be permitted a few additional assumptions, I think I can provide some evidence that bears on the point raised by the defense counsel.

DEFENSE ATTORNEY: More assumptions, Dr. Zed! Why don't you just assume that my client is guilty and be done with it?

JUDGE: The counsel for the defense will refrain from such outbursts in the future. Continue, Dr. Zed.

ZED: Thank you, your Honor. I'm afraid that this may become rather complicated, but I'll do my best. The defense counsel is partially right about the nature of the assumptions we shall have to make in order to apply what is called Bayesian inference. It is an analytical method based on a theorem first proposed by Thomas Bayes, an eighteenth century English clergyman, who . . .

JUDGE: You may spare us the details of Reverend Bayes's personal life, Dr. Zed.

ZED: I'm sorry, your Honor. Well, as I was saying, this approach assumes that one doesn't approach a decision problem such as this without some a priori ideas about the relative merits of the alternatives. Bayesian analysis provides us with a means of evaluating these predispositions in light of evidence and arriving at a decision that takes into account, both the more subjective, a priori judgments we have and the more objective available evidence. This should become clearer as we go along.

A problem such as the one confronting us here would be laid out in the following way.

Alternative	Prior Probability	Likelihood	Posterior Probability
A_1	Pr_1	L_1	Po_1
A_2	Pr_2	L_2	Po_2

A_1 and A_2 are the decisional alternatives available to us; in this case they correspond to innocent or guilty. Pr_1 and Pr_2 are the probabilities of being true that we attach to the first and second alternatives, respectively, *prior* to evaluating the evidence. These are sometimes referred to as credibility values, and they must sum to 1.0. These prior probabilities reflect our bias concerning the alternatives, and their values may be derived from past empirical evidence, less systematic observations, or even intuition.

After setting our prior probabilities, we make some empirical observations and compute the likelihoods, L_1 and L_2, that we would obtain the observed result if first A_1 and then A_2 is assumed to be true. Using Bayes's theorem, we can compute the posterior probabilities, Po_1 and Po_2, for each alternative. These reflect the relative credibility of the two alternatives. These values can be derived from the following formuli.

$$Po_1 = \frac{Pr_1 L_1}{Pr_1 L_1 + Pr_2 L_2}$$

$$Po_2 = \frac{Pr_2 L_2}{Pr_1 L_1 + Pr_2 L_2}$$

Let me see if I can make this clear at an intuitive level with a simple example. Suppose that we are confronted with a choice between two alternatives and we believe that each has a probability of 1/2 of being true. Suppose further that we conduct an experiment and find that the observed outcome is as likely to occur if the first alternative is true as it is if the second alternative is true. Obviously, under these circumstances we would have no reason to change our a priori credibility assessments, as the experimental outcome is equally confirmative of the two alternatives.

Now, what would be the reasonable thing to do if the outcome of the experiment were twice as likely to occur if the first alternative was true than if the second was true? The logic of Bayes's theorem dictates that we should raise our level of confidence in the first alternative to two-thirds and lower our level of confidence in the second to one-third. You can verify this for yourself by setting $Pr_1 = Pr_2$ and $L_1 = 2L_2$ in the formuli I gave earlier. I hope that this gives you an intuitive understanding of the procedure I propose to use in this case.

First we need to specify the alternatives. Let's designate A_1 as the alternative that [Nation X] is one of the less war-prone nations, which, in line with my earlier testimony, I will equate with a rate of war involvement of 1/50, or an average of one war per 50 years. The second alternative, A_2, stipulates that [Nation X] is one of the more war-prone nations that we previously identified as having a war involvement rate of 1/10.

Now we come to the difficult problem of setting our levels of confidence in these two alternatives, expressed as the probabilities Pr_1 and Pr_2. I think that we can safely argue that Pr_2 must be greater than zero. That is, if we felt that the assertion that [Nation

X] was one of the more war-prone nations had no credibility whatsoever, then there would be no point in conducting this trial, for no amount of evidence could convince us otherwise. Thus, although we say that a defendant is "presumed innocent until proven guilty," this cannot mean that we assign a probability of zero a priori to the conclusion that the defendant is guilty. More likely, we mean that the innocent alternative should be assigned a higher value than the guilty alternative. Mathematically, we have established that $Pr_2 > 0$ and $Pr_1 > Pr_2$, which still leaves us with a large number of values to choose from. I will work with three values for Pr_2 reflecting different degrees of confidence in the innocence of [Nation X]. On the pessimistic side I will posit that the probability that [Nation X] is one of the more war-prone is one-third and on the optimistic side one in a hundred. In between these two values, I have selected 1/10 as the a priori probability of guilt. I could have selected other values, but these should serve our purposes.

Now let us turn to the computation of the likelihood values. If we make the same assumptions of stationarity and independence that we made before, then we can proceed in the following way. First we ask what is the likelihood that a nation with a rate of war involvement of 1 war per 50 years would experience exactly 14 wars in 150 years? Substituting the appropriate values into the Poisson formula provides us with the answer.

$$\frac{e^{-150/50}(150/50)^{14}}{14!} = .000003$$

Similarly, we can find out what the probability is that a nation with a war involvement rate of one war per ten years would experience 14 wars in 150 years. That probability is equal to

$$\frac{e^{-150/10}(150/10)^{14}}{14!}$$

which is .102436. As we can see, the probabilities are quite different, the latter being 30,000 times greater than the former. Now let's consider the posterior probabilities of guilt for each of the three conditions posited above.

Under the pessimistic presumption, we assumed that the a priori probability of guilt was one-third. Using the formula for posterior probabilities just given, we find that the values for Po_1 and Po_2 are .00006 and .99994, respectively. If we put all this information in a tabular form, it looks like this.

Alternative	Prior Probability	Likelihood	Posterior Probability
Innocent	2/3	.000003	.00006
Guilty	1/3	.102436	.99994

This means that, given our prior presumptions about guilt and innocence and the available evidence, the second alternative has a great deal more credibility than the first. If we lower the a priori probability of guilt to one-tenth and perform the calculations again, we obtain the following results.

Alternative	Prior Probability	Likelihood	Posterior Probability
Innocent	9/10	.000003	.0003
Guilty	1/10	.102436	.9997

As we can see, the second alternative is still a great deal more credible than the first.

Let's reset the a priori probability of guilt at only one in a hundred. The decision table would look like this.

Alternative	Prior Probability	Likelihood	Posterior Probability
Innocent	99/100	.000003	.003
Guilty	1/100	.102436	.997

I could go on to show you in this particular case that, even if the prior probability of guilt were set at 1 in 10,000, the posterior probability of guilt would still be about three-fourths. In other words, our initial belief in the innocence of the defendant would have to be very, very strong, for us to discount the evidence to the contrary.

Returning now to the point that the counsel for the defense raised, these probabilities, given that the assumptions are valid, may be interpreted as the probabilities that the defendant nation is innocent or guilty and *not* merely the probabilities that we would make errors in selecting one alternative over the other. In order to derive these former probabilities, we had to make some additional assumptions, but as I'm sure you'll appreciate, this is always necessary when information is lacking.

DEFENSE ATTORNEY: I have no further questions of this witness, your Honor.

JUDGE: Dr. Zed, have you made similar calculations for the other nations?

ZED: I have, your Honor.

JUDGE: May I see your list?*

ZED: Of course.

JUDGE: This looks interesting, Dr. Zed. I want to thank you for your helpful testimony and. . . .

ZED: I'm sorry to interrupt, your Honor, but it occurred to me that probation is sometimes considered in cases like this. Is that correct?

JUDGE: That is one of the alternatives if the defendant is found guilty. Why do you ask?

ZED: Well, I think probability theory can be useful in setting the length of such a probationary period.

JUDGE: Please proceed, Dr. Zed.

ZED: Thank you. If we are willing to make the same assumptions as before—primarily the stationarity and independence assumptions—we can take advantage of an interesting property of the Poisson distribution. As it turns out, if we are dealing with a phenomena whose occurrence accords with that predicted by the Poisson distribution, which, I will remind you, deals with the distribution of the total number of events that occur during a given period of time, then the time intervals that separate such events will be exponentially distributed. That is, the exponential distribution provides a probabilistic answer to the question, how long need one wait if one is observing a sequence of war involvements occurring in time in accordance with a Poisson probability law at the rate of R war involvements per year in order to observe the first subsequent war involvement? This sounds rather more complicated than it is, but a simple example should clarify the situation. If a nation is involved in a war in a particular year, the exponential distribution tells us the likelihood that it will or will not become involved in another war within a specified number of subsequent years. The exponential distribution is a distribution of waiting times between events that occur in accordance with a Poisson distribution.

Now to be more specific, the probability that a nation, with a

* Unfortunately, this list was also not among the transcript materials, but I believe that I have been able to produce a reasonable facsimile of Zed's compilation. It is included here as Exhibit 3.

rate of war involvement R, will *not* become involved in a war during t years is simply e^{-Rt}, and the probability that its first subsequent war involvement will occur within t years is $1-e^{-Rt}$. This means, for example, that a less war-prone state, with a war involvement rate of 1/50, has a probability of approximately .82 of *not* having a war involvement during a decade and a probability of .18 that it will become involved in at least one war during the same period. In contrast, a more war-prone state, with a rate of war involvement of 1/10, has only a .37 probability of avoiding war altogether during a decade and a .63 probability that it will have at least one war involvement during the ten-year span.

As I see it, the idea behind a probationary period is that, if the guilty party does not repeat his offense within a prescribed period of time, he is judged to be reformed. If, however, the convicted party engages in the prescribed behavior during the probationary period, a reexamination of the case is deemed necessary. Now, the decision as to whether the convicted party is reformed or not is subject to the same two types of errors we mentioned earlier. On the one hand, we may decide, after a certain period of exemplary behavior, that a nation has lowered its war propensity when nothing of the sort has really happened. Or, on the other hand, because it is possible for a truly reformed nation to become involved in a war, we might decide that such a nation is unreformed and erroneously subject it to harrassment. Poetically speaking, in the first case we mistake a saint for a sinner and, in the second, a sinner for a saint. Now what I propose to do is to use the exponential distribution to determine the probabilities of committing these errors in relation to probationary periods of different lengths.

First, let's consider a short probationary period, say five years. If we were to say that a convicted nation that avoids war for five years has reformed, how often can we expect to be wrong? Well, this is equivalent to asking what the probability is that a more war-prone nation, with a rate of war involvement of 1/10, would *not* become involved in a war during the five years. This is simply

$$e^{-(1/10)(5)}$$

or about .61. Now let's turn the matter around and look at it the other way. Because we know that even a less war-prone state has some likelihood of becoming involved in a war during a given period of time, we also can see that it is possible for a nation that has reformed, and has become less war-prone, to nevertheless involve itself in a war. If this were to happen within the probationary period, then we would be committing an error if we concluded that the nation had not reformed. The probability that we would commit such an error with a five-year probationary period is simply the probability that a less war-prone state would have at least one war involvement during that period or

$$1. - e^{-(1/50)(5)} = .10$$

In short, then, we can see that a five-year probationary period would permit about 61% of the unreformed more war-prone states to escape detection, whereas 10% of the truly reformed would be considered unreformed. What I have done is to compute these probabilities for longer probationary periods. They are as follows.

Length of Probationary Period in Years	Probability that Reformed Nation is Judged Unreformed if War Occurs	Probability that Unreformed Nation is Judged Reformed if No War Occurs
5	.10	.61
10	.18	.37
15	.26	.22
20	.33	.14
25	.39	.08
30	.45	.05
35	.50	.03
40	.55	.02
45	.59	.01
50	.63	< .01

As you can see, your Honor, the longer the probationary period, the smaller the probability that an unreformed more war-prone state will escape detection, but the larger the probability that reformed nations will not be recognized. I'm sorry that I cannot give you any more specific advice as to the length of the probationary period, your honor, but, as you can see, it depends on the risks that you are willing to run.

JUDGE: Dr. Zed, you have given the Court a great deal to think about. I admit that I had not seen these vital issues of war and peace cast in these terms. Your testimony is greatly appreciated. I assume that you will remain available if further testimony is required at some future date.

ZED: Yes, your Honor.

JUDGE: Very well, gentlemen. It has been a long day and I'm sure that you, like me, need time to consider this testimony. Court is recessed until 10 o'clock, Monday morning.

Exhibit 1. Inequalities in the War-Proneness of Nations

Nations with More Wars than Expected

Nation[1]	Years[2]	Expected Wars[3]	Observed Wars[4]	Probability of Fewer Wars[5]
France	148	4.9	19	>999.9
United Kingdom	150	5.0	19	>999.9
Turkey	150	5.0	17	>999.9
Russia	150	5.0	15	999.8
Italy	150	5.0	12	994.5
Austria-Hungary	103	3.4	8	975.8
India	19	0.6	3	973.2
China	106	3.5	8	972.1
Bulgaria	58	1.9	5	953.3
Japan	99	3.3	7	949.0
Spain	150	5.0	9	931.9
Israel	18	0.6	2	878.1
Yugoslavia	85	2.8	5	842.4
Greece	134	4.5	7	835.3
Rumania	88	2.9	5	826.3
Hungary	47	1.5	3	791.9
Egypt	29	1.0	2	748.0
Germany	130	4.3	6	731.1

[1] Nations are listed in order of decreasing war proneness.
[2] Extreme caution should be exercised in evaluating the war proneness of those nations that existed for less than two decades during the 1816-1965 period.
[3] Based on a frequency of one war per 30 years and rounded to the nearest tenth.
[4] Taken from Table 11.2 in J. David Singer and Melvin Small, *The Wages of War*, pp. 273-280. Both interstate and extrasystemic wars are included.
[5] Probabilities have been multiplied by 1,000 and rounded to the nearest tenth. They may be interpreted as the proportion of "typical" nations that would have had *fewer* war involvements during the same period of national existence.
[6] Nations are listed in order of increasing war proneness.
[7] Probabilities have been mulitptied by 1,000 and rounded to the nearest tenth. They may be interpreted as the proportion of "typical" nations that would have had *more* war involvements during the same period of national existence.

Exhibit 1. Inequalities in the War-Proneness of Nations (Cont)

Nations with More Wars than Expected (Cont)

Nation[1]	Years[2]	Expected Wars[3]	Observed Wars[4]	Probability of Fewer Wars[5]
Ethiopia	63	2.1	3	649.6
United States	150	5.0	6	616.0
Syria S. Korea	17	0.6	1	568.0
Papal States Mongolia	45	1.5	2	557.8
N. Korea	18	0.6	1	548.8
Two Sicilies Canada Australia	46	1.5	2	546.8
Finland	47	1.6	2	535.9
Pakistan	19	0.6	1	521.4
Lebanon Jordan Philippines	20	0.7	1	514.0
Holland	145	4.8	5	470.3
Baden Bavaria Wuerttemburg	55	1.8	2	453.1
Meck.-Schwerin	25	0.8	1	435.1
Hanover	29	1.0	1	380.8

Nations with Fewer Wars than Expected

Nation[6]	Years[2]	Expected Wars[3]	Observed Wars[4]	Probability of More Wars[7]
Switzerland Sweden	150	5.0	0	993.3
Venezuela	125	4.2	0	984.5
Haiti	107	3.6	0	972.7
Portugal	150	5.0	1	959.6
Uruguay	84	2.8	0	939.2
Dominican Republic	79	2.6	0	928.1
Ecuador	112	3.7	1	886.7
Iran	111	3.7	1	883.8
Cuba	64	2.1	0	881.4

Nations with Fewer Wars than Expected (Cont)

Nation[6]	Years[2]	Expected Wars[3]	Observed Wars[4]	Probability of More Wars[7]
Denmark	145	4.8	2	860.6
Colombia	134	4.5	2	826.4
Chile	127	4.2	2	794.1
Albania	47	1.6	0	791.0
Argentina	125	4.2	2	785.3
Costa Rica Panama Liberia Afghanistan Nepal	46	1.5	0	784.0
Tuscany	45	1.5	0	776.9
Ireland	44	1.5	0	769.1
Luxemburg	42	1.4	0	753.4
Bolivia	118	3.9	2	751.9
Guatemala	117	3.9	2	746.9
Thailand	79	2.6	1	738.8
Yemen	40	1.3	0	736.1
Saudi Arabia	39	1.3	0	727.5
Brazil	140	4.7	3	685.0
Paraguay	70	2.3	1	676.6
Mexico	135	4.5	3	657.7
Nicaragua	66	2.2	1	645.4
Belgium	131	4.4	3	634.7
Austria	30	1.0	0	632.1
Peru	128	4.3	3	616.7
Norway	56	1.9	1	556.6
Estonia Latvia Lithuania	23	0.8	0	534.9
Iceland	22	0.7	0	519.2
Hesse Gd. Ducal Saxony	52	1.7	1	516.0
Hesse Electoral	51	1.7	1	506.8
Modena	19	0.6	0	468.6
S. Africa New Zealand	46	1.5	1	453.2
Ceylon	18	0.6	0	451.2

Nations with Fewer Wars than Expected (Cont)

Nation[6]	Years[2]	Expected Wars[3]	Observed Wars[4]	Probability of More Wars[7]
Korea				
Burma				
Morocco	74	2.5	2	447.6
Indonesia	17	0.6	0	432.0
Taiwan				
Czechoslovakia	42	1.4	1	408.2
Poland	41	1.4	1	396.5
Honduras	67	2.2	2	386.2
Libya	14	0.5	0	372.2
El Salvador	91	3.0	3	360.3
Cambodia	13	0.4	0	351.0
E. Germany	12	0.4	0	329.7
Laos				
N. Vietnam				
S. Vietnam				
Iraq	34	1.1	1	313.1
W. Germany	11	0.4	0	306.2
Tunisia	10	0.3	0	282.7
Sudan				
Parma				
Ghana	9	0.3	0	259.2
Malaysia				
Guinea	8	0.3	0	233.2
Cyprus	6	0.2	0	181.3
Mali				
Senegal				
Dahomey				
Mauritania				
Niger				
Ivory Coast				
Upper Volta				
Togo				
Cameroun				
Nigeria				
Gabon				
Cent. Af. Rep.				
Chad				
Congo Braz.				
Congo Kins.				
Somalia				
Malagasy				
Sierra Leone	5	0.2	0	152.6

Nations with Fewer Wars than Expected (Cont)

Nation[6]	Years[2]	Expected Wars[3]	Observed Wars[4]	Probability of More Wars[7]
Tanzania				
Kuwait				
Jamaica	4	0.1	0	123.9
Trin.-Tobago				
Uganda				
Burundi				
Rwanda				
Algeria				
Kenya	3	0.1	0	95.2
Zambia	2	0.1	0	63.5
Malta				
Zanzibar				
Malawi				
Gambia	1	0.0	0	31.7
Maldive Islands				
Singapore				

Exhibit 2. Error Probabilities in the Rendering of Verdicts

Nation[1]	Wars/Years[2]	Verdict Guilty: Probability of National Injustice[3]	Verdict Innocent: Probability of Global Injustice[4]
France	19/148	<.0001	.83
United Kingdom	19/150	<.0001	.82
Turkey	17/150	<.0001	.66
Russia	15/150	<.0001	.47
Italy	12/150	.0001	.18
Austria-Hungary	8/103	.0013	.20
China	8/106	.0015	.17
Spain	9/150	.0038	.037
Japan	7/99	.0045	.14
Bulgaria	5/58	.0067	.31
India	3/19	.0070	.70

[1] Nations are listed in order of increasing probability of national injustice.
[2] Source is the same as given in Exhibit 1.
[3] Probability that the nation, if convicted, would be erroneously labeled a more war-prone nation.
[4] Probability that the nation, if exonerated, would be erroneously labeled a less war-prone nation.

Exhibit 2. Error Probabilities in the Rendering of Verdicts (Cont)

Nation[1]	Wars/ Years[2]	Verdict Guilty: Probability of National Injustice[3]	Verdict Innocent: Probability of Global Injustice[4]
Greece	7/134	.021	.021
Yugoslavia	5/85	.030	.074
Rumania	5/88	.033	.062
Germany	6/130	.049	.011
Israel	2/18	.052	.46
Hungary	3/47	.070	.15
United States	6/150	.084	.0028
Egypt	2/29	.12	.21
Ethiopia	3/63	.13	.050
Holland	5/145	.17	.0014
Papal States Mongolia	2/45	.23	.061
Two Sicilies Australia Canada	2/46	.24	.056
Finland	2/47	.24	.051
El Salvador	3/91	.28	.0058
Syria S. Korea	1/17	.29	.18
Bavaria Baden Wuerttemburg	2/55	.30	.027
N. Korea	1/18	.30	.16
Pakistan	1/19	.32	.15
Lebanon Jordan Philippines	1/20	.33	.14
Honduras	2/67	.39	.0095
Meck.-Schwerin	1/25	.40	.082
Morocco	2/74	.44	.0051
Hanover	1/29	.44	.055
Peru	3/128	.47	.0003
Belgium	3/131	.49	.0002
Iraq	1/34	.49	.034
Mexico	3/135	.51	.0001
Brazil	3/140	.53	.0001

Exhibit 2. Error Probabilities in the Rendering of Verdicts (Cont)

Nation[1]	Wars/ Years[2]	Verdict Guilty: Probability of National Injustice[3]	Verdict Innocent: Probability of Global Injustice[4]
Poland	1/41	.56	.017
Czechoslovakia	1/42	.57	.015
S. Africa New Zealand	1/46	.60	.010
Hesse Electoral	1/51	.64	.0061
Hesse Gd. Ducal Saxony	1/52	.65	.0055
Norway	1/56	.67	.0037
Guatemala Bolivia	2/117	.68	.0001
Argentina	2/125	.71	.0001
Chile	2/127	.72	.0001
Nicaragua	1/66	.73	.0014
Colombia	2/135	.75	<.0001
Paraguay	1/70	.75	.0009
Denmark	2/145	.79	<.0001
Thailand	1/79	.79	.0004
Iran	1/111	.89	.0002
Ecuador	1/112	.89	.0002
Portugal	1/150	.95	<.0001

Exhibit 3. Posterior Probabilities of Guilt for Various Prior Probabilities

Nation[1]	Wars/Years[2]	Prior Probabilities[3]		
		1/3	1/10	1/100
France	19/148	>999.9	>999.9	>999.9
United Kingdom	19/150	>999.9	>999.9	>999.9
Turkey	17/150	>999.9	>999.9	>999.9
Russia	15/150	>999.9	>999.9	999.5
Italy	12/150	998.7	994.0	938.1

[1] Nations are listed in decreasing order of the posterior probability of guilt.
[2] Caution must be exercised in evaluating the war records of nations with less than two decades of existence.
[3] Probabilities have been multiplied by 1,000 and rounded to the nearest tenth.

32   Methodological Perspectives

Exhibit 3. Posterior Probabilities of Guilt for Various Prior Probabilities (Cont)

Nation[1]	Wars/Years[2]	Prior Probabilities[3]		
		1/3	1/10	1/100
Austria-Hungary	8/103	981.0	919.7	510.1
China	8/106	975.9	900.1	450.3
Bulgaria	5/58	937.9	770.3	233.6
India	3/19	931.8	752.4	216.4
Japan	7/99	931.7	752.0	216.1
Spain	9/150	857.1	571.4	108.1
Israel	2/18	747.6	396.9	56.5
Yugoslavia	5/85	635.1	278.9	34.0
Hungary	3/47	592.7	244.4	28.6
Rumania	5/88	577.9	233.3	26.9
Egypt	2/29	551.3	214.5	24.2
Greece	7/134	463.3	161.0	17.1
Syria S. Korea	1/17	390.9	124.8	12.8
N. Korea	1/18	372.0	116.3	11.8
Pakistan	1/19	353.5	108.4	10.9
Lebanon Jordan Philipines	1/20	335.5	100.9	10.1
Gambia Maldive Islands Singapore	0/1	315.8	93.0	9.2
Zambia Malta Zanzibar Malawi	0/2	298.8	86.5	8.5
Ethiopia	3/63	288.0	82.5	8.1
Kenya	0/3	282.3	80.4	7.9
Jamaica Trin.-Tobago Burundi Rwanda Algeria Uganda	0/4	266.4	74.7	7.3
Papal States Mongolia	2/45	254.6	70.5	6.9
Meck.-Scherwin	1/25	252.8	69.9	6.8

Exhibit 3. Posterior Probabilities of Guilt for Various Prior Probabilities (Cont)

Nation[1]	Wars/Years[2]	Prior Probabilities[3]		
		1/3	1/10	1/100
Sierra Leone Tanzania Kuwait	0/5	251.0	69.3	6.7
Canada Two Sicilies Australia	2/46	239.6	65.5	6.3
Cyprus Mali Senegal Dahomey Mauritania Niger Ivory Coast Upper Volta Togo Cameroun Nigeria Gabon Cent. Af. Rep. Chad Congo Braz. Congo Kins. Somalia Malagasy	0/6	236.3	64.3	6.2
Finland	2/47	234.1	63.6	6.1
Guinea	0/8	208.6	55.3	5.3
Hanover	1/29	197.3	51.8	4.9
Ghana Malaysia	0/9	195.7	51.3	4.9
Germany	6/130	192.4	50.3	4.8
Parma Sudan Tunisia	0/10	183.5	47.6	4.5
W. Germany	0/11	171.8	44.1	4.2
E. Germany Laos N. Vietnam S. Vietnam	0/12	160.7	40.8	3.9
Cambodia	0/13	150.2	37.8	3.6
Iraq	1/34	141.4	35.3	3.3
Libya	0/14	140.3	35.0	3.3

Exhibit 3. Posterior Probabilities of Guilt for Various Prior Probabilities (Cont)

Nation[1]	Wars/Years[2]	Prior Probabilities[3]		
		1/3	1/10	1/100
Bavaria Baden Wuerttemburg	2/55	133.0	33.0	3.1
Indonesia Taiwan	0/17	113.7	27.7	2.6
Ceylon Burma Korea	0/18	105.9	25.7	2.4
Modena	0/19	98.6	23.7	2.2
Poland	1/41	85.9	20.5	1.9
Czechoslovakia	1/42	79.9	18.9	1.8
Iceland	0/22	79.2	18.8	1.7
Estonia Latvia Lithuania	0/23	73.6	17.3	1.6
S. Africa New Zealand	1/46	59.3	13.8	1.3
Honduras	2/67	55.5	12.9	1.2
United States	6/150	45.5	10.5	1.0
Austria	0/30	43.4	10.0	0.9
El Salvador	3/91	41.2	9.5	0.9
Hesse Electoral	1/51	40.6	9.3	0.9
Hesse Gd. Ducal Saxony	1/52	37.6	8.6	0.8
Morocco	2/74	32.4	7.4	0.7
Norway	1/56	27.6	6.3	0.6
Saudi Arabia	0/39	21.6	4.9	0.5
Yemen	0/40	20.0	4.5	0.4
Luxemburg	0/42	17.1	3.8	0.4
Holland	5/145	14.7	3.3	0.3
Ireland	0/44	14.6	3.3	0.3
Tuscany	0/45	13.5	3.0	0.3
Nicaragua	1/66	12.6	2.8	0.3
Costa Rica Panama Liberia Afghanistan	0/46	12.5	2.8	0.3

Exhibit 3. Posterior Probabilities of Guilt for Various Prior Probabilities (Cont)

Nation[1]	Wars/Years[2]	Prior Probabilities[3]		
		1/3	1/10	1/100
Nepal				
Albania	0/47	11.5	2.6	0.2
Paraguay	1/70	9.2	2.1	0.2
Thailand	1/79	4.5	1.0	0.1
Cuba	0/64	3.0	0.7	0.1
Belgium	3/131	1.8	0.4	<0.1
Peru	3/128	1.5	0.3	<0.1
Mexico	3/135	1.3	0.3	<0.1
Guatemala	2/117	1.1	0.2	<0.1
Bolivia	2/118	1.0	0.2	<0.1
Dominican Rep.	0/79	0.9	0.2	<0.1
Brazil	3/140	0.9	0.2	<0.1
Uruguay	0/84	0.6	0.1	<0.1
Argentina	2/125	0.6	0.1	<0.1
Chile	2/127	0.5	0.1	<0.1
Iran	1/111	0.4	0.1	<0.1
Ecuador	1/112	0.3	0.1	<0.1
Colombia	2/135	0.3	0.1	<0.1
Denmark	2/145	0.1	<0.1	<0.1
Haiti	0/107	0.1	<0.1	<0.1
Portugal	1/150	<0.1	<0.1	<0.1
Venezuela	0/125	<.01	<0.1	<0.1
Sweden	0/150	<0.1	<0.1	<0.1

2

The Measurement of System Structure

James Lee Ray
University of New Mexico

One of the distinctive features of the *Correlates of War* project has been its emphasis on the importance of system structure in accounting for international war. Many researchers have looked to national attributes, dyadic relationships, and internation interactions as possible explanatory variables, but few have looked to the characteristics of the international system itself. Several of the papers in these two volumes reflect that emphasis and also give some indication as to its fruitfulness. My purpose in this paper is to put the idea of system structure into theoretical context, examine the diverse ways in which it may be understood, and then spell out some of the issues and strategies involved in measuring it. In doing so, I hope to provide colleagues working in the field of global politics with a more integrated overview of system structure as we see it and a clearer understanding of the relationship among some of the separate studies that have emerged from the project or are now under way.

Before turning to a discussion of the theoretical usefulness and promise of the concept, a brief definitional aside would seem to be in order. We can think of few words that are so casually and imprecisely used as "system" and "structure"; this semantic permissiveness has even gone so far as to see them used interchangeably. Thus any pattern, order, or regularity—real or imagined—in the referent world may well be graced with the label "system" or "structure." We mean, of course, to use them rather more carefully here. By *system*, we mean an aggregation of social entities that share a common fate (Campbell, 1958), or are sufficiently interdependent to have the actions of some consistently affect the behavior and fate of the rest. In addition, our definition of system is clearly distinct from those that focus on "systems of action" and thus fail to specify which social entities constitute the system (Singer, 1971). By the *structure* of the system we mean the way in which relationships are arranged, but this definition leaves unclear the distinction between two kinds of relationships, that is, those based on *comparisons* between and among states or other entities and those based on *links or bonds* between them. For example, if we refer to the concentration of military-industrial capability in the international system, we are focusing on a structural attribute based on comparisons of the attributes of states. However, if we focus on the bipolarity of the system, we are then discussing a structural attribute which arises out of the links and bonds among states. It should also be pointed out that these two kinds of structural attributes are related in the sense that variation in one may produce variation in the other. For example, a concentration of military-industrial capability in the hands of two dominant states in the system may well lead to its bipolarization.

Use of Structural Concepts

It has long been the custom of scholars who analyze social systems to attach great importance to their structure. From Aristotle through Marx and beyond, social thinkers have assumed and/or theorized that the structure of social systems has an important impact on the behavior of constituent units, as well as on the fate of the system as a whole. For example, Marx argued that a focus on the structural links between those who own the means of production and those who engage in that production is crucial to the understanding of any society. Contemporary social scientists generally find this somewhat incomplete and suggest that structural patterns based on the distribution of power, prestige, income, education, religious beliefs, and ethnic group membership must also be taken into account (Barber, 1968). Disagreement about the relative importance of various structural attributes has persisted, but most observers have agreed on the explanatory importance of social structure.

Coincident with, and perhaps as a consequence of the system analysis focus that has emerged in the study of international politics, there has been an interest in system structure that borrows from the conceptual repertoire of sociologists. Whereas scholars of international politics have long been concerned with such concepts as polarity and the "balance of power," emphasis on such concepts as status inconsistency, structural isomorphism, and vertical mobility is, for the most part, a recent trend and one that we would like to encourage.

This is so, first, because we think that such variables will be crucial to a scientific understanding of war. For example, we believe that knowledge about the impact of structural variables should allow scholars to make theoretically interesting and data-based decisions about "cut points" that delineate time periods during which relationships and processes may differ. We have, for example, rather consistently found relationships that exist between variables in the nineteenth century but that disappear, or change direction, when we shift our focus to the twentieth century. This is interesting, but also disturbing. Until we can identify the factors that account for these intercentury differences, it will be difficult to predict how far into the future present relationships will persist. Structural variables seem to us to be prime candidates for a key role in the explanations of changes in relationships. Concentrating on such variables should help us to explain those changes that we discover empirically and to predict and discover other changes about which we are still ignorant.

Furthermore, we believe that system structural variables will be important as explanatory and/or control variables in system level models of conflict and war and that variation in a single nation's role or location within the system structure might have a significant impact on its war proneness. And even though we are particularly concerned with questions concerning international war, we should also point out that structural variables may have an important impact on other interesting phenomena in international politics. For example, the relationship between bipolarity and levels of, and rates of change in, defense budgets might be explored more fully; as might the effect of a nation's role in alliance structures on its rate of industrialization (Bueno de Mesquita, 1973). One might also hypothesize that votes in the United Nations are affected by a state's place in the system structure or that levels of interaction between and among states will be a function of various structural factors (Galtung, 1964, 1966; Gleditsch, 1967).

Types of Structural Attributes

In this section, we will categorize structural attributes of the international system, to permit the full range of these to be appreciated and also to facilitate discussion of the measurement problems as presented in the next section. We have already mentioned one distinction that we find useful, that is, the distinction between structural attributes based on comparisons among states and those based on linkages and bonds. Both kinds of structural variables order states (or, of course, other social entities) either *vertically* or *horizontally*.

To elaborate, comparison of the resources of states allows one to order them vertically, and these rank orders can be analyzed to determine the extent to which power, or military-industrial capability, is concentrated in the system. One might want to develop a composite index of capability in the manner of Singer, Bremer, and Stuckey (1972), or focus on the distribution of the various resources one at a time. Linkage-based variables, such as those based on the exchange of diplomatic missions (Brams and Alger, 1967; Singer and Small, 1966; Small and Singer, 1973), also order states vertically. By now it is a rather well-established procedure to treat the number of states that establish diplomatic missions in the measured state's capital city as an indicator of that state's diplomatic importance (Wallace, 1973; East, 1972). Once these diplomatic importance scores have been assigned, their effect on individual states can be explored, and the impact of the distribution of diplomatic importance on the system can be analyzed (Ray, 1974). States are also ordered vertically by the number of alliance bonds they form (Singer and Small, 1966; Small and Singer, 1969) and by the number of IGO (intergovernmental organization) memberships they maintain (Wallace and Singer, 1970). Both these variables also have their system level counterparts, of course, that focus on the number of alliance bonds in the system, on the one hand (Singer and Small, 1968), and the number of IGO memberships in the system, on the other.

As for structural variables that order states horizontally, one type is generated by comparing the distribution of states across categories of nominal variables. For example, one structural variable would focus on the percentages of states that fall into different categories of types of regime, such as personalist, centralist, and polyarchist (Wilkenfeld, 1968). Linkages such as alliance bonds, diplomatic bonds, and common IGO memberships also order states horizontally into *clusters*. The form, number, and relationships between and among these clusters can be analyzed in turn to determine the extent to which the system is *polarized*, which opens the way to empirical analysis of the questions concerning the relative stability of multipolar versus bipolar patterns (Deutsch and Singer, 1964; Waltz, 1967; Rosecrance, 1966).

In short, comparison-based and linkage-based interunit relationships order those units vertically and horizontally. Additional structural characteristics of the system arise as a result of differences among these relationships at one point in time or in their changes over time. For example, differences in the distribution of military-industrial capability and diplomatic importance lead to status inconsistency, both on the system and the national level. Comparisons of the clusters that emerge from trading ties, on the one hand, and the formation of alliances, on the other, can also yield interesting information about the system. If these clusters are isomorphic, then the structural order is clear, and it should be relatively predictable which states will be on whose side in the various conflicts that arise in the system. If, contrariwise, the clusters are quite different, one might reason that the system members are highly cross-pressured, that the structural order in the system is unclear, and that the alignments among states on different issues will be relatively unpredictable. Changes in interstate relationships over time, whether comparison based or linkage based, also have implications for the structural clarity of the system. Generally speaking, rapid changes in those structural variables that rank order states will indicate that those states are exhibiting rapid *vertical mobility;* they may be moving up or down the capability or the diplomatic importance dimensions, for example. Similarly, rapid changes in those structural variables that order states horizontally into categories or clusters would indicate substantial *lateral mobility*. States might be changing alliance partners with unusual frequency or breaking and forming diplomatic bonds in unusually large numbers, again making for reduced predictability.

A final important set of variables is based on comparisons of those concepts that order states vertically (i.e., stratify them) and those that order them horizontally, into clusters. Galtung (1966) has tested the hypothesis, for a variety of post-World War II spatial-temporal domains, that a variety of interstate relationships will depend on the rankings of those involved. In an egalitarian system, states of various ranks would be equally likely to interact with, and establish bonds with, each other. In a feudal, or oligopolistic, system, however, top dogs would interact with each other more frequently than those with lower ranks, and those lower-ranked states would interact with each other less than they would with the top dogs. Galtung found that the system was more "feudal" than egalitarian for the time period he analyzed. This might well be expected, but it would be interesting to know, if the post-World War II system is more feudal than the prewar system, how much variation there is between the feudal and the egalitarian extremes and what effect this variation has on the stability or the war proneness of the system. The answers to all of these questions would begin with an analysis and comparison of the strata and the clusters of the international system.

Measuring Structural Attributes

Let us focus first on that class of structural variables that order states vertically into strata. The first of these that comes to mind would probably be "power," or military-industrial capability. Not much need be said here about the measurement problems involved with this variable, as we have already discussed it elsewhere (Ray and Singer, 1973). Suffice it to say that the project has based its measure of military-industrial capability on six indicators: (1) total population, (2) urban population, (3) iron and steel production, (4) fuel consumption, (5) military personnel, and (6) military expenditures. We felt that these tap three important dimensions of the concept of "power," namely, the demographic, industrial, and military dimensions. We have experimented with giving more weight to some of these indicators and less to others, as well as with weighting some of them differently for different time periods, and this remains a continuing concern of the *Correlates of War* project.

The measurement of the concept of "diplomatic importance" has involved the project in a process that has been enlightening to us as well as others but—we hope—that has now run its course. Here we will briefly describe this process to help foster an understanding of the measure as it now stands. Originally, it was proposed (Singer and Small, 1966) that the number of states that establish diplomatic missions in a given state's capital would serve as a good indicator of that state's diplomatic importance. Most governments, it is noted, do not establish diplomatic missions in the capital cities of every other state in the system. In fact, in the past 155 years, the capital city of the average state has been the site of missions from only 45% of the other states in the system. This less than universal exchange is an indication that states make recurrent choices among their peers in the system when they establish missions, depending, inter alia, upon the latters' diplomatic importance to the sending state. Therefore, one can reason that the more missions a state has in its capital, the larger the number of states that consider it to be sufficiently important to warrant the establishment of a diplomatic mission.

When this measure was originally presented, the number of missions received was weighted in various ways. For example, for each ambassador, minister, or *charge d'affaire* accredited to a given capital, the host state received 3, 2, and 1 points, respectively. In short, a state was given more credit for receiving representatives of higher rank. However, this refinement was later discarded, not only because in recent years nearly all missions are headed by ambassadors, but also because the extra information had virtually no effect on the rankings of the states. Another refinement of the measurement in the first article that was abandoned in the second article reflected the importance of nations sending the particular missions. A state received an increment to its importance score based on the number of missions in the capital of the state that *sent* the mission. This procedure also failed to make an empirically important difference in the measure.

One more problem concerning the data on diplomatic missions deserves brief mention. When the data set was first compiled, about 10% of the diplomatic bonds were reported as asymmetrical. That is, the data sources indicated that, in some instances, state A had sent a mission to state B but that B had not reciprocated. Later, we concluded that it would be more accurate to assume that all diplomatic bonds were symmetrical, even if no official record of the second mission could be found. Most recently, however, the evidence convinces us that a few diplomatic bonds were indeed asymmetrical and that most of them have now been identified. Therefore, the data set now in use includes asymmetrical bonds, and the diplomatic scores reflect such asymmetries.

As suggested earlier, an actor experiences status inconsistency when its score on one dimension (such as military strength) is high and its status or rank on another (such as diplomatic importance) is low. These scores may rest on ordinal or interval scales, each with some possible dangers. For example, Wallace (1973) shows that an indicator of status inconsistency that rests on two interval scales will be inflated if one of the distributions is positively skewed and the other is negatively skewed. Given this problem, plus the reasonable assumption that decision makers are often more attentive to mere differences in rank than to the interval distances between ranks, one may use the former alone to tap this phenomenon. Thus, he measures status inconsistency at the system level by adding the differences between each of the states' ranks on strength and importance, and then normalizes this sum by dividing it by $n^2 + n$, where n is the number of states in the system, to control for variation due to fluctuation in system size. Ray (1974) discusses a possible modification of this index on the assumption that differences between higher ranks are likely to be more important than differences between lower rank positions. For example, a state that ranks first on a military-industrial dimension and fifth on a diplomatic importance dimension is likely to perceive itself (and be perceived) as more status inconsistent than a state whose rank scores on those same dimensions are 16 and 20, respectively. Ray incorporates this idea into his index of status inconsistency by basing the index on the differences between the squares of reverse rank scores. (Assigning reverse rank scores involves giving the highest score to the state which scores highest on the ranking criterion. For example, if there are 10 states in the system, and state A has the highest score, its normal rank score would be 1, but its reverse rank score would be 10.)

A comparison of stratification patterns by different criteria does not necessarily confine us to the concept of status inconsistency. One might, for example, be interested in the more general concept of structural clarity as it pertains to the classical balance of power model. This implies that states must make rather fine judgments with regard to the relative power of all the states in the system, and, if these judgments are mistaken, the balance may be lost. One could reasonably hypothesize, therefore, that such judgments would be more difficult if states are ranked differently on the several dimensions of military-industrial capability. That is, if a state has the largest population, *and* the largest industrial capacity, *and* the largest military establishment in the system, there is not much doubt that this state is the most powerful in the system. On the other hand, if a state has the largest population, but only the fifth largest industrial capacity and the tenth largest military establishment, it might very well be difficult to calculate just how powerful this state is. If we carry this problem to the system level and imagine that most of the states in the system rank differently on the different power dimensions, it makes sense to argue that this lack of structural clarity might lead to confusion in the system and, hence, war. It would, of course, make equal sense to argue that such a situation would lead to uncertainty about the outcome of any war and, therefore, reluctance by decision makers to commit their states to war.

How would one measure this aspect of structural clarity? What is needed is a measure of rank order correlation that is applicable to more than two rank orders, of which Kendall's W (Hays, 1963, p. 657) is a useful, if not widely known, example. One could rank order the states at, say, five-year intervals according to the various indicators of military-industrial capability, calculate Kendall's W as an index of the similarity of these rank orderings, and then analyze the relationship between these scores and the war proneness of the system.

Clusters and Poles

The most prominent structural concepts that are used to order states horizontally are clustering and polarization. No measurement problem has evoked more disagreement and a wider variety of approaches among those associated with the *Correlates of War* project than that involving the detection of clusters, and the degree of polarization in the international system. Although this indicates the difficulty of the task, the greater difficulty seems to be in choosing among the many possible approaches.

Two basic choices are to be made. First, one must decide what kinds of bonds—and what kinds of information about these bonds— will be analyzed to establish the strength of the relationships between pairs of nations. This information will typically be recorded in a nation-by-nation matrix, at which time one must decide which of the various matrix decomposition techniques will be used.

Composing the Matrix

With regard to the first of these choices, there are several ways in which the clustering of nations can be manifested. Nations might reveal commitments to one another, or at least agreement and cooperation on issues in the international political system, by their voting patterns in the League or the United Nations (Alker and Russett, 1965) or by the number of common IGO memberships they maintain (Wallace and Singer, 1970). The degree to which nations trade with each other might also be taken as an indication of the strength of bonds among them, as might the exchange of diplomatic missions or the signing of formal alliance agreements.

Which of these dimensions is most relevant to the measurement of the extent to which the nations in the international system are clustered, or polarized? If one is particularly concerned with questions about the war proneness of the international system, Bueno de Mesquita (1975) argues that military alliances are the most relevant indicator. There is a serious problem with concentrating on this indicator alone, however, as many states—including many highly important ones—go along for years without belonging to any alliances. One solution to this problem might be to concentrate on bonds established by the exchange of diplomatic missions, as this indicator is sensitive enough to include interactions among *all* the states in the system. However, it can be argued that an exchange of diplomatic missions involves a commitment between states of such a minor nature that focusing on such exchanges alone will mask clustering patterns. Two groups of states might, for example, be quite antagonistic toward one another (and this might be revealed in the structure of alliance bonds) but still maintain a large number of diplomatic bonds between them. In short, the trouble with focusing on alliance bonds as an indicator of clustering in the system is that too many states are excluded from view. But the trouble with focusing on diplomatic bonds is that the presence of such bonds does not indicate any real commitment between states (and therefore may exist between nations that belong to different clusters), and the absence of such bonds may indicate either substantial antagonism (states usually withdraw recognition from each other only as a result of substantial disagreement) *or* simple lack of interest and contact between the states involved. These two cases, of course, have quite different implications for the clustering structure of the system.

Ideally, then, for the purpose of detecting clusters in the international system, one should be able to differentiate between the absence of a link (be it a diplomatic bond or an alliance bond) that (1) is the result of antagonism and (2) is the result of mere indifference or lack of contact. One could move in this direction in the manner of Savage and Deutsch (1960), who interpreted the relative strength of trading bonds by comparing the actual amount of trade between nations with that which might be expected given the assumptions of their null model. This would be easier and more fruitful for diplomatic bonds than alliances, because alliances are relatively rare. Any null model of the probability of the formation of an alliance bond between two states would predict the absence of such a bond in the vast majority of cases, and the development of the model would not provide sufficient differentiation among pairs of nations to be worthwhile. However, in the case of diplomatic bonds, a null model might help distinguish, at least in a general way, between the absence of a bond caused by antagonism and that caused by indifference.

One might, for example, reason that the probability of any given pair of nations exchanging diplomatic missions is a function, first, of the geographic distance between them. Bolivia and Paraguay, barring some political conflict between them, will probably exchange diplomatic missions; Bolivia and Afghanistan probably will not. Also, the probability that a given pair of states will exchange diplomatic missions is a function of their joint diplomatic importance in the system as a whole.

Perhaps other factors that might predict an exchange of diplomatic missions between a pair of states could be included in this null model. In any case, once such a model were fully developed, one could use, for example, discriminant analysis to specify whether or not a given dyad would be expected to exchange missions. This would, finally, allow one to distinguish between pairs of states that fail to exchange missions because of a lack of contact and those which, under "normal" conditions, would be expected to exchange missions.

This would be one way to deal with the general problem of what kind of information concerning the strength of internation bonds should be included in the nation-by-nation matrix to be analyzed. Another way to deal with the same problem focuses on available information regarding the different types of diplomatic bonds that states form. For example, states may exchange officials of such lowly status as "trade agents" or "vice consuls," or they may exchange minister plenipotentiaries or full ambassadors. Similarly, alliance bonds may vary in strength, according to the strength of the commitments made by signatories, and differentiate among defense pacts, neutrality or nonaggression pacts, and ententes.

This may be the sort of information that should be included in any effort to detect clusters of states in the international system, because it would help to differentiate degrees of commitment between states, but again there are problems. As noted, states are much more likely to exchange ambassadors now (as opposed to officials of lower rank), meaning that the ranks of officials that head diplomatic missions are not comparable over time. Similarly, with regard to alliances, Wallace (1973) argues that differences between defense pacts, neutrality pacts, and ententes are not consistent enough across time to allow one to rank them as to the degree of commitment they entail.

It may be possible to (1) satisfy the need for information about differing degrees of commitment among pairs of states and (2) meet the objections of those who insist that discriminating among types of alliance bonds and diplomatic bonds is unjustified. We could develop a continuum of commitment between states that would rely only on the distinction between the presence and the absence of diplomatic and alliance bonds. Pairs of states would then fall into three categories: (1) those joined by both alliance and diplomatic bonds, (2) those joined by diplomatic bonds only, and (3) those joined by neither alliance nor diplomatic bonds. Another logically possible category would embrace states that belong to the same alliance while having no diplomatic missions in the others' capital, but this must be close to a null set. This procedure could be refined by relying on the null model referred to earlier. In effect, this would replace the third category above with two categories, of which both would contain states without alliance or diplomatic bonds. But our null model would allow us to differentiate between those pairs that do *not* have diplomatic bonds even though, given the geographic distance between them and their diplomatic importance, such bonds would be expected, and those pairs in which the absence of a bond *is* expected. The former pairs would be assumed to be farther apart in the clustering structure of the system than the latter pairs of states.

There are at least two ways to measure the strength of bonds between states that do not rely solely on the direct official links between them. First, it can be argued that the relationship between two states is reflected in the number of links necessary to establish contact between them. If states A and B are not directly linked to each other, but are both linked to state C, they have a second-order link between them. If A and B not only have no link to each other, but also no links to common third states, then they are separated by an even greater distance.

Second, the relationship between two states is reflected in the manner in which they relate to all other states in the system. The more alliance partners they share, for example, the stronger the bond between the two states may be. If one state in the pair has alliance partners not shared by the other, it is reasonable to assume that there is a corresponding weakening of the link between the two states. Here again, however, it is possible for reasonable men to disagree. Wallace (1973) takes into account only those alliance partners shared by each of two states in determining the strength of bonds between them, but Bueno de Mesquita (1975) also takes into account that set of states that is allied to one, but not the other, of the measured pair of states, as well as those states with which neither of that pair is aligned. There are plausible reasons for ignoring this information, and they will be discussed in the following paragraphs.

Decomposing the Matrix

The choice of indicator, whether or not to discriminate among bonds of different strength, and what information to include concerning the relationship of the measured pair of states to others in the system are all decisions that must be made to compose the nation-by-nation matrix. Whatever choices are made, the matrix will contain coefficients pertaining to each pair of states and reflecting the strength of the bond between them. To that matrix can be applied a variety of cluster detection techniques, many of which have found at least one advocate among those involved with the *Correlates of War* project. It is to these techniques that we now turn our attention.

There is little doubt that the simplest, most straightforward clustering technique available is McQuitty's typal analysis (1957). We will not describe the procedure here, except to say that it is simple enough that the analysis can be done easily and quickly by hand; no computer, or even a calculator, is necessary. In using this method as one step in his measure of polarization, Bueno de Mesquita defends it on the grounds that it is easy and inexpensive to compute and that it keeps between-cluster discriminations as large as possible.

The most damaging argument that can be made against typal analysis is that it is *too* simple. Why should we use it to maximize between-cluster discriminations if it does this by brute force and in a way that may possibly distort the data. In any event, McQuitty (1957), Smoker (1968), and Lankford (1974) have all found that typal analysis and factor analysis yield similar results, with the latter particularly interesting in this regard. Having used McQuitty's typal analysis, factor analysis, direct factor analysis, and multidimensional scaling to detect clusters in the same data matrix, Lankford concludes (p. 303) that "the great similarity between factor analysis and McQuitty's method shows the latter is a good approximation of the most cohesive groups." He nevertheless concludes that factor analysis of the correlation matrix remains the most efficient method of cluster identification. Following that reasoning, Bremer (1972) uses factor analysis to detect clusters in formal alliance bonds from 1816 to 1965 "because of personal preference and experience and because of the potential analytical power of the method."

On the other hand, Wallace (1973) explicitly rejects factor analysis as a method of cluster detection in his study of the relationship between polarization and international war. He has two basic reasons for doing this, the first of which is that factor analysis requires that the measure of the strength of inter-nation bonds be at the ratio level. He does not believe that his measure, based on alliance bonds, meets this requirement. Second, he argues that factor analysis requires too many difficult decisions to be made before the final results are generated. "At several stages in its complex sequence of operations, a priori decisions must be made as to how the algorithm shall proceed.... The need to make such crucial theoretical decisions at the very outset weighs heavily against the procedure, given the underdeveloped state of our knowledge" (p. 585).

The first of these arguments, concerning the requirement of ratio level measures is, perhaps, overstated. Rummel (1970, p. 17) states that it is based on a misconception: "factor analysis can be meaningfully applied even to nominally scaled data of a yes-no, or presence-absence type, the lowest and least demanding rung of the measurement ladder." ("Direct" factor analysis would be particularly appropriate for the kind of matrix Rummel refers to here. See Wright and Evitts, 1961; MacRae, 1960.)

The second argument by Wallace against factor analysis is more important, and more damaging. Selection of the number of factors to be extracted and rotated is a complex matter, leaving the door open to arbitrary intervention by the investigator. Rummel (p. 18) admits that the idea of arbitrariness in factor analysis has arisen largely from problems associated with rotating factors, that this sometimes involves "an intuitive or manual determination," and that therefore "rotations will then vary to a certain degree with the intuition of the investigator." As Wallace implies, our knowledge concerning matters of clustering in the international system is not well developed; this may be a good reason for avoiding factor analysis, assuming, of course, that a better alternative is available. His candidate is smallest space analysis (SSA), a multidimensional scaling procedure developed by Guttman (1968) and Lingoes (1966, 1965). Wallace prefers this procedure because it only demands ordinal level measurement and because the solutions it generates depend on fewer intermediate assumptions and decisions than those provided by factor analysis. Finally, the SSA solutions are usually less complex, involving only two or three dimensions.

In criticism of SSA, we would make the following points. It is true that some intuitive, perhaps arbitrary, choices must be made in the course of factor analysis. However, SSA does not deliver us entirely from this problem. The selection of the "appropriate" number of dimensions to be generated, for example, is not automatic. Shepard (1972, pp. 9-10), a pioneer in the development of "nonmetric" multidimensional scaling, suggests that the decision should be guided by whether or not the resulting representations generated by the algorithm are "interpretable and visualizeable." He further suggests that, with the appropriate number of dimensions, the departure from monotonicity should not be "too large." None of these are particularly operational or robust criteria.

Second, although SSA does allow one to plot states visually in n-dimensional space, it does not lead to clear differentiation of clusters. It is often difficult to decide, just by looking at the location of a state in space, which cluster it belongs to, and which other states belong in that same cluster. Typal analysis allows these decisions to be made easily, perhaps too easily. Mihalka (1974) uses Johnson's (1967) hierarchical clustering algorithm to approach this problem but admits that, even with this additional tool, the clusters are sometimes not very distinct.

It is also interesting to note that Lankford (1974, p. 303) in the study mentioned, comparing five different cluster detection techniques, found that the multidimensional scaling method did not do well, producing clusters dissimilar to those produced by the other four. However, he used the "classical" or "metric" approach to multidimensional scaling developed by Torgerson (1958) rather than the nonmetric variety of which SSA is an example (Shepard, 1972).

Bueno de Mesquita criticizes Wallace's use of SSA on the grounds that this technique requires an indicator of *distance* between states; Wallace's index of distance is only sensitive to the number of common alliance partners that both states share, whereas the former utilizes a coefficient of *similarity* that also includes information about those states with which only one, or neither, of the measured pair of states is aligned. Wallace claims that the exclusion of this latter information is a virtue of his index, differentiating it from similarity measures, but they both seem to agree that SSA requires coefficients that can be interpreted as measures of distance, not similarity. If this were true, and if this meant that Wallace were forced by his choice of technique to ignore the information that Bueno de Mesquita is able to incorporate into his measure of polarity, then this would be an unfortunate handicap for Wallace. However, Lingoes (1972, p. 53) himself says of SSA that "any matrix of real numbers may be analyzed by this technique provided that the formal requirements are met ... and the substantive requirement that the values make sense as measures of *similarity* or *dissimilarity*" (emphasis added). Therefore, it is probably unfortunate that Wallace does not include the information used by Bueno de Mesquita, but it does not appear that his choice of the SSA algorithm required this.

None of the clustering techniques used by those associated with the Correlates of War project has established itself as clearly superior. It seems to us that this will not happen until there is substantial progress on three related, but distinguishable fronts. First, the different methods will have to be applied to the *same* referent world matrices, as opposed to matrices of *different* coefficients pertaining to the same states, and the intuitive plausibility of the different results then compared. Second, ideal, simplified matrices, with relatively clear structures, should be contrived and then subjected to the different clustering techniques to see which produces the most sensible interpretation of these clear structures. (The factor analytic technique has been investigated in this way by applying it to data concerning cups of coffee; see Cattell and Sullivan, 1962.) Finally, the results of the different measures should be subjected to "criterion validation." "If an indicator of a variable proves to be related to measures of other variables in predicted ways, our confidence in its validity increases. The greater number of such 'tests' an indicator passes . . . , the greater its criterion validity (Gurr, 1972, p. 47)." In short, the different measures of clustering and polarity must be incorporated into models addressed to international war to see which relates most consistently, in the hypothesized way, to the outcome variable.

Measuring Changes over Time

All the variables we have discussed, of course, change over time, and all these changes can be monitored for direction and magnitude. Perhaps the most prominent of the variables that are generated in this fashion are vertical mobility and lateral mobility, both discussed earlier. Measurement of vertical mobility has been discussed carefully by Wallace (1973). A system level measure of *vertical* mobility, as well as a measure of changes in the concentration of military-industrial capability, are presented by Singer, Bremer, and Stuckey (1972), and the measurement problems associated with these concepts seem relatively simple.

Measurement of *lateral* mobility, however, may not be so simple. Generally speaking, we would want an index of lateral mobility to reflect the extent to which a state is changing its place in the structure of the system by making or breaking, for example, diplomatic bonds, alliance bonds, or bonds in the form of common IGO memberships. One way to do this is simply to count the number of such bonds that are made or broken. But this procedure is obviously less than ideal, because it ignores the fact that some bonds are much more important than others in their implications for the lateral mobility of a state. If state A forms an alliance bond with a state that is already aligned with most of state A's allies, this does not indicate much lateral mobility on the part of state A. But, if A forms an alliance with a state in an entirely different cluster, this does indicate substantial lateral mobility on the part of A, even though the simple number of bonds formed is the same as in the previous case. Obviously, what is needed here is some system of weighting the bonds that are made or broken according to some criterion that would reflect the relative importance of these bonds.

This, of course, is exactly what a clustering technique will provide. If SSA were used, states could be placed in two-dimensional space, and comparing each state's location in that space at two points in time would provide an indication of its lateral mobility. Thus, if a state forms an alliance bond with another that is already aligned with its allies, this will not affect greatly its location in space, and the lateral mobility index will be appropriately low. Conversely, if that same state forms a bond with another that is clearly in a different cluster, this will have an impact on its location in the SSA-defined space, and the lateral mobility index that is sensitive to this will be high.

However, it should be clear that a state could receive a high lateral mobility score without breaking or making bonds of any kind or having other states break or make bonds with it. This is because a state's location in space as defined by a technique such as SSA is a function of what the other states in the system do. If those states break and make a sufficient number of bonds with each other, even if none of these involve the state whose lateral mobility we are measuring, this may result in a substantial change in the location of that state in the SSA space and, therefore, a large lateral mobility index score. Do we want an individual state to receive such a score when it has not made or broken any interstate bonds itself? Perhaps it will be necessary to distinguish between active lateral mobility brought about by the actions of the state itself (or at least by actions in which it was directly involved) and passive lateral mobility brought about by the actions of other states in the system.

Conclusion

Scholars interested in the operation of social systems have long been convinced that the *structure* of those systems must play a key role in explanatory models. The field of international politics has recently been marked by an increased appreciation of this notion. In this paper we have defined several categories of variables that focus on structural characteristics of the international system, as well as the roles and the relationships of states and other entities within that system's structure. Our purpose was to clarify distinctions among these variables and to discuss briefly some of the research possibilities they present.

We have also discussed some of the measurement problems posed by research that relies on these variables. The *Correlates of War* project has generated the data on which several measures of structural characteristics of the international system can be based, and researchers associated with the project have also devised and experimented with a number of indices of different structural variables. We have analyzed here the rationale behind some of the coding procedures used to generate various data sets, as well as the design of different indices. Although this discussion revealed that the project's approach to these problems has not always been monolithic, we hope, nevertheless, that it provides a basis for a clearer understanding of the relationship among some of the separate studies that have emerged from the project.

If this discourse has been at least partially successful, its readers are now more aware of the structural attributes of the international system that may be important to an understanding of international politics. If it inspires an inclination to investigate the impact of these variables, so much the better. In any case, many of the measurement problems involving structural variables have only been touched on here, and none were resolved entirely. They will continue to be a major concern to those involved with the *Correlates of War* project and, we hope, an expanding number of interested scholars.

II

Accounting for the Onset of War

3

National Capabilities and War Proneness

Stuart A. Bremer
Science Center, Berlin

An analysis of war participation over the last century and a half clearly reveals that most nations fight few wars and that a few nations fight most wars (Singer and Small, 1972). Why is this so? What factors lead some nations to resort to large scale military violence rather frequently, while the majority are able to avoid it for long periods of time? One answer rests on the observation that nations differ markedly in power, and on the assumption that the possession of power and its violent application are inevitably linked. Thus, the argument runs, because a few nations are very powerful and most are weak, war participation will tend to be concentrated in the few who are powerful; the purpose of this paper is to examine the relationship between national power and national war experience.

There are several theoretical arguments that lend credibility to the hypothesis that more powerful nations are more war-prone. It may be that they are powerful precisely because they have frequently and profitably used violence to build and maintain their power base. Nation building and empire building have frequently involved the application of military force. Alternatively, it may not be the desire to acquire material capabilities that drives the powerful to war, so much as the more subjective need to preserve the *reputation* of being powerful. Because the ability to influence other national actors rests, in part, on this reputation, powerful actors must, the argument runs, respond to the slightest insult firmly and forcibly. Inevitably, conflict situations arise where it is uncertain as to who is the more powerful actor, and war serves as the empirical test (Blainey, 1973).

A third explanation as to why the powerful should be more war-prone rests on their assumed prominence in the structure and functioning of the international system. To preserve and protect the international order, the powerful are frequently moved to intervene in disputes that are only marginally related to their central concerns. These are not inconsistent explanations, of course. It may be that the desire to acquire material gains, the need to preserve a reputation, and the obligation to serve as the policemen of the world all work simultaneously to produce disproportionate war participation by the powerful nations of the world.

Despite the plausibility of these theoretical arguments, the empirical evidence is inconsistent and incomplete. Based on a survey of recent empirical work, McGowan and Shapiro (1974) concluded that there is a positive association between foreign conflict involvement and such commonly used indicators of national power as military personnel, military expenditures, and total population. Rummel (1968), on the other hand, found little relationship between foreign conflict behavior and indicators of national power, including population, GNP, military personnel, and defense expenditures. More recently, Rosecrance et al. (1974) reported little association between a variety of capability indicators and cooperation and conflict for the five European major powers during the period 1870 to 1881. Thus the question remains, are more powerful nations more likely to become engaged in conflict?

This study differs from those just cited in two important ways. First, we will be looking at only one form of conflict behavior—war—rather than at less intense forms of such as threats, protests, expulsion of diplomatic representatives, and the like, that are included in some of the prior empirical work. The second major difference stems from the much longer time span that this study uses. Whereas prior empirical work focused chiefly on the period of the late 1950s and 1960s, we will be concerned with examining the connection between power and war involvement for the period 1820 to 1964. Thus, although the behavioral domain is smaller in this study, the temporal domain is considerably larger than in previous studies. Let us first turn to the problem of measuring national power.

Measuring National Power

A principal reason that the empirical evidence is incomplete and inconsistent stems from the difficulty of arriving at a satisfactory operationalization of national power. Extensive theoretical discussions concerning the meaning and measurement of power (Bell et al. 1969), although interesting, have not done much to resolve the operationalization problem. The problem stems from the fact that most, if not all, scholars conceptualize power as a relationship whereby one actor is able to exercise control over the behavior of another (Singer, 1963). This type of behavior is difficult—some would say impossible—to observe directly, leaving us in a situation in which there is no completely satisfactory way of operationalizing a key concept.

One approach, adopted by both the traditional and scientifically oriented scholars, is to assess national power by examining a set of indicators of national attributes. The assumption is that nations that possess more of those things that can be used to punish or reward other nations do in fact exercise power over those who have less of those things. Thus, one nation is assumed to be more powerful than another if it possesses superior amounts of selected capabilities. Because we will be relying on an assumption of this nature in what follows, a more precise statement of the question we are interested in would be, do nations with greater capabilities differ from lesser nations with respect to war experience? This leads in turn to the question of what specific indicators of national capability will be used in the analyses that follow.

Indicators of National Capability

Recognizing that material capabilities are essential ingredients in national power, we still face a number of conceptual and empirical problems. Among these are (1) which specific indicators of national capability are we to measure and compare?, (2) how may they best be combined in order to arrive at a unidimensional indicator of national power?, and (3) how valid are these indicators, given the extensive changes over time and the sizable differences between nations on a variety of other dimensions?

Some capability dimensions reflect a national power base which is already usable for influence or coercion; others show a nation's capacity to produce tools of influence in a short period of time and with only minimal changes in social or economic structure; still others reveal capability in its raw form—as resources that could be converted into usable instruments of influence, but only after years of social change and mobilization. Our aim is to devise a set of such dimensions that reflect all three variants of national power base: long-range potential for power development, intermediate-range potential, and realized power. In the present study we emphasize demographic resources to reflect a nation's long-range potential (Davis, 1954), industrial activity to reflect its intermediate potential, and military forces and equipment to reflect its readily usable power (Knorr, 1970; Vansant, 1971). Each of these general dimensions is, in turn, represented by two separate but related indicators.

The demographic dimension consists of a nation's (1) total and (2) urban population. The *total population* measure is simply the best estimate of the number of people living within the nation's boundaries on January 1 of the observation year. The nation's *urban population* is measured as the number of people living in cities with a population of at least 20,000.

The industrial dimension is based on (1) the production of iron or steel and (2) the amount of fuel consumed during the observation year. From 1820 until 1894, the iron and steel production measure consists of the metric tons of *iron* produced; in 1895, reflecting the changed base of industrial activity, we shifted to metric tons of *steel* produced. *Fuel consumption* is measured as the metric tonnage of coal, oil, electricity, and gas consumed in the nation, expressed in coal-equivalent terms. In the present data set, fuel consumption data are utilized only from 1885.

The military dimension is composed of (1) military personnel and (2) military expenditures. *Military personnel* is a measure of the total number of people (excluding reserves) serving in the nation's armed forces on January 1 of the observation year. *Military expenditures* include all government allocations for military purposes, including maintenance of armed forces and acquisition of material. The expenditures are transformed into a common currency (British pounds sterling until 1919, U.S. dollars from 1920 to the present) by the best available estimate of real (market) exchange rates.

Any reader could suggest a number of other factors that have obvious relevance to various aspects of national power. Knowledge of the level and sophistication of social organization, the prevalence of higher and technical education, the amount of popular support for the national government or regime, and class, ethnic, or other cleavages, for example, would refine and improve our estimate of the degree to which a nation's population already represents realized power potential. If we included the manufacture of such technology-dependent products as plastics or chemicals and supplies of crucial raw materials, we might improve our indicator of intermediate potential. And, if we measured the training and morale of military forces and the possession of advanced weapons systems, we might more closely reflect the nation's actual, realized potential.

Our answer to these suggestions consists mainly of emphasizing the *general* nature of the six factors we chose. We cannot deny that additional factors are relevant, but we do assert that (1) they tap subdimensions of power bases which are highly correlated with those that we *do* utilize and would not, in all probability, appreciably change the results; (2) data to measure the factors we do utilize are generally more reliably available, and for longer periods of time, than some possible substitutes; and (3) these six factors are relevant to national power throughout the century and a half of this study, whereas some of the conceivable alternatives are relevant only for shorter periods.

Relationships Among the Basic Indicators

Before we can turn to the examination of the relationships among our six basic indicators, we need to say a word about the extent of the data set we will be using in the following analyses. It consists of observations roughly every five years on six indicators (five, until the addition of fuel consumption in 1885) for those nations considered "central" in an interaction sense to the interstate system of the period in question. Not until 1920 does this data set widen its range to include available data for *all* nations in the interstate system. A more complete data set, with *annual* observations on all six indicators for all nations in the system, was at the time this book was in progress nearly finished and should shed more light on some of the analyses reported here. In analytical terms, the problem rests on the necessary assumption that all nations whose capabilities are not measured for a given observation would score lower, if their capabilities *were* measured, than any presently measured nation. In practice, because *relative* rank position on the various indicators we use is of principal interest to us and because the nations considered politically and diplomatically "central" and therefore measured in our data set also tend to be the same nations that score highest on the demographic, industrial, and military dimensions, that assumption seems a reasonable one.

For any one point in time, we can compute the rank order correlation between how the nations stand with respect to a pair of indicators. Because we have many half-decade observation periods, it is clear that to adequately describe the association between any two of our six measures, we need to compute a correlation for each observation period. Because we have 29 periods for five of our variables and 21 periods for fuel consumption, this results in 395 rank order correlation coefficients.

To meaningfully assess the interrelationships among our six basic indicators, we have selected the median value of the correlations between each pair of variables as the most characteristic of their association over time; these are reported in Table 3-1.

An examination of this table reveals that, with a few exceptions, nations tend to rank similarly on our six indicators. Within each of the three capability dimensions—military, demographic, and economic—the correlations are .65, .72, and .80, respectively, between the appropriate pairs of indicators. The military and demographic groups of indicators are strongly correlated, whereas the correlations between each of these groups and the economic group are somewhat lower. Although some of these associations are intriguing—such as the rather modest correlation between iron and steel production and

Table 3-1. Median T_b Rank Order Correlations Between the Basic Capability Indicators

Milex.	1.00					
Milper.	.65	1.00				
Tpop.	.72	.63	1.00			
Upop.	.81	.55	.72	1.00		
I&S	.50	.26	.36	.54	1.00	
Fcon.	.65	.44	.50	.70	.80	1.00
	Milex.	Milper.	Tpop.	Upop.	I&S	Fcon.

military personnel (.26)—we want to resist the temptation to dwell on these values at the expense of more important matters. The main conclusion that we want to draw from this table is that our six basic indicators seem to be tapping some common underlying dimension. With this in mind we now turn to the description of an index that, it is hoped, captures this common element.

A Composite Index of National Capability

Although a variety of multidimensional scaling techniques could have been used to extract a dimension common to the six indicators, we have elected here to use a simpler, more straightforward approach. The Composite Index of National Capability (CINC) is based on the nation's average percentage share of the six capability resources, and it is computed as follows. For each of the six factors, we ascertain how much of the resource or activity is present in a particular observation year, then calculate the percentage share held by each relevant nation during that observation year. For example, if there were a total of 100 million people on active military duty in all the observed nations in a given year, a nation with an armed force of 2 million would have a "share" of 2% that year. Each nation's score on each of the six indicators is transformed in this fashion into percentage shares, and then each dimensional pair of them is averaged, yielding its mean demographic, industrial, and military scores.

The three averages are then further combined into a single composite score, reflecting each nation's *average* percentage share of all three pairs of factors. A nation will thus score high on CINC if it has great long-range, intermediate, *or* realized potential, and it will score even higher if it is high on more than one of these types of potential. In principle, the national CINC scores could range from 0% to 100%, but in practice even the top-ranked nation seldom scores above 30% of the system's composite share. Table 3-2 shows how the nations ranked on CINC at several points during the last century and a half. As it indicates, the "top dogs" on this particular index are Britain from 1820 until the turn of the century and the United States from 1900 through 1965.

A visual examination of the fluctuating ranks on CINC suggests that the index has substantial face validity. The emergence of China and its rapid power growth, especially in the 1940s and 1950s, can be traced, as can Germany's rise in the late nineteenth century, its

Table 3-2. Computed National Ranks on Composite Potential Index Roughly Every 25 Years

	1820	1845	1870	1895	1913	1920	1938	1960
1	U. Kingdom	U. Kingdom	U. Kingdom	U. Kingdom	U.S.A.	U.S.A.	U.S.A.	U.S.A.
2	Russia	France	France	U.S.A.	Germany	U. Kingdom	U.S.S.R.	U.S.S.R.
3	France	Russia	Germany	Germany	U. Kingdom	Germany	Germany	China
4	Aust-Hung.	U.S.A.	Russia	China	Russia	France	U. Kingdom	U. Kingdom
5	Turkey	Aust-Hung.	U.S.A.	Russia	China	U.S.S.R.	Japan	W. Germany
6	Spain	Turkey	Aust-Hung.	France	France	China	France	France
7	Prussia	Prussia	Turkey	Aust-Hung.	Aust-Hung.	Japan	China	India
8	Sweden	Spain	Italy	Turkey	Italy	Italy	Italy	Japan
9	Holland	Belgium	Spain	Italy	Japan	Poland	Poland	Italy
10	U.S.A.	Holland	Belgium	Japan	Turkey	Spain	Belg/Luxemb.	Poland
11	Sardinia	Sweden	Holland	Spain	Spain	Czechoslovakia	Czechoslovakia	Canada
12	Portugal	Switzerland	Sweden	Belgium	Serbia	Belg/Luxemb.	Spain	Brazil
13	Denmark	Portugal	Portugal	Sweden	Belgium	Rumania	Canada	Czechoslovakia
14	Switzerland	Sardinia	Switzerland	Holland	Switzerland	Canada	Brazil	Spain
15		Denmark	Denmark	Portugal	Holland	Greece	Rumania	E. Germany
16		Greece	Greece	Switzerland	Sweden	Yugoslavia	Argentina	Belg/Luxemb.
17				Rumania	Bulgaria	Argentina	Holland	S. Korea
18				Denmark	Rumania	Switzerland	Turkey	Pakistan
19				Greece	Portugal	Turkey	Mexico	Indonesia
20				Serbia	Greece	Mexico	Yugoslavia	Turkey
21					Denmark	Brazil	Afghanistan	Yugoslavia
22					Norway	Holland	Australia	Rumania
23						Sweden	Sweden	Australia

24	Afghanistan	Hungary	Argentina
25	Iran	Thailand	Mexico
26	Australia	S. Africa	Holland
27	Thailand	Saudi Arabia	N. Vietnam
28	Portugal	Iran	Taiwan
29	Chile	Greece	S. Africa
30	Hungary	Switzerland	N. Korea
31	Nepal	Austria	U.A.R.
32	Lithuania	Portugal	Switzerland
33	Austria	Chile	Sweden
34	Denmark	Denmark	Iran
35	Bulgaria	Colombia	Hungary
36	Colombia	Mongolia	Nigeria
37	Norway	Finland	Austria
38	Peru	Lithuania	Thailand
39	Bolivia	Cuba	Philippines
40	S. Africa	Bulgaria	Greece
41	Finland	Latvia	S. Vietnam
42	Latvia	Norway	Colombia
43	Venezuela	Peru	Israel
44	Uruguay	Iraq	Burma
45	Salvador	Ireland	Bulgaria
46	Estonia	Venezuela	Chile
47	New Zealand	New Zealand	Venezuela
48	Ecuador	Uruguay	Denmark
49	Guatemala	Estonia	Cuba
50	Haiti	Bolivia	Iraq

fall after World War I, its climb once again as World War II approached, and its disappearance as a political unit after that war. The growth in the postwar period of its two successor states—East and West Germany—is also evident. Competition for first rank among the United Kingdom, the United States, and Germany on CINC before World War I, between the United States and the Soviet Union during the interwar period, and among the United States, the Soviet Union, and China in recent years is also visible in the series.

In deriving CINC, the assumptions regarding the additivity and equal weight of the component dimensions are no doubt important ones. Had we introduced different weights for the various dimensions, we would have generated rankings somewhat different from those that emerged. Although we are not wed to the equal weight assumption, it seemed the most defensible choice in the absence of any compelling theoretical reason to weight some capability factors as more important than others. In a preliminary and descriptive study of the type reported here, we thought it best to minimize both the number and the complexity of such assumptions.

It is also important to emphasize that our analyses will take account only of *rank* position, rather than utilizing the interval data that dictates that rank. The hypotheses we will examine suggest only that the amount of war experienced by nations in different rank groups will differ, rather than that the amount of war experienced by a nation will be directly and linearly proportional to its standing on the Composite Index.

Measuring War Experience

Having outlined the procedures and rationale behind our indicators of national strength, we must do the same for our outcome variable. Before we can examine the war proneness of nations of different power ranks, we must specify how we will measure the amount of war that nations experience or inflict on others. In this paper we will present indicators of both the frequency with which nations get into war and the duration, severity, and intensity of that involvement. Because the procedures, reasoning, and resulting data sets are fully presented in *The Wages of War* (Singer and Small, 1972), we may settle here for a brief summary.

First, our focus here is only on *international* wars, which we define as wars involving at least one sovereign state member of the system and leading to at least 1,000 battle-connected deaths among combatant personnel. During the 145-year span covered by this study, there were 91 such wars, of which 49 involved at least one system member on each side. In addition, there were 42 colonial or imperial wars, defined as those in which a sovereign system member is opposed to a national entity that is outside the interstate system.

Second, we will limit our attention to six specific measures of war experience, as spelled out in Table 3-3. The first two measures, rate of war entries and initiations, indicate the relative frequency of different types of war involvements. A war entry is only coded as a war initiation when the nation was the first to undertake large-scale military activity against another. The third measure, average length of war, will enable us to ascertain whether more powerful nations experience longer or shorter wars than their less powerful counterparts. The fourth, fifth, and sixth measures will tell us whether more powerful nations have more or less severe war experiences than the less powerful in absolute terms (battle deaths per war) and relative terms (battle deaths per capita and battle deaths per personnel). The latter measures involve normalizing the battle deaths total for a particular nation in a particular five-year period by its prewar population and prewar standing army respectively. We will now turn to the

Table 3-3. Definition of Measures of National War Experience

Measure	Definition
1. Rate of war entries	Number of war involvements normalized by length of observation period
2. Rate of war initiations	Number of war initiations normalized by length of observation period
3. Average length of war	Months of war fought divided by number of war involvements in an observation period
4. Battle deaths per war	Total battle deaths divided by number of war involvements in an observation period
5. Battle deaths per capita	Average percentage of population lost in wars during the observation period
6. Battle deaths per personnel	Average percentage of pre war armed forces personnel lost in wars during the observation period

procedures for combining *individual* war experiences in order to derive *power rank* war experiences.

The war experience of a power rank is defined as the accumulated war experiences of the several nations that occupied a given rank in the power hierarchy over an extended period of time. A simple example should make this clearer. Suppose we had three nations—A, B, and C—which ranked in the following way in three time periods.

Rank	1820-1825	1825-1830	1835-1840	Rank War Experiences
1	A(1)	B(1)	C(1)	3
2	B(0)	C(1)	B(1)	2
3	C(0)	A(0)	A(0)	0

Suppose further that the number of war involvements for the three nations during each of the three five-year intervals were those given in the parentheses. The rank war experience would be the accumulated war experience of all three nations as indicated on the right-hand side of the table. Thus we assume that a nation holds the same rank from January 1 of the year of observation until December 31 of the year preceding the next observation, usually five years later. Because rank position on this type of indicator changes quite slowly, it is not likely that this assumption will lead to seriously distorted results. And because the number of ranked nations grows over time, the accumulated war experience is normalized by the length of time that the rank is occupied during the 145-year period under study. This enables us to readily compare the war experiences of power ranks.

National Capabilities and War Experience

Having explained the measures of national capability and war activity to be used in the following analyses, we can turn to the general question of the degree to which war experience depends on, and relates to, power rank. First, we examine the results stemming from the use of the composite capability index, and, then, we will consider the pattern that emerges for each of the six separate indicators.

Composite Capability and War Experience

Table 3-4 presents a summary of the war experiences of the nations that occupied the first 50 ranks over the entire span of time. The war measures are listed across the top of the table and for each rank the number of observation periods and the appropriate values for the war measures are given left to right. For example, nations that occupied rank number 1 experienced an average of .62 wars per half-decade—approximately one war every eight years—and initiated .07 wars per half-decade—which amounts to two initiations during the entire period. On the average, this resulted in 19 months of fighting per war, and, as a consequence of these wars, first-ranked nations lost an average of 15,028 personnel per war involvement. These losses averaged .111% of their prewar populations and 15.7% of their prewar armed forces.

An examination of the war experiences for each rank would be extremely tedious and not terribly rewarding, but, before we suggest some summary measures that might be helpful in testing the central hypothesis, we should note two interesting findings with respect to the top ranks. Rank 1 has the highest relative frequency of war *involvements*, which constitutes partial confirmation of our hypothesis that war involvement is rank dependent, but rank 2 has the highest relative frequency of war *initiation*. In fact, almost one-half of the war involvements recorded for rank 2 were cases in which wars were initiated by the second-ranked nation. Furthermore, among the top five ranks, rank 1 has the lowest rate of initiation (2 out of 18), and rank 2 has the highest rate (6 out of 13). To the extent that initiation is a valid indicator of who "forces" a dispute into war, this finding would be consonant with the theoretical positions of those like Organski (1968) who emphasize the inherent conflict between the top dog and the number 2 nation in the power hierarchy. The reasoning is that to overtake number 1, number 2 will be more aggressive in the conduct of its foreign policy, although not necessarily with respect to nation number 1. Of course, this interesting finding does not constitute direct evidence for this position, but rather is only consonant with some of its basic tenets.

An overall examination of Table 3-4 reveals a general downward trend in the magnitude of our war measures as we move from the higher ranks to the lower. This tendency is perhaps clearest with the frequency of war involvement, and Figure 3-1 shows the basic shape

Table 3-4. War Experience by Rank on the Composite Capability Index, 1820-1964

Rank on Composite Index	Years Observed	War Involvements Per Half-Decade	War Initiations Per Half-Decade	Average Length of War	Battle Deaths Per War	Battle Deaths as % of Population × 100	Battle Deaths as % of Pre War Personnel
1	145	.62	.07	19.2	436.	11.1	15.7
2	145	.45	.21	20.4	194.	28.5	31.4
3	145	.52	.10	21.4	442.	36.4	31.3
4	145	.59	.10	18.0	88.	16.1	18.0
5	145	.38	.14	31.1	221.	38.5	29.6
6	145	.41	.14	21.0	54.	7.8	9.4
7	145	.21	.07	28.6	552.	44.9	175.6
8	145	.38	.14	14.2	84.	21.0	23.4
9	145	.21	.10	33.3	84.	23.6	28.5
10	145	.31	.00	28.7	50.	12.8	12.8
11	145	.17	.03	28.2	13.	5.5	4.5
12	145	.14	.00	16.4	25.	32.8	52.5
13	145	.10	.00	43.0	36.	36.1	103.8
14	145	.10	.03	6.0	2.5	7.7	7.5
15	135	.19	.04	17.4	60.	18.3	21.4
16	130	.12	.04	6.7	109.	52.9	29.0
17	95	.06	.00	3.3	31.	74.4	53.3
18	95	.29	.00	15.2	3.2	5.1	8.6
19	70	.36	.14	14.4	7.6	7.9	6.5
20	70	.29	.07	22.4	9.3	11.7	5.3
21	60	.08	.00	6.3	5.2	18.5	16.7

22	55	.18	.09	38.3	22.	47.5	141.3
23	45	.00	.00	0.0	0.0	0.0	0.0
24	45	.00	.00	0.0	0.0	0.0	0.0
25	45	.11	.00	43.6	40.	43.5	100.0
26	45	.11	.00	0.9	25.	25.5	14.7
27	45	.22	.00	54.5	214.	104.1	243.5
28	45	.00	.00	0.0	0.0	0.0	0.0
29	45	.11	.00	6.4	10.	14.1	14.3
30	45	.11	.00	0.0	3.	1.3	3.0
31	45	.00	.00	0.0	0.0	0.0	0.0
32	45	.11	.11	37.3	525.3	536.1	297.1
33	45	.11	.00	34.5	0.1	0.0	0.2
34	45	.22	.00	19.1	8.2	8.1	8.1
35	45	.11	.00	30.9	0.1	0.1	0.4
36	45	.00	.00	0.0	0.0	0.0	0.0
37	45	.22	.00	2.3	0.3	25.0	3.8
38	45	.11	.00	26.4	0.1	0.1	0.6
39	45	.22	.00	21.4	41.4	52.6	62.1
40	45	.11	.11	2.7	0.5	1.1	1.1
41	45	.33	.11	13.9	3.4	3.0	8.4
42	45	.00	.00	0.0	0.0	0.0	0.0
43	45	.11	.00	1.8	2.0	6.9	14.3
44	45	.00	.00	0.0	0.0	0.0	0.0
45	45	.11	.11	2.7	1.0	3.2	2.5
46	45	.11	.00	71.8	17.5	108.1	144.2
47	45	.00	.00	0.0	0.0	0.0	0.0
48	45	.00	.00	0.0	0.0	0.0	0.0
49	45	.11	.00	27.3	0.1	0.1	0.6
50	45	.11	.00	36.4	80.8	320.0	2000.0

of the frequencies of war experience for groups of 5 from the 50 ranks on the Composite Index for the entire period. Ranks 1 through 5 had an average of .48 war experiences per half-decade, or nearly one every ten years. The pattern is clearly for lower-ranking nations to show less frequent war activity, although it is less than perfect. The minimum frequency shown on this figure is .05 war experiences per half-decade, or an average of only one war every 100 years.

A somewhat stronger test of the hypothesis that national war experiences are related to the possession of capability involves correlating each of the war measures with the composite capability index. By using a rank order correlation (τ_b) we can ascertain the degree to which the relationship between the war variables and power rank is a monotonic one, but not necessarily linear.

Table 3-5 presents the correlation values for the entire time span and the separate centuries. The frequency of war involvement and

Figure 3-1. Average Number of War Experiences Per Half-Decade, 1820–1964, by Rank Position on Composite Potential Index

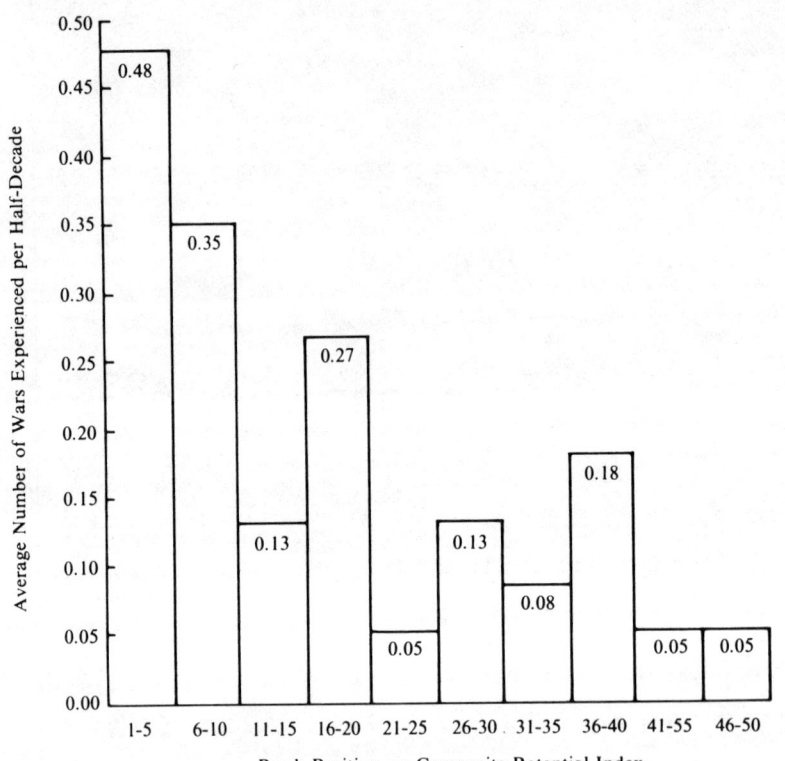

war initiation per half-decade are both highly correlated with capability rank, with some evidence to suggest that the relationship is stronger in the nineteenth century than in the twentieth. In general, it appears that more powerful nations experience and initiate more wars than their less powerful counterparts.

Considering the nature of these war involvements, however, we find only a modest association between relative capability and the duration of war participation. Contrary to what might be expected, the possession of substantial capabilities does not lead to shorter war involvements but, rather, if anything, to longer wars. There are no substantial intercentury differences in this relationship.

On the other hand, although not necessarily longer, the war involvements of high-ranking nations are certainly bloodier, in absolute terms, than low-ranking nations. In both centuries we find a fairly high positive correlation between power ranking and the average number of battle deaths per war. However, the correlations drop noticeably when we normalize these losses by population size and prewar standing army, suggesting that proportionally higher-ranked nations do not lose substantially more than lower-ranked nations, although this would appear to be less true in the nineteenth century than in the twentieth.

In general, then, we can expect that a nation that ranks high on capability to (1) have more war involvements, (2) initiate war more

Table 3-5. Correlations Between War Experience Indicators and Composite Index Rank

War Measure	Entire Period	Nineteenth Century	Twentieth Century
Rate of war involvement	+.60	+.74	+.65
Rate of war initiation	+.64	+.74	+.48
Average length of wars	+.26	+.18	+.28
Battle deaths per war	+.64	+.60	+.62
Battle deaths per capita	+.37	−.03	+.34
Battle deaths per personnel	+.37	+.05	+.34

NOTE: All correlation coefficients are Kendall's T_b.

frequently, and (3) sacrifice more of its population in these wars than a nation that ranks lower.

Before turning to a consideration of the more specific capability indicators and war experience, there is one additional observation to be made. A visual inspection of the war involvement frequencies for those ranks that have been observed for 100 years or more (ranks 1 through 16) suggested that the association between war involvement and rank might be linear, and a regression of war frequency on composite capability rank tended to support this observation. The estimated values of the intercept and slope, respectively, were .12 and −.007, with a resulting r^2 of .65. Figure 3-2 presents a plot of the line of predicted values stemming from this equation and the observed values. The relationship is quite striking; the likelihood of war involvement is directly and positively related to power rank. Put another way, if a nation moves up one rank it can expect, on the average, to become involved in .035 additional wars per half-decade, or about one per 150 years.

Unfortunately we do not have sufficient observation points to estimate the relationship for the lower ranks. Clearly, the regression equation cannot be extended, as the relative war frequency would go below zero before rank 50 was reached. What is likely is that the line levels off at the lower ranks with a value a little above zero.

Figure 3-2. The War Proneness of Capability Ranks

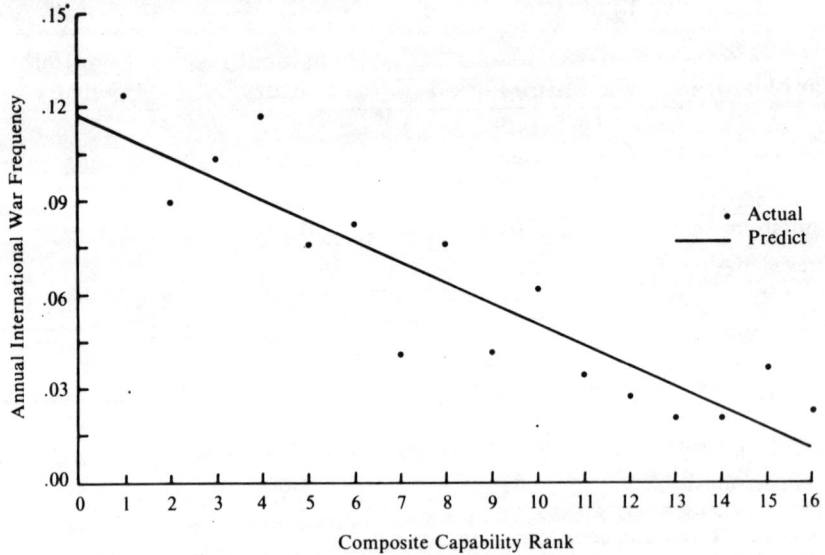

Individual Capability Indicators and War Experience

In the preceding section we saw that certain aspects of war activity are strongly associated with rank on CINC. In this section we will examine each of the six indicators in groups of two to discern whether the results obtained above are largely attributable to some subset of the six indicators. In addition, by briefly examining each indicator we can determine whether these striking results are a consequence of the index construction procedures, rather than a reflection of more fundamental tendencies.

Demographic Dimension

The rank order correlations (τ_b) between the war experience variables and our demographic indicators are given in Table 3-6. Turning first to total population, we find that nations with larger populations relative to other nations tend to be involved in and initiate more wars. This is equally true in both centuries. However, these wars are neither noticeably longer or shorter than those of lower-ranked nations, although once again we see they are bloodier in absolute terms. Controlling for the size of the population and prewar standing army substantially reduces this association, as we found before. And, once again, no sharp intercentury differences are apparent.

Moving to the urban population, we find substantially similar albeit somewhat weaker associations. War involvement and initiation are both positively associated with urbanization, although the association between urbanization and initiation is noticeably weaker in the twentieth century. Nations with larger urban populations do not tend to fight longer wars, in either century, although these war involvements tend to be more costly in absolute terms for the more urbanized nations. As before, however, these losses are not disproportionate when normalized by either population or prewar armed forces.

In general, then, the relationships found using the *composite* indicator are duplicated when we restrict ourselves to only the demographic variables.

Table 3-6. Correlations Between War Experience Indicators and Demographic Rank

War Indicator	Total Population			Urban Population		
	Entire Period	Nineteenth Century	Twentieth Century	Entire Period	Nineteenth Century	Twentieth Century
Rate of war involvement	+.55	+.61	+.56	+.53	+.66	+.50
Rate of war initiation	+.45	+.67	+.40	+.41	+.67	+.32
Average length of wars	+.05	+.10	+.17	+.02	+.28	+.12
Battle deaths per war	+.51	+.59	+.55	+.38	+.54	+.43
Battle deaths per capita	+.19	−.13	+.15	+.03	−.23	.00
Battle deaths per personnel	+.18	+.23	+.16	.00	−.13	−.01

NOTE: All correlation coefficients are Kendall's τ_b.

Economic Dimension

In an earlier section we noted that the variables that tap the economic dimension of the composite index—fuel consumption and iron and steel production—were only moderately associated with the demographic and military variables. We expect, therefore, that the associations between rank on the economic dimension and the war experience variables to be somewhat different. They may, of course, be weaker or stronger.

An examination of Table 3-7 reveals that the relationships are, in fact, somewhat weaker than those previously found. Turning first to iron and steel production, we see that nations that rank high on this variable tend to become involved in and initiate more wars than those who rank low. However, it is also apparent that this is largely a twentieth century phenomenon. We do not find any strong relationship between iron and steel production and the duration of war involvements in either century, however. Nor do we find notable associations between high rank and the war severity measures, either in absolute or relative terms.

Shifting our attention to the fuel consumption variable, we find generally still weaker associations than those found in the iron and steel analysis. High rank on fuel consumption is moderately, but positively, correlated with war involvement and initiation, without a noticeable difference between the centuries. However, there does appear to be a notable positive correlation between the length of war involvements and fuel consumption in the nineteenth century only, and a moderate positive association between battle deaths per war involvement and fuel consumption rank in the twentieth century. But, as we have seen previously, controlling for population size or prewar armed force size reduces this association. Caution must be exercised in interpreting the nineteenth century results, because the fuel consumption series begins in 1870 rather than 1820 as our other indicators do. Thus, the nineteenth century associations are based on only six half-decade observations.

As a whole, then, the economic variables exhibit the same—albeit weaker—pattern of associations reported above. Nations with relatively large economic output—as reflected in iron and steel production and fuel consumption—are more likely to become involved in and initiate wars, but the wars themselves are not substantially different in character.

Table 3-7. Correlations Between War Experience Indicators and Economic Rank

War Indicator	Iron and Steel Production			Fuel Consumption		
	Entire Period	Nineteenth Century	Twentieth Century	Entire Period	Nineteenth Century	Twentieth Century
Rate of war involvement	+.54	+.28	+.55	+.39	+.43	+.43
Rate of war initiation	+.51	+.08	+.45	+.31	+.33	+.27
Average length of wars	+.02	+.29	+.20	+.07	+.50	+.13
Battle deaths per war	+.30	+.07	+.36	+.41	+.18	+.43
Battle deaths per capita	+.14	-.02	+.10	-.17	-.07	+.17
Battle deaths per personnel	-.01	+.33	-.03	+.19	-.07	+.18

NOTE: All correlation coefficients are Kendall's τ_b.

Military Dimension

Finally, we turn to the military variables—expenditure and personnel—and, as is apparent in Table 3-8, with two interesting exceptions, the pattern of associations is the same as we observed earlier. The intercentury differences are generally small, and the familiar association between war involvement and initiation and high standing on a capability dimension is clearly present. Large armies and high defense expenditures do not, however, make for shorter war involvements. The severity indicators, on the other hand, reveal associations that diverge slightly from what was previously found. Whereas the composite index and several of the component indicators exhibited a moderate to strong positive association between capability and the average number of battle deaths suffered in wars, both military variables are weakly correlated with this measure of severity. On the other hand, the composite and several of the other component variables were weakly correlated with the relative measures of severity, whereas the military variables are both positively associated with battle deaths as a percentage of prewar armed forces size. The implication of this relationship is that large armies and high levels of defense expenditures are associated with higher mortality rates in warfare, although we hasten to reiterate that this is based on the prewar army rather than the number of troops involved in the actual fighting.

The overall findings with respect to the military variables may be relevant to the problem of deterrence. Over the past 150 years, there is no evidence to support the contention that the possession of military capability in large quantities ensures peace. On the contrary, the evidence suggests that, regardless of whether nations arm to prevent war or to wage war, in the long run there is a positive association between the possession of military capability and its ultimate use.

Conclusion

Let us restate our major findings. First, nations that rank high on indicators of aggregate capability are involved in and initiate more wars than do nations that have a lower standing. In addition, nations

Table 3-8. Correlations Between War Experience Indicators and Military Rank

War Indicator	Military Expenditures			Military Personnel		
	Entire Period	Nineteenth Century	Twentieth Century	Entire Period	Nineteenth Century	Twentieth Century
Rate of war involvement	+.59	+.61	+.63	+.52	+.51	+.55
Rate of war initiation	+.42	+.54	+.33	+.40	+.43	+.39
Average length of wars	-.11	+.27	+.06	+.06	+.21	+.17
Battle deaths per war	+.05	-.41	+.04	-.02	-.17	-.03
Battle deaths per capita	-.01	-.23	-.06	+.03	+.18	+.04
Battle deaths per personnel	+.54	+.54	+.58	+.52	+.51	+.54

NOTE: All correlation coefficients are Kendall's τ_b.

with larger amounts of aggregate capability have more severe war experiences, as reflected in the tendency for their wars to have higher battle death totals. However, larger amounts of aggregate capability do not, on the average, enable their possessor to reduce the duration or intensity of their war experiences. These findings seem to be equally true in the nineteenth and twentieth centuries. It is interesting to note that capability rank accounts for some aspects of war but not others. In particular, it accounts for the occurrence of wars quite well, but it tells us very little about the severity or magnitude of the war that follows.

On the other hand, it is not altogether surprising that capability is differentially associated with war experience. The duration of a war is probably determined more by the *relative* capability of the contending parties rather than the *absolute* levels with which this paper has dealt. Other things being equal, we would expect, for example, that wars involving nations of roughly equal capability should be longer than those involving nations of more disparate capabilities. Similarly, the level of relative losses—battle deaths normalized by population size or prewar armed forces—appears also to depend more on relative rather than absolute levels of capability. Recent research on this question (Cannizzo, Chapter 8) supports the common sense notion that the more disparate the capabilities of the combatants, the smaller the relative losses of the stronger side and the larger the relative losses of the weaker side.

What are the major implications of these findings? First, they tend to cast doubt on the long-run sensibility of policies that rest on the assumption that the preservation of peace depends on the accumulation of human and nonhuman resources. We are often told that a nation which seeks peace should prepare for war. Yet the historical evidence suggests that it is precisely the nations that have the greatest actual and potential military capability that are disproportionately involved in war.

At the risk of committing an historical fallacy, it would seem to be worthwhile to consider the more specific implications. The nations that, as of this writing, stand at the top of the composite index are as follows:

1. United States
2. Soviet Union
3. China
6. West Germany
7. France
8. Japan

4. India
5. United Kingdom
9. Italy
10. Indonesia

If history is a reliable predictor of future events, it is very likely that one of these "top ten" nations will become involved in an international war within the next decade.

This brings us to an unanswered question which flows logically from the preceding analysis. If nations with greater aggregate capabilities are more likely to become involved in wars, who are their opponents? Are they other more powerful nations or are they significantly weaker? For example, given that the first and second ranks have the highest frequency of war involvement, one null model would predict that these are the most likely pair of antagonists. Is this historically true? Additional research is needed at the dyadic level to answer these questions.

4

Status, Capabilities, and Major Power Conflict

Charles S. Gochman
University of Pittsburgh

Social conflict may be defined as a struggle over claims to status, power, and scarce resources, often involving an attempt to injure or eliminate opponents (Coser, 1968). A particularly brutal form of such conflict is the organized group violence known as *war*. Although it is one of the most destructive types of human behavior, it is also one of the most poorly understood. There are, of course, many explanations as to why wars occur, but they are often simply the product of selective recall rather than of systematic investigation. We have "learned," for example, that World War I resulted from the inflexibility of the German mobilization system, or as Taylor (1972, p. 20) puts it, it was "imposed upon the statesmen of Europe by railway timetables." And we "know" from World War II that "peace in our time" cannot be achieved through appeasement. Recognizing the extent to which causal explanations of war often rest on these selective perceptions of historical events, it is not surprising that Singer and Small (1974) have found in recent state of the world messages unsupportable assumptions about the causes of war and the conditions for peace. What is alarming, however, are the ominous implications of misguided policies; the major power settlement forced on a defeated Germany at the conclusion of World War I stands as a stark reminder that understanding *why* wars occur is a prerequisite to the development of effective measures for preventing them.

An Approach to Understanding War

It seems to me that, if we are to understand the "why" of war, we must begin with the assumption that there are historical regularities that help to account for their incidence, as well as their magnitude and duration. For, if wars are viewed merely as aberrations resulting from the idiosyncracies of human nature, there is little point in seeking either global explanations or generalizable solutions. Assuming, however, that historical regularities do exist, we should direct our efforts toward identifying (1) those factors that alter the probability that a nation will become involved in war and (2) those points in the escalation and deescalation process at which these factors come into play. One of the most effective strategies for doing this is to construct and test alternative models that reflect the best available information from both history and the social sciences. Ultimately, our goal is to define the critical experiment that will allow us to select from among our contending models. It is, of course, not to be expected that any single "theory" will adequately explain the many different types of wars (e.g., civil, colonial, imperial, interstate), and it will probably be necessary to construct different classes of models. It is also to be recognized that, at the earliest stages of development, our theoretical arguments will have to be parsimonious. But, as we test our models, we will discover regularities for which our theoretical arguments poorly account, and by means of a combined deductive-inductive procedure we will gradually improve our "theories" and come to understand the processes by which nation-states become involved in military conflict.

It is within this context that I have begun to develop and test several contending models of major power war involvement; although these models are competing, they are not necessarily contradictory, as they have many areas of overlap. What distinguishes one from the other is the "motivating force" that is alleged to be the impetus toward conflict. In the pages that follow, I present four of the more plausible—but certainly not the only—theoretical arguments accounting for interstate conflict and report some results from preliminary tests on three of these. Considerable time has been consumed in collecting data and constructing indicators, but much refining of the research design, analytic techniques, and, even, theoretical concepts still remains. Nevertheless, I think that this paper contains a number of insights and findings that are of interest to the academic and policy communities, and thus present it here despite its unfinished state. The reader is forewarned that, in places, I have employed unorthodox statistical procedures, but, in doing so, I believe that I have come a bit closer to accurately representing and testing the theoretical notions that I shall put forth in the following paragraphs. Before presenting the theoretical arguments and the empirical evidence, let me offer one final caveat. Although I shall posit the nation-state as actor, it is not my intention to anthropomorphize. The nation "acts" only in the sense that national decision makers more or less accurately perceive and react to their environment. And, when I speak of France or Germany as "acting," I use this only as a verbal shorthand. Having said this, let me turn to the theoretical arguments.

Some Alternative Models

Although historians and social scientists have suggested hundreds of different factors as sources of conflict among humans, only a handful of them appear repeatedly in the literature of these disciplines. Most prominent among these are three that Coser includes in his definition of social conflict, presented in the opening sentence of this paper: struggles over claims to (1) status, (2) power, and (3) scarce resources. Three of the alternative explanations for interstate military conflict that I proffer below are the politico-military analogs to these struggles. A fourth serves as a "base line" against which to compare the first three. It is worth repeating that these four explanations are offered, not because they are the only possible ones, but because they are highly plausible and are among those most frequently suggested by both diplomatic historians and political scientists.

To emphasize the distinctions among the four explanations, I present each in a very simplified form that highlights the different motivating forces that are alleged to drive nations toward military confrontation. It is these motivating forces that distinguish one explanation from the next and from which the models derive their names.

The first of these is the "inequity" model; elsewhere (Gochman, 1975, 1976) I have referred to this as the "fair share" model. The underlying argument is that each state is entitled to particular benefits from the other members of the interstate system in accordance with some recognized standard, and, when a state does not receive its "fair share" of benefits, conflict arises. In my own work, including the research presented here, I have examined this in terms of status inconsistency. Formulated this way, if a state is not attributed the degree of importance (or, in the sociologist's terminology, status) commensurate with its material capabilities, it should attempt to demonstrate its dissatisfaction in the most visible manner available in international politics—namely, by a threat or show of military force. I reason, as does Galtung (1964), that differential treatment resulting from status inconsistency leads to frustration and that a powerful state that is attributed too little importance is likely to perceive that it possesses the capabilities to alter its low status. Indeed, it is not infrequent that we read or hear political commentaries that account for the international behavior of Hitler's Germany, Mao's China, or any number of other states in just such terms. Thus, according to the first hypothesized explanation, *the failure to receive an equitable share of system benefits—in this case, attributed importance—motivates a government to use, or threaten to use, military force.*

A second explanation of interstate conflict is a primitive realpolitik conception that I call the "capability" model. This model underlies the writings of Kautilya and Machiavelli, and, if one is willing to oversimplify his thesis, it can be found in the works of Morgenthau. According to the "capability" argument, dissatisfaction and, ultimately, aggressive behavior are *not* the result of states' receiving less than an equitable share of system benefits; indeed, the argument eshews the principle of fair share. The proponents of the "capability" argument subscribe to the realist contention that statesmen "think and act in terms of interest defined as power" (Morgenthau, 1960, p. 5). Powerful states become engaged in conflict because they attempt to expand the areas over which they exercise control or because their own reputation for power makes them the target for other expansionist states. In short, nations attempt to aggrandize as much as they can; *the more powerful they are, the more likely they are to threaten or use military force.* If one desires a demonstration of this fact, the proponents argue, one need only observe the international behavior of the United States and the Soviet Union throughout the post-1945 period; see also Bremer in Chapter One.

A third contending explanation might be labeled the "necessity" model. In this model, the motivating force toward conflict involvement is objective national need, manifested in the need for raw materials, overseas markets, investment opportunities, living space, or a host of other possibilities. Many parallels might be drawn between the "necessity" model and the concept of "lateral pressure" introduced by North and Lagerstrom (1971). Hence, one variant of the necessity model might stipulate that nations, in the continuous process of development, require certain essential raw materials. If these materials are not available at home or cannot be purchased at reasonable prices abroad, considerable pressure is placed on national decision makers to find other means for obtaining them. Under such pressure, decision makers may well turn to the threat or use of military force to obtain the necessary materials. Explanations of Japanese international behavior just prior to World War II have often played on this theme. Thus, the necessity explanation posits that *the states that have the most critical objective needs are the ones most likely to threaten or use military force.*

Finally, a fourth explanation as to why nations become involved in interstate military conflict might be called the "opportunity" model. In this model, the motivating factor is not inequity, capability, or necessity, but simply the existence of an international environment that is conducive to conflictual behavior. The opportunity model is predicated on a Hobbesian world view. The interstate system, comprised as it is of sovereign states devoid of any superordinate global authority, is seen as a world of anarchy in which states are *at all times* predisposed to conflict involvement. In such a world, only a (transient) restraining domestic or international situation gives pause to what would otherwise be perpetual conflict. Thus, the opportunity explanation differs from the preceding three in that it does not require that a *particular* motivating force be present before a state will threaten or use military force. Rather, it assumes that *states are always predisposed to use or threaten to use military force;* only the presence of certain restraining contextual variables prevents the predisposition from continually being manifested. In the multivariate data analyses hereafter, the opportunity model will serve as a base line against which the other models can be compared.

A Bivariate Test of the Inequity and Capability Models

In the data analyses that follow, we shall examine only three of our four models—the inequity, the capability, and the opportunity. The necessity model presents serious problems for the construction of valid indicators and is left for subsequent work, including that now underway by Choucri and North (1975).

We begin the investigation with simple, bivariate analyses in which we ascertain the statistical association between the hypothesized motivating forces and the threat or use of military force, without introducing any extraneous contextual variables. That is, in these bivariate analyses, we assume that all factors other than the motivating forces are of only marginal importance in accounting for variance in national conflict behavior. This assumption is obviously not consonant with the opportunity model, which stipulates the central importance of restraining contextual variables. The bivariate analyses, therefore, cannot offer a direct test of this model, but subsequent multivariate analyses will.

Focusing, then, on the two models—the inequity and the capability—that do accord with the aforementioned bivariate assumption, we ask a very simple question of each. We ask of the inequity model, "Are the most *status inconsistent* states the most likely to become involved in military conflicts?," and we ask of the capability model, "Are the most *powerful* states the most likely to become involved in military conflicts?"

Identifying the Spatial-Temporal Domain

To investigate these questions, we focus on the set of states that comprise the major power subsystem from 1820 to 1970. The temporal domain encompasses a large number of military conflicts and permits sufficient time for regularities in the data to become visible. In addition, the selection of a 150-year time span permits tests of intercentury differences, a phenomenon that has been found to recur in several former studies of interstate war.

The selection of major powers as the entities to be examined is based on several factors. First, and most important, there is the conceptual criterion. The concept of attributed importance (or status) is likely to be salient to major powers in that they have the capacity to gather and process information that would make them aware of their position vis-à-vis other states. And, if (as hypothesized in the inequity model) status inconsistency is a source of dissatisfaction with existing arrangements, major powers are more likely than other states to believe that they are capable of altering the international order by means of armed conflict. Second, there is the question of relevance: Major powers account for a large proportion of the conflict behavior in the international system. Finally, there is the pragmatic consideration that, at least for the nineteenth century, data for the major powers are more readily available and are of higher quality than for any other set of states.

The major powers and the appropriate years for inclusion in this exclusive club were identified through a mail questionnaire sent to 24 diplomatic and military historians. The 20 who responded agreed almost unanimously on the following list (with the exception of Japan's inclusion during 1960-1970):

State	Inclusive Years
Austria-Hungary	1820-1918
Prussia/Germany	1820-1918, 1925-1945
Russia/USSR	1820-1917, 1922-1970
France	1820-1940, 1945-1970
United Kingdom	1820-1970
Italy	1860-1943
Japan	1895-1945, 1960-1970
United States	1899-1970
China	1950-1970

For the remainder of this study, the term "major power" will refer to these states for the designated years. Parenthetically, it may be noted that the historians' judgment coincides (excepting only Japan, 1960-1970) with the countries and dates suggested by Singer and Small (1972).

Operationalizing the Predictor Variables

Only two predictor variables—status inconsistency and national capabilities—are used in this preliminary test of the inequity and capability rationales, but both have managed to generate a good deal of discussion in the social science literature. Let us therefore take a moment to discuss how these concepts have been operationalized for this set of analyses. Readers who are interested in a more detailed explanation of the scaling techniques employed to construct the indicators of the predictor variables can find this in Gochman (1975).

According to the inequity rationale, *status inconsistency* arises when a nation fails to receive attributed importance commensurate with its material capabilities. We thus need a measure of a state's capabilities (or power base) and a measure of its attributed importance. Because power base is widely held to be a multidimensional concept, I tap three different facets: total and urban population as indicators of demographic capability, fuel consumption and iron and steel production as indicators of industrial capacity, and military personnel and expenditures as indicators of military might. It is, however, unlikely that these indicators are either measured on a true interval or ratio scale or are directly comparable to one another. For example, it is not likely that spending 20% of the world's military expenditure makes a state twice as powerful as one that spends only 10%, nor is it likely that having one-fourth of the world's population is equivalent to producing one-fourth of the world's iron and steel. But if we assume that the indicators do tap the concept we wish to measure and that they are at least ordinally scaled, we could transform them so as to maximize their comparability. I have done this by using a nonmetric scaling technique called Guttman-Lingoes CM-III that maximizes the average intercorrelation among the indicators for all major powers during each year, subject to the restriction that the rank order of the nations on these indicators be preserved. We may think of this procedure as regressing "power base" on its six indicators so as to maximize the fit (R^2).

To obtain a measure of attributed importance, I count the number of permanent diplomatic missions (at the rank of diplomatic agent or higher) received by each major power, and then weight these missions by the importance of the *sending* states. The basic procedure is the same as that used by Singer and Small in their 1966 article, although the particular sociometric technique differs. Diplomatic missions are used as a measure of attributed importance because (1) they play a central role in the communication network of the international system (Modelski, 1972); (2) they represent, in a sense, a systemwide plebiscite on the importance of the receiving state (Small and Singer, 1973); and (3) they have been employed in all previous quantitative studies examining the association between status inconsistency and international war (East, 1972; Midlarsky, 1969; Ray, 1974; Rosecrance et al., 1974; von Riekhoff, 1973; and Wallace, 1973). The importance of the *sending* states is defined as their centrality in the international diplomatic network and is determined by using a sociometric matrix technique (Festinger, 1949) to compute the number of direct and indirect diplomatic links between the partners in all pairs of states in the interstate system.

Finally, the six rescaled indicators of capability and the single indicator of diplomatic importance are used to determine each major power's annual status inconsistency score. The "fair share" rationale that underlies the inequity model implies that we should be able to predict a state's attributed importance on the basis of its capability scores. This suggests that we should simply regress diplomatic importance on the six transformed capability scores and define status inconsistency as the difference between the score we predict for each state and the one we "observe" for it. An analysis of covariance, however, showed that it would be inappropriate to use a single regression equation to represent the relation between capability and diplomatic importance for the entire 150 years under examination. Therefore, regressions are performed within approximate ten-year time slices. These regressions demonstrate that the indicators of capability are highly correlated with the indicator of diplomatic importance and that, over time, the labor intensive indicators of capability (e.g., total population) have contributed less and the capital-intensive indicators (e.g., fuel consumption) more to the association between the two variables.

The index of *national capabilities* used to test the capability model is computed from the six capability indicators that have already been constructed via a scaling method called Conjoint Measurement, version III. Whereas the CM-III procedure maximizes the intercorrelation among the indicators, it does not tell us how to weight the indicators if we wish to combine them into a single index. To ascertain such a weighting scheme, I performed a principal components analysis on the six indicators and used the factor score coefficients from the first factor (i.e., the factor that accounts for the most variance in the intercorrelation matrix of the capability indicators) to represent the relative contribution of each indicator to the overall index. The factor scores were correlated .97 (Pearson r) with the mean unweighted CM-III scores.

Operationalizing the Outcome Variable

It is important to note that almost all quantitative studies of international conflict that have examined long spans of time have focused on the most deadly form of military engagement, that is, war. Unlike these other studies, the models outlined above do *not* specify that *war* will occur, but rather that certain attributes or conditions make states more likely to threaten or to use military *force* to achieve their aims. Whether or not the resulting military confrontations will subsequently erupt into wars is a separate issue.

Thus, to test the models that were specified at the outset, we need to identify all interstate military conflicts (not merely wars) involving one or more major powers during the past 150 years. Although several scholars have compiled lists of conflicts and disputes for various brief periods (Bloomfield and Leiss, 1969; Butterworth, 1976), no adequate data set existed when I undertook this research, and so the greater part of one year was consumed in collecting and constructing this conflict data set. For a case to qualify for inclusion, it had to satisfy three criteria. First, the military conflict had to be between members of the *interstate* system, that is, it had to be between national political entities that independently controlled their own armed forces and received diplomatic recognition from any two members of the interstate system (see Singer and Small, 1966). Second, one of the states using, or threatening to use, military force during the conflict had to be a *major power*. Finally, the conflict had to be government directed, nonaccidental, and nonroutine. This last criterion ruled out such events as inadvertent actions by subordinates, activities by groups over which the government had no effective control, participation in IGO (intergovernmental organization) peace-keeping operations in which national troops were not under direct control of the donor government, and the supplying of advisors and noncombat support to allies.

The procedures by which the data were collected, as well as the categories into which the data were classified, are described elsewhere (Gochman, 1975). Suffice it to say that 134 interstate conflicts were identified in which one or more major powers explicitly threatened or actually employed military force against other members of the interstate system. An additional 37 cases were identified in which major powers used military force to intervene in civil conflicts occurring in other countries. These latter cases are excluded from the current analyses because the factors that motivate such intervention in other country's factional disputes are likely to be different from those that lead to confrontations between states *qua* states. This is, of course, an empirical question, but, given the complex nature of the research design, I thought it best to avoid introducing any additional confounding effects and thus leave the testing of this proposition to a subsequent paper. Also excluded are those interstate conflicts that erupted during the years 1914-1918 and 1939-1945, valid measures of the predictor variables could not be obtained during the course of the two world wars. Although it is not possible to precisely ascertain the extent to which these latter omissions affect the findings of this paper, those findings do not appear to do violence to my historical recollection of the two periods.

Finally, I should note that, for the findings reported in the following paragraphs, the outcome variable is *participation* in, not *initiation* of, interstate conflict. It could be argued that the outcome variable should be initiation of conflict, as the hypotheses to be tested specify that particular factors *motivate* states to threaten or use military force. Yet there are historical instances in which the state that is the target of the initiator (i.e., the state against which the first explicit threat or use of military force is directed) appears to have been no less anxious, and no less culpable, for the conflict than the initiator itself. The Franco-Prussian war of 1870-1871, militarily initiated by France, is a good illustration of this. Fortunately, the initiation/participation distinction proves to be of minimal importance for the current analyses. The major powers initiate more than 80% of the interstate conflicts in which they participate, and the findings reported hereafter are not significantly altered if initiation rather than participation is used as the outcome variable, or vice versa. Thus, even though both sets of analyses were run, to avoid redundancy, only the coefficients for conflict participation are reported.

Testing the Models

In the initial sweep through the data, we are asking only one basic question: "Are the most status inconsistent major powers (or, for the capability model, the most powerful major powers) most likely to become involved in military conflict?"

The simplest way to examine this question, and the one we shall employ, is to place each state, each year, into one of two categories. In one category are those that, during any given year, are "underrecognized" (i.e., are attributed less diplomatic importance than their capabilities would merit); in the second category are those that are "overrecognized." Similarly—and to test the capability model—we can divide the states into those that, during any given year, are *more* powerful than the major power subsystem mean and those that are *less* powerful than the mean. If a considerably larger proportion of underrecognized (as opposed to overrecognized) states become involved in conflict or if a considerably larger proportion of the more powerful (as opposed to less powerful) states become involved in conflict, then we would deem this to be supporting evidence for the appropriate model. Put visually, the more closely the distribution of cases (i.e., the X's) approximates one of the patterns below, the more confident we can be that the inequity or capability model accurately depicts major power conflict behavior.

	Inequity				Capability	
	No Conflict	Conflict			No Conflict	Conflict
Over-recognized	X			Less Powerful	X	
Under-recognized		X	or	More Powerful		X

As is evident from Table 4-1, however, the empirical evidence does *not* approximate the hypothesized pattern. Looking at these contingency tables, we can see that for the entire 1820–1970 period

Table 4-1. Joint Frequency Distribution of Motivating and Outcome Variables for Inequity and Capability Models, 1820–1970

	Inequity (1820–1970)				Capability (1820–1970)		
	No Conflict	Conflict			No Conflict	Conflict	
Over-recognized	79.9% (318)	20.1% (80)	398	Less Powerful	82.2% (301)	17.8% (65)	366
Under-recognized	77.1% (326)	22.9% (97)	423	More Powerful	75.4% (343)	24.6% (112)	455
	644	177			644	177	
	$Q = +0.08$				$Q = +0.20$		

there is very little relationship between either status inconsistency or power, on the one hand, and involvement in interstate military conflict on the other. Those major powers that are underrecognized in a given year have only a slightly greater likelihood (22.9%) of becoming involved in an interstate military conflict in that year than those major powers that are overrecognized (20.1%). The Yule's Q, a measure of the independence of cell frequencies, confirms this point. Similarly, those major powers that are more powerful than the subsystem mean in a given year have only a moderately greater likelihood (24.6%) of becoming involved in an interstate military conflict in that year than those major powers that are less powerful than the mean (17.8%); again the Yule's Q reflects a relatively weak relationship. If, as in Table 4-2, we divide our cases by century (1820–1899, 1900–1970), the relationships remain unchanged, with the capability model continuing to receive slightly more support than the inequity model.

It might be noted that the absence of a clear pattern in the contingency table analyses is not an artifact of our having dichot-

Table 4-2. Joint Frequency Distribution of Motivating and Outcome Variables for Inequity and Capability Models, by Century

	Inequity (Nineteenth Century)				Capability (Nineteenth Century)		
	No Conflict	Conflict			No Conflict	Conflict	
Over-recognized	82.3% (172)	17.7% (37)	209	Less Powerful	84.8% (139)	15.2% (25)	164
Under-recognized	78.9% (187)	21.1% (50)	237	More Powerful	78.0% (220)	22.0% (62)	282
	359	87			359	87	
	$Q = +0.11$				$Q = +0.22$		
	Inequity (Twentieth Century)				Capability (Twentieth Century)		
	No Conflict	Conflict			No Conflict	Conflict	
Over-recognized	77.2% (146)	22.8% (43)	189	Less Powerful	80.2% (162)	19.8% (40)	202
Under-recognized	74.7% (139)	25.3% (47)	186	More Powerful	71.1% (123)	28.9% (50)	173
	285	90			285	90	
	$Q = +0.07$				$Q = +0.24$		

omized the predictor variables. If, for example, we had divided the predictor variables into three categories (i.e., overrecognized, appropriately recognized, and underrecognized or less powerful than, approximately equal to, and more powerful than the subsystem mean), no clearer patterns would have emerged.

It may be, however, that by "lumping" together the data for all major powers we are masking substantial national differences. That is, some major powers may conform to the inequity model, some may conform to the capability model, and yet others may conform to neither. By not differentiating among the major powers, we may fail to uncover these nation-specific associations. And indeed, for our spatial-temporal domain, this turns out to be the case. For example, we can see from Table 4-3 that the inequity model appears to be a rather good predictor of U.S. conflict behavior (producing a Q score of +.87), and the capability model does reasonably well for the United Kingdom in the twentieth century ($Q = +.62$).

In Table 4-4 are presented the Yule's Q coefficients for all the major powers, for the entire 1820-1970 period and for each century. A number of observations can be made about the coefficients in this table. First, the Q scores for the total 1820-1970 period are, for the most part, not very different from the corresponding Q scores for the individual centuries. There are, however, a few instances (e.g., the inequity model: Italy) in which there appear to be intercentury differences in a state's conflict behavior. Given these possible differences, we will continue to conduct separate analyses for the two centuries. Second, a comparison of the Q scores for "all states"

Table 4-3. Joint Frequency Distribution of Motivating and Outcome Variables for the United States and United Kingdom, Twentieth Century

	Inequity (United States, Twentieth Century)				*Capability* (United Kingdom, Twentieth Century)		
	No Conflict	Conflict			No Conflict	Conflict	
Over-recognized	97.1% (34)	2.9% (1)	35	Less Powerful	84.4% (27)	15.6% (5)	32
Under-recognized	70.8% (17)	29.2% (7)	24	More Powerful	55.6% (15)	44.4% (12)	27
	51	8			42	17	
	$Q = +0.87$				$Q = +0.62$		

Table 4-4. Q Scores from Contingency Table Analyses of Inequity and Capability Models for the Major Powers, Total Period and by Century

Nation (N)	Inequity			Capability		
	Total Period	Nineteenth Century	Twentieth Century	Total Period	Nineteenth Century	Twentieth Century
All states (821)	+0.08	+0.11	+0.07	+0.20	+0.22	+0.24
United States (60)	+0.86		+0.87	x		x
United Kingdom (139)	+0.08	+0.20	−0.04	+0.42	*	+0.62
France (139)	+0.06	+0.30	−0.16	+0.34	x	+0.45
Germany (108)	−0.07	0.00	−0.18	+0.50	+0.26	*
Austria-Hungary (94)	−0.07	−0.08	−0.30	−0.55	−0.49	x
Italy (74)	−0.03	+0.63	−0.20	x	x	x
Soviet Union (136)	+0.35	+0.34	+0.58	*	*	*
China (21)	+0.43		+0.43	−0.11		−0.11
Japan (50)	−0.35		−0.41	x		x

x = Q score could not be computed because state was always either "less" or "more" powerful than subsystem mean.
* = Q score was +1.00, but there were too few data points in a row of the table to view the coefficient as a stable estimate.

versus those for the individual major powers illustrates that there is considerable variability in the degree to which the states conform to the hypothesized inequity and capability models of conflict involvement. In a number of instances, the difference in the distribution of cases for "all states" and for an individual major power (e.g., the inequity model: United States) is unlikely to have occurred by chance alone or have been the result of measurement error. Finally, some of the nine major powers appear to conform more closely to one rationale for conflict involvement than to another. The United States and nineteenth century Italy, for example, appear to be better represented by the inequity model, whereas the United Kingdom appears to be more closely approximated by the capability. Yet, in evaluating the generalizability of the inequity and capability rationales, our judgment must be tempered by the fact that most of the major powers conform consistently to neither model. If, for the sake of simplicity, we can say that a Q score with an absolute value of less than 0.25 is weak, one ranging from 0.25 to 0.49 is moderate, one ranging from 0.50 to 0.74 is moderately strong, and one greater than or equal to 0.75 is very strong, then we have only one very strong and two moderately strong coefficients among the 15 nation/century-specific Q scores computed for the inequity model and four very strong and one moderately strong among the 9 that can be computed for the capability model. And, it will be noted, all four very strong coefficients (denoted by *'s) for the capability model are likely to be quite unstable estimates.

Summarizing the Bivariate Findings

Contingency table analysis, of course, is only one of the more simple approaches to investigating these two models of conflict involvement. We might also examine the bivariate association between predictor and outcome variables by employing more powerful statistical techniques that necessitate that the predictor variable be measured on an ordinal or interval scale. I have undertaken such analyses, and the statistical results have not been very different from those that have already been reported. In fact, it is fair to conclude on the basis of bivariate analyses that neither the inequity nor the capability model, as presently operationalized, does particularly well in accounting for major power involvement in interstate military conflict. Each model may have some applicability to different states or different periods of time, but there does not seem to be any simple pattern underlying these associations. For example, (on the basis of the contingency table analyses) we might be tempted to say that the inequity model holds for states that are latecomers to the ranks of the major powers, but Russia may belie this explanation. Similarly, the nineteenth century Italian case upsets the interpretation that the inequity model applies to the most populous major powers. On the other hand, we probably should not have expected that a bivariate association would be sufficient to "explain" the aggressive behavior of major powers. For, while possessing great material capabilities or receiving less than a fair share of system benefits may motivate states to become involved in military hostilities, there are, undoubtedly, a number of factors that place constraints on national behavior. Indeed, considering that we have so far ignored the domestic and international environment within which major powers act, even our modest statistical findings are surprisingly robust. What is really called for is a more complete specification of our models—a specification that incorporates these contextual factors (see Snyder, Bruck, and Sapin, 1962).

A Multivariate Test of the Inequity,
Capability, and Opportunity Models

What, in effect, is being suggested in the preceding paragraph is that receiving little recognition or being very powerful may *predispose* a state to engage in conflict, but whether it actually manifests such behavior depends on the effects of additional contextual factors (to the identity of which we shall turn in a moment). If this argument is correct, then we would expect the distribution of cases, within the 2 × 2 contingency tables that we have been examining, to approximate the following:

	Inequity			*Capability*	
	No Conflict	Conflict		No Conflict	Conflict
Over-recognized	X		Less Powerful	X	
Under-recognized	X	X	More Powerful	X	X

or

That is, if a state is *not* predisposed to engage in conflict (if, for example, it is overrecognized or less powerful than the subsystem mean), then, *regardless* of contextual factors, it will avoid participating in military conflict. Consequently, we would expect no cases of conflict involving overrecognized or "less powerful" states. On the other hand, if a state *is* predisposed to conflict involvement (if, for example, it is underrecognized or more powerful than the subsystem mean), then the probability of involvement *depends* upon the effects of contextual variables. An underrecognized or "more powerful" state will become involved in conflict if there are no domestic or international environmental constraints to inhibit its behavior and, conversely, it will avoid conflict if such environmental constraints are present.

A reexamination of Table 4-3 reveals that both American and twentieth century British conflict participation approximate, to a greater or lesser degree, the hypothesized distributions just suggested. Indeed, nearly half of the nation/century-specific distributions for the inequity model and fully two-thirds of the distributions for the capability model approximate these distributions. Four of them (i.e., those identified by an * in Table 4-4) actually conform precisely to the hypothesized capability distribution. Although this in no way proves that the inequity or capability model has any validity—after all, we have not even identified the alleged inhibiting factors—it at least suggests that a more completely specified model that incorporates both (1) an impetus that predisposes states to conflict involvement *and* (2) contextual factors that constrain aggressive behavior may improve the models' ability to account for the conflict behavior of major powers.

This forces us to ask, "What are some of these factors that might alter the probability that those states, predisposed to conflict involvement, will actually manifest aggressive behavior?" Or, put another way, "What aspects of the domestic and international environment of major powers are relevant to their conflict behavior?" A perusal of the social science literature suggests three promising areas for investigation: physical, psychocultural, and structural.

First, in the area of physical capabilities, there would seem to be a prima facie case for believing that a state's conflict participation might be associated with *changes* in its potential power. In particular, it seems reasonable that decision makers would feel that their states are less vulnerable to external threat and more able to achieve external objectives when national capabilities are rising, and just the opposite when capabilities are declining. Thus, it might be hypothesized that *a state, predisposed to conflict involvement, will be more likely to become engaged in a military conflict if its capabilities are rising and, conversely, it will be less likely if its capabilities are declining.* Organski (1968, Ch. 14) posits just such behavior when he discusses the threat to international peace posed by an ascending challenger to the existing power hierarchy.

A second area to which we might turn for contextual influences on conflict behavior is in the psychocultural realm. In particular, we might speculate that states—or, more precisely, statesmen and their respective populaces—learn from prior war experiences. Psychologists tell us that experience serves as a source of expectations concerning the consequences of future behavior and that such behavior is shaped by prior reward and punishment (see Berkowitz, 1962; Mowrer, 1960; and Skinner, 1974). Historians (e.g., Shy, 1971) and political scientists (e.g., Raser, 1965) have suggested the applicability of learning models to nation-states. If we consider wars to be punishing experiences—some wars being more punishing than others—then we can surmise that decision makers consider both the costs of their prior war experiences and the will of the people to support subsequent military ventures before engaging in activities that might initiate a new war. *The more costly the previous wars, the less likely are decision makers to press for new confrontations.*

A third area in which we might look in our search for mediating influences on conflict behavior is among structural relationships. Anthropologists, psychologists, and sociologists have all found that aggressive behavior can be inhibited or displaced when individuals have multiple competing loyalties that place cross-pressures on them and raise the spectre of social disapproval (see, for example, Colson, 1953; Coser, 1956, 1968; Rule and Percival, 1971; and Worchel, 1966). At the level of the nation-state, Galtung (1968) has hypothesized that multiple competing affiliations among states can produce cross-pressures that ameliorate aggressive behavior and, thereby, reduce the likelihood of military conflict. Thus, we might hypothesize that *the more cross-pressured a state, the smaller is the probability that it will become involved in conflict.*

Finally, this emphasis on the moderating influence of cross-pressures suggests that the mere *opportunity* to have multiple competing relationships may have a moderating effect on conflict involvement. This calls to mind the rather extensive literature on interstate system polarity. This literature usually contrasts bipolarity, a situation in which two opposing blocs leave little room for realignment, to the more flexible multipolar system in which multiple competing relationships are possible. Although there is no theoretical consensus on whether bipolarity (Waltz, 1964), multipolarity (Deutsch and Singer, 1964), or some mixture of the two (Rosecrance, 1966) is more conducive to peace, the advocates of multipolarity are, perhaps, more numerous. For our purpose, we shall hypothesize that *a bipolar system increases the likelihood that a single cleavage will demarcate and exacerbate potential conflicts, whereas a multipolar system reduces the likelihood of such conflicts.*

Operationalizing the Contextual Variables

To briefly reiterate, we have found that neither being status inconsistent nor possessing great capabilities is, by itself, sufficient to explain why major powers become involved in interstate military conflict. I have postulated that it is also necessary to consider those contextual factors that may serve to reduce the likelihood that states, predisposed to conflict involvement, will actually manifest violent behavior. Drawing from the social science literature, I have suggested four such factors: declining national capabilities, costly prior war experiences, cross-pressures produced by multiple competing affiliations, and potential cross-pressures associated with system multipolarity. Traditionally, all four factors have been prominent elements in efforts to identify the causes of war (see, for example, Blainey 1973).

To empirically investigate whether these modifications will improve the inequity and capability models fit to major power conflict behavior, it will be necessary to construct operational indicators of each of the contextual factors. Let me therefore take a moment, before turning to our final set of data analyses, to explain how each of these factors has been operationalized. The reader who is interested in a more detailed discussion of the indicator construction is referred to Gochman (1975).

The indicator of *change in national power capabilities* is simply the difference between a state's power capabilities score in one year and its score in the preceding year. The annual capabilities scores that are subtracted from one another are standardized scores (z scores) already derived for the preliminary test of the capability model. Thus, the indicator measures the change in a state's capabilities relative to that of the other major powers.

The indicator of the perceived cost of *prior war experience* is a bit more complex. It is comprised of (1) a measure of the cost of previous war involvements and (2) a decay factor that reflects the likelihood that the salience of these costs will recede with the passage of time. As a measure of cost, I follow Richardson (1960) and Rosen (1971, 1972), and use battle deaths per million population. As a decay factor, I employ an inverse logistic function such that the indicator of cost approaches zero after 15 years. The decay function reflects what psychologists have discovered about long-term memory (see, for example, Hovland, 1951, and Wickelgren, 1972) and the noted empirical association between logistic curves and biological, economic, sociological, and historical phenomena (see Bailey, 1967; Coleman, 1964; Hart, 1945; Lotka, 1956; and Taagepera, 1968).

As an indicator of *multiple competing affiliations* (and, what I shall infer to be cross-pressure), I measure the extent to which each major power is tied to all other major powers on two relevant dimensions: the economic and the military. These dimensions are selected not only because they are highly visible, but also because they appear to be both central to international interactions and major factors in the credibility of national commitments (Russett, 1963). For each major power, each year, I construct a "trade-by-alliance" contingency table, representing its principal trade partnerships and formal military alliances with the other major powers, and compute a Kendall's τ_b statistic (with corrections for empty cells, if any). The resulting τ_b value, with its sign reversed, is the indicator of cross-pressure. Thus, a *completely* cross-pressured state would be one that is "bonded" to all states in the subsystem but is neither (1) a formal military ally of any of its principal trade partners (defined as those that account for a minimum of 5% of its total imports and exports) nor (2) a principal trade partner of any of its military allies. A state that is *not at all* cross-pressured is one that trades principally only with its formal military allies and allies militarily only with its principal trade partners. The indicator of cross-pressure is constructed for only twentieth century years; adequate trade data are not available for the years prior to 1879, making construction of the indicator impossible for most of the nineteenth century.

Finally, the measure of *system polarity* that I will employ is essentially the same as that used by Singer and Small (1968). It is computed on the basis of military defense pacts among the major powers that are directed against other major powers and reflects the extent to which the major powers have lost their freedom to form new, logically consistent alliances in a given year; that is, the extent to which potential competing affiliations have been ruled out. By "logically consistent," I mean that decision makers of a state cannot reasonably commit their state to fight, simultaneously, on opposing sides in a military conflict. And, therefore, these decision makers cannot reasonably be cosignatories of two (or more) mutual defense alliances directed against one another. To take an example, if there are five major powers, divided into two opposing dyads and one unaligned state, there remain only two logically consistent alliance dyads that still can be formed. Because the members of the existing dyads cannot reasonably ally (against themselves) with either member of the opposing alliance, only the unaligned state is free to form new alliances. It can form an alliance with each member of one of the existing alliances but cannot, by the same reasoning, simultaneously form alliances with members of opposing alliance blocs. Hence, of the maximum of ten dyads that might be formed in a system of five states, only two alliance choices remain unmade. The system is, therefore, nearly bipolar—eight-tenths of its possible dyads having been used up—and this configuration is assigned a score of 0.8.

Testing the Models

Having constructed these indicators, we now turn to the multivariate data analyses. The spatial-temporal domain will again embrace the major power subsystem from 1820 to 1970. But, rather than employ contingency table analysis as we did in the bivariate investigation, we shall now use probit analysis, which can be thought of as an appropriate surrogate for multiple regression when, as in our study, the outcome variable is dichotomous (i.e., conflict/no conflict) rather than continuous.

We also reintroduce, at this point, the opportunity model that was described earlier and offer it as not only a plausible explanation of major power conflict behavior, but also an appropriate base line against which to compare both the modified inequity and the modified capability models. It will be recalled that the opportunity model posits that states are *always* predisposed to conflict involvement and whether they manifest this behavior depends entirely on the existing values of contextual variables. The modified inequity and capability models, on the other hand, posit that the manifestation of conflict behavior depends not only on the existing values of contextual variables, but also on the presence of particular predisposing factors. Thus, by comparing the three models, we will be able to tell whether the contextual variables *alone* are sufficient to account for major power conflict behavior, or whether the presence of a particular predisposing factor is also necessary.

To investigate the predictive power of the modified inequity and capability models, the following procedure is employed. Each major power's annual scores on the four contextual variables are multiplied by zero for those years in which the major power is *not* theoretically predisposed to conflict (i.e., when it is not underrecognized or not more powerful than the subsystem mean) and multiplied by one for those years in which it is predisposed. This procedure is consistent with the theoretical argument we have made—namely, that the value of the contextual variables is relevant *only* when the state is predisposed to conflict. Hence, when a state is not predisposed in accordance with the inequity or capability rationale, the value of all contextual variables is set to zero and we would expect, as depicted in the 2 × 2 tables earlier in this section, that no conflict would occur. Of course, for testing the opportunity model, the extant values of the contextual variables are always used, as this latter model posits that states are *always* predisposed to conflict.

Table 4-5 presents the estimated proportion of variance in each major power's conflict involvement that can be accounted for by the opportunity, modified inequity, and modified capability models. We see in Table 4-5, as we saw earlier in the bivariate analyses, that—even after we have controlled for relevant aspects of the domestic and international environment, such as changes in national capabilities, prior war experience, economic and military cross-pressures, and system polarity—neither the inequity nor the capability model in its modified form can adequately account for the conflict behavior of all states in either century. Rather, we find that each model has *some* predictive power for some states. The inequity model, for example, does moderately well in accounting for the conflict behavior of Austria-Hungary in the nineteenth century and for the United States, China, and particularly Japan in the twentieth. The capability model offers somewhat more modest fits to nineteenth century British and Austro-Hungarian as well as twentieth century German and

Table 4-5. Estimated Amount of Variance ($\hat{R}^2$) in Each Major Power's Conflict Involvement Accounted for by Opportunity, Inequity, and Capability Models

Nation	N		Opportunity		Inequity		Capability	
	Nineteenth Century	Twentieth Century	Nineteenth Century	Twentieth Century	Nineteenth Century	Twentieth Century	Nineteenth Century	Twentieth Century
United States		59		.14		.46		.14
United Kingdom	80	59	.25	.18	.09	.12	.25	.18
France	80	59	.00	.77	.02	.15	.00	.15
Germany	80	28	.12	.99	.21	—	.07	.41
Austria-Hungary	80	14	.08	.71	.47	—	.34	—
Italy	40	34	.06	.30	.13	—	—	.30
Soviet Union	80	56	.13	.31	.10	.18	.11	.10
China		21		.10		.42		—
Japan		45		.87		.81		—

Opportunity: $Y = b_0 + b_1 X_1 + b_2 X_2 + b_3 X_3 + b_4 X_4$

Inequity: $Y = b_0' + b_1' SX_1 + b_2' SX_2 + b_3' SX_3 + b_4' SX_4$

Capability: $Y = b_0'' + b_1'' PX_1 + b_2'' PX_2 + b_3'' PX_3 + b_4'' PX_4$

where Y = Interstate military conflict
X_1 = Δ Capabilities
X_2 = Prior war experience
X_3 = Economic-military cross-pressures in the twentieth century, zero otherwise
X_4 = System polarity
S = One if underrecognized, zero otherwise
P = One if more powerful than the subsystem mean, zero otherwise

NOTE: Germany, Austria-Hungary, and Italy are underrecognized on too few occasions during the twentieth century and/or engage in military conflict too infrequently when underrecognized to compute stable estimates. Italy during the nineteenth century and Austria-Hungary, Italy, and Japan during the twentieth century are more powerful than the major power subsystem mean on too few occasions and/or engage in military conflict too infrequently when more powerful than the mean to compute stable estimates.

Soviet conflict behavior. The question to ask, however, is not simply whether the modified inequity and capability models fit the empirical data, but whether these two models offer us any greater predictive power than does the more parsimonious opportunity model? That is, are the contextual variables alone sufficient to account for conflict behavior, *or* are the particular predisposing factors associated with the inequity and capability rationales needed to obtain better fits to empirical reality? The answer to this question is contingent upon the countries and time periods about which we are talking. For example, if we compare the inequity with the opportunity model, it is evident that the former gives us a modest increase in our ability to account for nineteenth century German conflict behavior and a sizable increase in our ability to account for nineteenth century Austro-Hungarian, twentieth century American, and twentieth century Chinese behavior. The capability model compares far less favorably with the opportunity model, with nineteenth century Austria-Hungary displaying the only increase in "explained" variance—and, even here, the increase is not as large as it was for the inequity model. Thus, it may be concluded that although the "fair share" rationale that underlies the inequity model increases our ability (vis-à-vis the opportunity model) to account for the conflict behavior of some major powers, the "power politics" rationale that underlies the capability model does not.

If we focus then on the inequity and the opportunity models, we note the following. Neither model individually (nor both models jointly) offers a very compelling explanation for ninetenth century major power conflict behavior. Indeed, for France, Italy, and Russia, the squared multiple correlation coefficients never exceed 0.13. But, for the twentieth century, the two models together offer considerable predictive (or, more accurately, "postdictive") power—accounting poorly only for British behavior. The opportunity model produces quite respectable fits with the pattern of conflict involvement for the five "old continent" major powers (France, Germany, Austria-Hungary, Italy, and the Soviet Union), and the inequity model seems applicable to the non-European latecomers to the major power ranks (the United States, China, and Japan). If the squared multiple correlation coefficients for Japan seem to belie this interpretation, it should be pointed out that Japan is underrecognized in 41 of her 45 major power years, and so the coefficient for the opportunity model is, for all practical purposes, a measure of the "fair share" rationale that underlies the inequity model.

When we turn from the overall goodness-of-fit of the models to the magnitude and direction of the probit coefficients themselves, the picture becomes more complex. It should be noted that to compare the strength, as well as the general direction of the associations between the contextual variables and conflict involvement, the probit coefficients are standardized. This is done by multiplying the unstandardized coefficients by s_x/s_y, where s_x is the standard deviation of the interactive term produced by multiplying the contextual variable by the dummy "predisposing" variable, and s_y is an estimate of the standard deviation of the outcome variable. Because this is a rather unorthodox procedure with probit coefficients, I have de-emphasized the precision of the estimates by simply indicating into which of five categories the coefficients fall.

The direction and magnitude of the probit coefficients are reported in Table 4-6. We see that, although there are some very sizable associations in the empirical data, there are also a large number of essentially zero relationships and the directions of a number of the nonzero relationships are quite different from the ones that were hypothesized to exist. By and large, no clear patterns emerge in Table 4-6. This, however, is not totally unexpected, given the way in which a major power during a specific century seems to adhere to one hypothesized model of conflict behavior as opposed to another. In an effort to reduce the amount of "noise" created by this situation, I present in Table 4-7 only one set of coefficients for each country in a given century; the set chosen (with the exception of that for Japan) is the one that accounts for the most variance in the country's conflict involvement. By examining the direction and magnitude of the probit coefficients from these "best fitting" models, we may be better able to discern patterns of associations that might be hidden in the welter of coefficients generated by models that only poorly fit the data. Indeed, in viewing the table, the reader may want to exclude from consideration the direction and magnitude of coefficients from even the best fitting models, if these models do not produce at least some minimum R^2, for example, 0.20 or 0.25.

Although Table 4-7 still contains a number of conflicting coefficients, there seem to be some basic underlying patterns in the data. Turning first to the nineteenth century, we find that the effects of the contextual variables are generally consistent, although fairly weak. During this earlier century, changes in national capabilities have basically no effect on the conflict involvement of the major powers. The single exception is Germany (Prussia), and contrary to

Table 4-6. Direction and Magnitude of Effects of Contextual Variables on Each Major Power's Conflict Involvement for Opportunity, Inequity, and Capability Models

		Opportunity Model				Nineteenth Century Inequity Model				Capability Model			
	N	Δ Cap.	War Exp.	Polar.	$\hat{R}^2$	Δ Cap.	War Exp.	Polar.	$\hat{R}^2$	Δ Cap.	War Exp.	Polar.	$\hat{R}^2$
United Kingdom	80	0	0	+	.25	0	0	+	.09	0	0	+	.25
France	80	0	0	0	.00	0	0	0	.02	0	0	0	.00
Germany	80	0	0	+	.12	−	−	+	.21	0	0	0	.07
Austria-Hungary	80	0	0	+	.08	0	−	0	.47	+	−	0	.34
Italy	40	0	0	0	.06	0	+	+	.13				
Soviet Union	80	0	0	0	.13	0	0	0	.10	0	0	0	.11

NOTE: Germany, Austria-Hungary, and Italy are underrecognized on too few occasions during the twentieth century and/or engage in military conflict too infrequently when underrecognized to compute stable estimates. Italy during the nineteenth century, and Austria-Hungary, Italy, and Japan during the twentieth century are more powerful than the major power subsystem mean on too few occasions and/or engage in military conflict too infrequently when more powerful than the mean to compute stable estimates.

Categories for probit coefficients:

+.50 ≤ ++
+.25 ≤ + < +.50
−.25 < 0 < +.25
−.50 < − ≤ −.25
  − ≤ −.50

(Continued on page 110)

Table 4-6. Direction and Magnitude of Effects of Contextual Variables on Each Major Power's Conflict Involvement for Opportunity, Inequity, and Capability Model (Cont)

		Opportunity Model					Twentieth Century Inequity Model					Capability Model				
	N	Δ Cap.	War Exp.	Cross-Press.	Polar.	$\hat{R}^2$	Δ Cap.	War Exp.	Cross-Press.	Polar.	$\hat{R}^2$	Δ Cap.	War Exp.	Cross-Press.	Polar.	$\hat{R}^2$
United States	59	0	0	0	+	.14	—	++	++	++	.46	0	0	0	+	.14
United Kingdom	59	0	+	+	+	.18	—	0	0	0	.12	0	+	0	+	.18
France	59	0	++	+	++	.77	0	0	+	0	.15	—	0	0	0	.15
Germany	28	0	—	0	0	.99						0	0	0	++	.41
Austria-Hungary	14	++			—	.71										
Italy	34	0	++	—	0	.30										
Soviet Union	56	0	—	0	+	.31	0	—	0	+	.18	0	—	0	++	.30
China	21	0	++	+	0	.10	+	++	0	—	.42	0	++	0	—	.10
Japan	45	++	0	+	—	.87	++	0	+	—	.81					

Table 4-7. Direction and Magnitude of Effects of Contextual Variables on Each Major Power's Conflict Involvement for Best Fitting Model

Nineteenth Century		Δ Cap.	War Exp.	Cross-Pressure	Polarity	$\hat{R}^2$
United Kingdom	Opportunity	0	0		+	.25
France	Inequity	0	0		0	.02
Germany	Inequity	−	−		+	.21
Austria-Hungary	Inequity	0	−		0	.47
Italy	Inequity	0	+		+	.13
Soviet Union	Opportunity	0	0		0	.13
Twentieth Century						
United States	Inequity	−	++	++	++	.46
United Kingdom	Opportunity	0	+	+	+	.18
France	Opportunity	0	++	+	++	.77
Germany	Opportunity	0	−	0	0	.99
Austria-Hungary	Opportunity	++	++	0	−	.71
Italy	Opportunity	0	−	−	0	.30
Soviet Union	Opportunity	0	++	0	+	.31
China	Inequity	+	++	0	−	.42
Japan	Inequity	++	0	+	−	.81

NOTE: Categories for probit coefficients are:

+.50 ≤ ++
+.25 ≤ + < +.50
−.25 < 0 < +.25
−.50 < − ≤ −.25
− ≤ −.50

our hypothesis, an increase in German capabilities relative to those of the other major powers is associated with a *decrease* in the probability of German conflict involvement. A glance at Table 4-6 reveals that this inverse relationship exists only for the German inequity model. Although underrecognized, Germany engages in two conflicts when her capabilities are rising—each time against an overrecognized major power (Austria-Hungary in 1850 and France in 1870-1871); in contrast, she engages in four conflicts when her capabilities are declining—three times against much weaker opponents (Denmark in 1848 and 1864 and Switzerland in 1856). Notwithstanding this prudent selection of foes, German behavior in these cases seems to be unique among the major powers; for all other major powers, changes in capabilities are unassociated with conflict involvement during the nineteenth century.

With respect to prior war experience, we again find that the behavior of one country runs counter to the hypothesized relationship. This time it is Italy and, again, it is only for the inequity model. Although underrecognized, Italy tends to be *more* likely to engage in conflict following her more costly war experiences. Given the relative mildness of these wars and her success in unifying the peninsula through war, the unexpected stimulating effect of prior experiences may be understandable. But, again, the exacerbating effect appears to be unique to Italy. The prior war experiences of the United Kingdom, France, and Russia are unassociated with their subsequent conflict involvements, and, as hypothesized, Germany and particularly Austria-Hungary are much less likely to engage in conflict following costly wars. Thus, on the whole, prior war experiences tend to have either no effect, or an inhibiting one on nineteenth century major power conflict involvement.

Finally, as hypothesized, system bipolarity tends to exacerbate, and multipolarity inhibit, major power participation in interstate conflict during the nineteenth century. Although the behavior of France, Austria-Hungary, and Russia does not appear to be affected by the polarity of the system, the United Kingdom, Germany, and Italy are all more likely to engage in conflict when major power alignments are polarized.

In general, then, increases in national capabilities tend to have no effect on the conflict involvements of the major powers during the nineteenth century, whereas prior war experience tends to have an inhibiting, and polarity an exacerbating, effect on major power conflict involvements.

Turning to the twentieth century, we find in Table 4-7 that the effects of the contextual variables are far more powerful than in the preceding century but that the direction of the effects is less clear. As hypothesized, there is a tendency for increases in a state's capabilities to enhance the likelihood of its getting into conflict. Although the conflict behavior of the United Kingdom, France, Germany, Italy, and the Soviet Union appears unaltered when these countries' capabilities increase relative to those of the other major powers, China and particularly Austria-Hungary and Japan are noticeably more likely to engage in conflict as their capabilities rise. The United States, on the other hand, as Singer and Small (1974) found when examining major power war involvement, tends to be more prone to conflict when her capabilities are declining relative to those of the other major powers. Once again this unexpected finding is for a state that adheres most closely to the inequity model, but, unlike Germany in the nineteenth century, the United States in the twentieth century is less prudent in selecting conflict opponents—thrice confronting the Soviet Union (1957, 1961, and 1962) and once confronting China (1958) while American capabilities are in *relative* decline. Overall, however, and despite the direction of the coefficient for the United States, increases in national capabilities tend to have no, or an exacerbating, effect on the conflict behavior of the major powers during the twentieth century.

Contrary to the relationship that was hypothesized to exist, prior war experience generally *increases* the likelihood of subsequent confrontations for major powers during the twentieth century. The United States, United Kingdom, France, Italy, and China are all more, rather than less, likely to engage in conflict following war experiences. Only Germany and the Soviet Union—nations devastated by world wars—display the hypothesized negative effect. This suggests that, for most major powers, the losses suffered in war are not sufficiently severe to outweigh perceived gains from conflict participation, that, in fact, wars may actually enhance the belief that military force is a useful means for obtaining one's objectives. Only catastrophic losses (in one case accompanied by occupation and in another by internationalized civil war) seem to produce the hypothesized inhibiting effect on major power conflict involvement during the twentieth century.

Somewhat surprisingly, the coefficients for cross-pressures show that, if anything, the existence of multiple competing affiliations stimulates, rather than constrains, conflict participation by the major powers during the current century. Only Italy exhibits the hypothesized negative association between cross-pressures and conflict involvement. Germany, Austria-Hungary, the Soviet Union, and China seem unaffected by economic and military cross-pressures, and the United States, United Kingdom, France, and Japan are *more* likely to become involved in conflict when the states with which they principally trade are not the same as those to which they are militarily allied. Apparently, such cross-pressures are insufficient to inhibit their involvement in conflicts. Indeed, multiple affiliations may actually *enhance* the probability of conflicts by increasing the number of states with which a major power has salient relationships. Because almost all relationships are comprised of some mixture of cooperative and conflictive interactions, this can lead, on the one hand, to increased commitments to come to the military aid of some states and, on the other, to a heightened awareness of incompatible interests between states. Either or both of these occurrences may well increase the probability of conflict involvement.

Finally, the coefficients in Table 4-7 reveal that system polarity has no clear, unidirectional effect on major power involvement in military conflict during the twentieth century. The two superpowers (the United States and Soviet Union), along with the United Kingdom and France, are more prone to become involved in conflict when the system is highly polarized; while the Asian powers (China and Japan), along with Austria-Hungary, are less conflict-prone in a bipolar world. Neither Germany nor Italy appears to be noticeably affected by the degree of system polarity. It is not clear why some states should be more, and other states less, conflict-prone in a bipolar system. Disregarding, for the moment, the coefficient for Austria-Hungary, one possible explanation is that the bipolarization of the interstate system has historically meant the alignment of opposing European (or Eurocentric) blocs in which Asian states have had little, if any, importance. If, as hypothesized, the antagonism between opposing bloc members in the bipolar world leads to increased conflict between the blocs, then it is the Eurocentric, and not the Asian, states that we would expect to be most exercised by the bipolar division of the system. Indeed, one might speculate that it is precisely during those periods in which the structure of international alignments is most diffused (i.e., least bipolar) that the Asian states are most visible and most active in international interactions—both cooperative and conflictive. A bipolar system would, therefore, be associated with an increased probability of conflict involvement for Eurocentric states and a decreased probability for Asian states. The negative coefficient for Austria-Hungary, of course, is not accounted for by this rationalization, but, given the fact that she remains a major power for only a few years after the turn of the century, the negative coefficient could reflect some particularistic factor related to Austria-Hungary's situation in the 14 years preceding the outbreak of World War I.

In general, then, we find that increases in national capabilities, prior war experiences, and economic-military cross-pressures tend to increase the probability of conflict involvement for major powers during the twentieth century, whereas system polarity increases the probability of involvement for Eurocentric states but decreases it for Asian states.

Summarizing the Multivariate Findings

The effects of the contextual variables have proven at points to be somewhat different, and usually more complex, than those that were hypothesized. We have found them to be less sizable in the nineteenth than in the twentieth century. And, during the latter century, the effects of two variables—prior war experience and economic-military cross-pressures—have generally been contrary to those that were predicted. Despite these discrepancies (for which interpretations have been offered), the magnitude of the multiple correlation coefficients for the best fitting models suggests that, at least during the current century, the posited contextual variables are relevant and important in accounting for major power conflict involvements. Although none of the three hypothesized models—the opportunity, the inequity or the capability—offers a particularly good explanation for nineteenth century major power conflict involvement, two of the models have sizable empirical support in the twentieth century. The opportunity model, which posits that states are *always* conflict prone, accounts for an average of 54% of the variance in the conflict involvement of the six European major powers during the twentieth century. And the inequity model, which posits that states are conflict-prone when they are not attributed importance commensurate with their capabilities, accounts for an average of 56% of the variance in the conflict involvement of the three non-European major powers. Considering the norm for social science research, these are not trivial results. Why one model should apply to one set of states, and the other model to another set, is far from evident. What *is* clear is that the states to which the opportunity model is most applicable are European major powers that have lengthy traditions of political leadership in world affairs, whereas the states to which the inequity model is most applicable (the United States, China, and Japan) are all tyros in the ranks of the major powers. Thus, one plausible conjecture might be that the opportunity model describes, as it were, the "traditional" pattern of major power behavior, whereas the inequity model captures the behavior of latecomers to the major power ranks—states that may be insecure about their new-found status or particularly sensitive to perceived attempts to exclude them from major power decision-making circles. The validity of this conjecture is subject to empirical verification. That is, if the nature of the motivating force underlying conflict involvement is associated with the length of time that a state is a major power, then the pattern of involvement for those major powers that currently adhere to the inequity model (i.e., the United States, China, and Japan) should gradually alter and come to resemble the traditional pattern of the European major powers.

What, however, are we to conclude about the poor showing of the capability model when compared with that of the inequity and opportunity models? It can, of course, be argued that the capability model is rather naïvely operationalized. But, if the association between material capabilities and conflict involvement is as high as many traditional scholars have suggested, should we not have expected to find at least some indication of the relationship, despite the simplicity of the model? Bremer (Ch. 3), for example, has shown that there is a very strong relationship between a state's rank on capabilities and its involvement in *war*, if not in subwar conflict. Why then do our findings appear to be different?

There is, of course, a rather simple statistical explanation. In limiting myself to the major powers as the spatial domain to be examined, I made it more difficult than it might otherwise have been to find an association between the level of a state's capabilities and its conflict involvement. I selected a small set of highly homogeneous states from a much more disparate population of states in terms of capabilities. As a result, the variance of the predictor variable—and, concomitantly, the likelihood of uncovering a strong statistical relationship—was much smaller than it would have been if I had chosen, for example, all the members of the interstate system as my spatial domain. But to say that, by reducing the variance of the predictor variable, I thereby lessened the chance of finding a *strong* statistical relationship does not mean that we should have found *none*. In preliminary investigations, such as the one reported here, "intraocular trauma" plays an important role; that is, if a strong relationship exists, it should probably hit the researcher between the eyes. Quite obviously, the analysis of the capability model produced no such trauma.

This statistical explanation, however, does suggest an equally simple (and related) theoretical explanation—namely, that the applicability of the opportunity model to *major power* conflict involvement does not preclude the possibility that the capability model might provide a quite satisfactory explanation of interstate conflict *in general*. The major powers constitute a small set of states that cluster at the top of the international power hierarchy, and, as such, the *capability* model would posit that these states would be extremely conflict-prone. The goodness-of-fit of the *opportunity* model to major power conflict involvements may merely indicate that once states reach such a high level of conflict proneness, differences in capabilities no longer differentiate among their conflict behavior. In other words, our findings do not rule out the possibility that the "power politics" rationale that underlies the capability model (i.e., that the more powerful a state, the more likely it is to threaten or use military force) is generally applicable to interstate conflict involvement. What our findings do indicate, however, is that the relationship between national capabilities and conflict proneness is not strictly monotonic for states at the upper extremity of the power hierarchy.

Conclusions and Implications

The theoretical arguments, data manipulations, empirical findings, and post hoc rationalizations presented in this paper have been both lengthy and intricate. In essence, however, they reduce to the thesis that interstate conflict involvement is a product of motivating and contextual factors: motivating factors that predispose national decision makers to threaten or use military force and contextual factors that constrain (or, conversely, exacerbate) this predisposition. Four different motivating factors (i.e., inequity, capability, necessity, and opportunity) have been posited, and three of them examined for the major powers of the nineteenth and twentieth centuries within the context of changing national capabilities, prior war experiences, economic and military cross-pressures, and varying degrees of system polarity.

I suspect that researchers always yearn for more powerful or more consistent findings than those that they uncover. I am certainly disappointed that my hypothesized models accounted so poorly for major power conflict involvement during the nineteenth century. On the other hand, the preceding set of preliminary analyses has produced what I consider to be extremely interesting results for major power conflict involvement during the twentieth century. The principal finding is that there have been two distinct patterns of conflict involvement for major powers during the current century. The traditional European major powers have been opportunists, predisposed to engage in conflict whenever contextual factors have been favorable to such behavior. The more recent major powers in North America and Asia seemingly have responded to inequities, being more likely to engage in conflict when the importance attributed to them by other members of the interstate system has been incommensurate with their material capabilities. This may have important implications for international politics in the years ahead.

In addition to this distinction between states motivated by opportunity and those motivated by inequity, we also have found some differences among the major powers with respect to the effects of contextual variables. Perhaps the two most theoretically interesting discoveries are that (1) only those states that suffer catastrophic losses in war are deterred by those experiences and (2) system bipolarity has an exacerbating effect on the conflict propensity of Eurocentric states, but not on the propensity of Asian states. This latter discovery is particularly revealing; we too infrequently appreciate the extent to which a state's position in the network of international interactions alters the way in which a given contextual factor (such as bipolarity) impinges upon it.

Finally, we have found that (1) increases in national capabilities and (2) increasing diversification of economic and military ties (and, presumably, cross-pressures) tend to enhance the probability of major power conflict involvement in the twentieth century. The United States is an important exception to the first of these two associations, being more prone to conflict involvement when her capabilities are declining relative to those of the other major powers. It would be interesting to explore, in a subsequent (and more refined) investigation, the extent to which the direction of the association between changing capabilities and conflict involvement is related to whether a state is a defender of (or challenger to) the international status quo.

For the nonce, however, rather than move off to some new investigation, it may be instructive to see what implications the preceding findings may have for international politics in the years immediately ahead. The journalistic literature abounds with speculation about the likelihood of the superpowers' or China's becoming involved in military conflict in the near future. Let us reflect on the state of world affairs in the mid-1970s and engage in our own speculation about the likelihood of such conflict involvement.

The world today is becoming continually less bipolar as the blocs forged at the conclusion of World War II begin to disintegrate under a range of economic and political pressures. The states of the Western alliance, confronted by resource scarcities, are unable to agree on a program for shared resource allocation. And, faced with economic recession, they are pursuing explicitly self-serving policies of international market expansion. Such economic behavior is occurring simultaneously with, and is partly a result of, the perception of a diminished military threat from the Soviet Union. Adding fuel to the fire are questions being raised by America's allies concerning the United States' ability and willingness in the wake of the war in Indochina to fulfill her security commitments to her European and Asian allies. As a result, America's allies have begun to seek an accommodation with the Soviet Union and her allies.

This process of "depolarization," of course, has not been one sided. If anything, the Sino-Soviet schism manifested itself sooner and has deteriorated further than any fissure in the Western bloc. The expanding military and industrial capabilities of China, as well as her proximity to the Soviet Union, have led Soviet and Chinese leaders to view one another through hostile lenses. At the same time, the Soviet Union's East European allies have become decidedly less preoccupied with West German "revanchism" and decidedly more cognizant of their need for Western industrial technology. Contacts between East European and Western states have been tempered by the vivid realization that too hasty a process of bridge building could resurrect a renewed demonstration of the Brezhnev doctrine, yet the détente policies of the superpowers themselves—culminating in agreements on strategic arms limitations, human rights, and food transfers—can only serve to encourage interbloc contacts between the superpowers' allies and undermine residual support for bipolar policies.

Accompanying this relentless movement away from bipolarity is the steady liberalization of trade policies between East and West. Many items that formerly were embargoed in East-West trade now flow freely. Western machine parts and vehicles for transportation move with increasing ease into East European, Soviet, and even Chinese ports, and discussions are underway that promise to increase the flow of Eastern mineral and energy resources to the West. This trade, cutting across military alliances, is still minute when compared with intrabloc trade, but at least Soviet-Western economic transactions, if not those between China and the West, promise to reach sizable proportions in the not distant future. Added to this is the increasing reliance of industrial countries on mineral and energy resources from Third World states. These trends toward East-West and North-South trade suggest that the set of states with which the major powers have important economic ties may become increasingly more diverse than the set of states with which they have formal military alliances.

On yet another dimension, world politics today is in flux. Although the absolute capabilities of the major powers continue to grow, the relative capabilities of some major powers vis-à-vis others have been declining. In recent years the relative capabilities of the United Kingdom and France have been decreasing, whereas those of China have been increasing, albeit erratically. The Soviet Union, too, has been on the rise. And the United States, though still expanding her capabilities, is not growing nearly so rapidly as in the past.

Finally, despite the recent American involvement in the war in Indochina, the world has been relatively free of direct major power war involvement during the past decade and a half. The Chinese have not engaged in large-scale war since the border conflict with India in 1962, and the Soviets have refrained since the Hungarian uprising in 1956. This is not to say that either Peking or Moscow has abandoned the use of military force—the Soviet invasion of Czechoslovakia in 1968 and the Sino-Soviet border skirmishes along the Ussuri River in recent years should quickly dispel any such notion. What it does point out is that Chinese and Soviet military losses in recent altercations have been minimal.

If the preceding paragraphs represent an accurate reading of the current state of world affairs, if the empirical findings reported in this paper are well founded, and if the patterns of conflict involvement that have persisted through the first three quarters of the twentieth century recur, then certain implications about the likelihood of Chinese, American, and Soviet participation in military conflicts may be drawn from this research.

For example, the Chinese appear to be operating in a very precarious environment. An examination of the coefficients in Table 4-7, in conjunction with the world scenario sketched above, suggests that almost all the contextual elements for the manifestation of military conflict are present today. Increasing Chinese power capabilities are likely to be conducive to Peking's use of force, as is the movement away from system bipolarity. The Chinese have not had any recent war experience that might induce them to reassert their military prowess, but recent border skirmishes will do nothing to discourage future conflict. Of course, our findings suggest that the Chinese will *not* be predisposed to conflict involvement unless they perceive that they are failing to receive an equitable share of system benefits, and the drift of international politics in recent years has been to rectify the 20-year policy of exclusion that has been directed at them by Western nations. The diplomatic recognition of China by Western countries, the admission of China into the United Nations, and the reopening of Sino-Western commercial relations have all signified a slowly increasing acceptance of China as a full-fledged member of the international community, although our raw data indicate that she is still underrecognized. Our findings suggest that a continuation of the policies of acceptance represents a positive step toward reducing the likelihood of Chinese military activities. Conversely, given the contemporary state of world affairs, any movement away from these policies could result in an increased likelihood of China using military force.

The United States also appears to be traveling along a path sprinkled with military enticements. As can be seen from Table 4-7, two of four contextual variables currently offer, and perhaps a third portends to offer in the near future, an environment conducive to the use of American military force. If past patterns are any guide to future behavior, the recent war experience of American forces in Indochina is likely to increase rather than reduce Washington's incentive to employ military force on future occasions. Similarly, trade liberalization policies that reduce the overlap between military allies and major trade partners are likely to diminish constraints on the use of American force. Third, any reduction in the relative military-industrial capabilities of the United States—a possibility raised by the recent decline in the growth rate of these capabilities and also strongly hinted at in statements by American leaders—will further increase the likelihood of conflict involvement. The contextual factor that might stem the tide toward military engagement is the loosening of the bipolar bloc system. It should, however, be noted that the pattern of conflict involvement for the United States conforms most closely to the inequity model, and it therefore can be expected that Washington should not be predisposed toward participating in conflict as long as American leaders perceive that the United States is receiving an equitable share of system benefits (which seems to be true today whether one looks at the statements of American national leaders or the raw data used in the current analyses). One caution, however, might be inserted: If a supposition outlined above is correct—namely, that the inequity model is applicable to states that are relatively new to the major power circle and are, therefore, particularly insecure about their new-found status— American conflict behavior in the near future may come to approximate more and more the behavior depicted by the opportunity model. Germany may offer an example of a state that underwent such a metamorphosis. In the nineteenth century, German conflict behavior, if only modestly, displayed characteristics of the inequity model, but, as we saw in Table 4-7, the behavior of twentieth century Germany is depicted well by the opportunity model. It is possible that the United States also might undergo such a change.

If our analyses are well founded, the contextual variables appear to be least conducive to Soviet conflict behavior. Table 4-7 suggests that neither the rise in Soviet military-industrial capabilities nor the increasing diversity of her military and economic ties is likely to have much effect on her conflict behavior, but the movement away from bipolarity should serve to constrain Moscow's use of military force. The rather lengthy hiatus since the last Soviet war involvement suggests that the constraining effects of prior Soviet war experience— and the twentieth century findings reported in Table 4-7 indicate that the Soviets are one of only two major powers restrained by such experience—may be wearing thin. Nevertheless, there still may be some residual effect from the devastating experience of the Soviet Union during World War II. Of course, the primary danger in Soviet behavior is the volatility inherent in the opportunity rationale. This rationale suggests that the Soviet Union is *always* predisposed to conflict involvement, and changes in the domestic and international environment could well trigger a military response.

It should be noted that the final segment of this paper has been highly speculative. I have outlined what conflict behavior might be expected *given* the assumptions of our models, the operationalizations of our indicators, and the predictive power uncovered by our data analyses. Such speculation offers no more than a crude estimate of possibilities—but an estimate based on patterns that have been manifested across, at least, three quarters of a century. The crudeness of our projections should not be a cause for despair; rather it should be an incentive to seek a more complete understanding of why interstate conflicts (and, particularly, wars) occur and, hopefully, to develop effective measures for preventing them.

5

Influence Strategies and Interstate Conflict

Russell J. Leng
Middlebury College

Once a foreign policy objective has been determined, the most difficult problems facing the national decision maker turn on the question of influence. "How," ask the decision makers from state A, "can we persuade, coerce, or even seduce the policy makers in state B to comply with our wishes?" However the question is put, influencing another nation's behavior is the critical problem of diplomacy. And it becomes all the more critical for the statesman who finds his nation embroiled in a conflict that poses the threat of war. Are there effective prescriptions for action in these situations? Or is this an area in which each decision maker can rely only on his own intuition?

At least one school of thought has offered a consistent response to these questions. Generally referred to as the "realist" school, its basic tenets appear as early as Thucydides's account of the Athenian-Melian dialogue in the Peloponnesian War, and they have been restated and elaborated throughout history by classical thinkers from Machiavelli to Clausewitz. The realist persuasion also has been identified with the views and practices of many of the world's most famous statesmen, including Metternich, Bismarck, Churchill, Stalin, and Kissinger, to name a few. Given the prominence of the approach, it is worth our while to take a closer look at how well it has worked. That is, when statesmen have acted in a manner consistent with the realist prescription, have they been successful in attaining compliance with their influence attempts? This chapter reports on an empirical investigation of that question.

The General Model

The understanding of internation influence employed in the investigation is based largely on a model developed by Singer (1963) and on this author's later research on conflict behavior; nevertheless, an attempt has been made to construct the model in a manner consistent with the work of other students of internation conflict behavior as well.

An *influence attempt* is assumed to be the central component of a communication process, whereby one of the parties to a dispute signals its desires and intentions to another. Singer (1963) has categorized the desired outcomes of influence attempts according to whether the target nation is asked to modify or reinforce existing behavior or undertake or refrain from undertaking some future action. Thus, there are four types of objectives associated with influence attempts: *modify, reinforce, persuade,* or *dissuade.* Singer's model also distinguishes among four types of accompanying inducements: *threat, promise, reward,* and *punishment.* These actions signal the actor's intentions should the target comply or not comply with the request.

Outcomes of influence attempts are described according to the degree to which the target complies with the actor's request. Compliance occurs when one actor accepts influence from the other to attain specific rewards or to avoid specific punishments controlled by the other. We will consider at this juncture five types of responses indicating the degree of compliance: to *comply* with the request, to *placate* the actor with an alternative response, to *ignore* the request by not acting, to *defy* the influencer with a threat or demonstration in the form of punishment, or to *combine* defiant and placating behavior in a *carrot and stick* response (Boulding, 1970).

We will not be concerned here with the actor's motives for

undertaking the influence attempt, or with his reasons for choosing one type of influence attempt over another, except to assume that the actor is attempting to influence the target to perform the requested action.[1]

Two other simplifying assumptions should be mentioned. First, the study deals with internation influence attempts as if they were occurring in dyadic conflicts, even though few of these cases are truly dyadic. In addition to the principal antagonists chosen for our purposes, a number of large and small actors enter into, and exit from, many of the conflicts at different time intervals, with each actor involved to a different degree and for its own reasons.[2] The behavior of these third parties undoubtedly exerts some influence on the two principals, but it will be ignored here. Second, the complexities of decision making, domestic politics, and other variables that are thought to play a part in determining a nation's conflict behavior are, likewise, temporarily ignored. This is a more drastic simplification, but it is quite consistent with the assumptions of the realist model being tested, that is, that statesmen are motivated by a calculation of "national interest measured in terms of power" (Morgenthau, 1972).

The Realist Model

The most explicit modern statement of the realist persuasion can be found in the writings of Hans J. Morgenthau, perhaps the most influential American student of international politics in the second half of this century. Morgenthau postulates that politics may be understood by observing objective laws which have their roots in human nature (1973, p. 4). He echoes Hobbes in asserting that man is "born to seek power" (1946, p. 168) and concludes that the power drive determines the nexus of man's political relationship with other men. Political power is viewed by Morgenthau as a psychological relationship among men—the influence which one man is able to exert over the minds and actions of another man. Hence, the famous realist definition of politics:

> Politics is a struggle for power over men, and whatever its ultimate aim may be, power is its immediate goal, and the

modes of acquiring, maintaining, and demonstrating it determine the technique of political action (1946, p. 195).

There is a qualitative and quantitative extension of the power drive in politics among nations. Whereas the nation-state is ideologically and physically more powerful than its individual citizens or their other associations, it is free from effective restraints from above. In "a world where power counts," the "supreme virtue" is *prudence,* that is, a rational calculation of the advantages of alternative courses of action (1973, p. 10). Such a calculation requires a judgment of the relative power of adversary nations and one's consequent ability to influence their actions. And the most crucial dimension of a nation's power is the military force at its disposal (1973, p. 27).

Deciding when and how to attempt to influence a target nation must be based, inter alia, on the power that the would-be influencer can bring to bear. On the other side of the coin, the target nation's decision as to whether or not it should comply with an influence attempt assumes a calculation of the cost in power which comes with compliance, as opposed to the costs and risks of defiance. This has led another generation of political realists, the "conflict strategists," to view conflict behavior as a special form of bargaining behavior (Schelling, 1960, 1966; Kissinger, 1958; Kahn, 1960, 1968).

One of the most explicit expositions of this view is Thomas Schelling's *The Strategy of Conflict* (1960). Schelling conceives of internation conflicts as games of strategy, wherein each participant's best course of action depends on what it expects its adversary to do. Assuming that the participant nations act rationally,[3] that is, that their behavior is "motivated by a conscious calculation of advantages, a calculation that in turn is based on an explicit and internally consistent value system" (1960, p. 4), it is possible, Schelling contends, to develop a theory of "intelligent, sophisticated conflict behavior—of successful behavior" in a game-winning sense.[4]

The key to success lies not only in applying the requisite amount of power to induce the adversary to comply, but also in making the proferred inducements *credible.* If each adversary bases its choice of action on what it expects the other to do, the actor who seeks to attain compliance with its influence attempt must convince the target that it will carry out its threats or promises. Credibility depends not only on the actor's power to carry out rewards and punishments, but also on its commitment to act.

The conflict strategists do not assume explicitly that the most successful inducements are negative, but their work has placed emphasis on "correct behavior" for the "exploitation of potential force" or, more completely, the use of threats and punishments to achieve compliance with the influencer's request (Schelling, 1960, pp. 69–78). In its most brutal form it is what Schelling has called the "diplomacy of violence," the use of force to inflict enough pain and suffering to induce a recalcitrant adversary to comply with one's wishes. The goal, nevertheless, is to achieve the adversary's compliance short of the actual application of military force (1966, p. 3).[5] The realist paradox is that one must prepare for war to achieve peace; the conflict strategists' extension of this is that one must threaten war to avoid it, or escalate it to end it.

Critics of this approach offer a countermodel (which I will refer to as the "counterrealist" model) that posits that, in the course of serious disputes, statesmen do not necessarily behave rationally to pursue the national interest in terms of power, but that there are strong psychological and social pressures to respond to threats with defiance and counterthreats, and that such situations naturally tend to escalate to war (see Carr, 1939, for an early statement). One could argue that, when *both* parties to a dyadic conflict are intent on employing the "diplomacy of violence" successfully and believe they are capable of doing so, the situation is analogous to a poker game in which the sky is the limit. As Deutsch (1968, p. 129) has pointed out, the realist prescription contains a hidden assumption of *asymmetry* with regard to both the relative capabilities of the adversaries, and their motivation to win.

As each player commits more and more of his resources and reputation to winning the game, the costs of losing grow. The objective of winning tends to dominate all other values, and the result is not just a stalemate, but an escalation of the conflict that stems from each side's determination to make its commitment to winning more credible. The scenario is akin to the "fight" process generalized by Rapoport (1960) from Richardson's (1960) model of an arms race. In light of recent history, this is a plausible alternative description of what happens when one applies the more specific prescriptions of the conflict strategists. It also is consistent with the results of an earlier study of five internation conflicts occurring between 1850 and 1965 (Leng and Goodsell, 1975).

This investigation, then, will focus on influence attempts in serious dyadic disputes and consider the effectiveness of behavior prescribed by the realists and conflict strategists.[6] When statesmen do behave as prescribed by these theorists, does the behavior produce the desired results? Does the prudent exploitation of potential power result in the adversary's compliance without leading to war? Or do such influence attempts more often predict to defiance, escalation, and war?

The central assumptions of the realist model just described may be summarized in a general proposition:

> In the course of a serious dyadic dispute, the degree of nation B's compliance with an influence attempt by nation A will be positively associated with (1) the degree of inducement employed by nation A and (2) the credibility of nation A's stated intention to carry out the inducement(s) minus (3) the cost of compliance to nation B.

This can be broken down into the following bivariate hypotheses for the purposes of this study.

> *Hypothesis 1.* The greater the cost of compliance to target nation B, the lower the degree of compliance by B.
>
> *Hypothesis 2.* The greater the degree of inducement by A, the higher the degree of compliance by B.
>
> *Hypothesis 3.* The greater the credibility of A's inducements, the higher the degree of compliance by B.

The *counter*realist model implies that the realist prescription will not have the rate of success that Hypotheses 2 and 3 suggest, particularly when the adversaries are evenly matched. But the explicit proposition is that, when the realist prescription fails, it is likely to lead to counterthreats and war. This leads to the following bivariate hypotheses:

> *Hypothesis 4.* The greater the degree of negative inducements employed by nation A, the greater the likelihood that target nation B will respond with defiance.
>
> *Hypothesis 5.* The greater the *credibility* of negative inducements used by nation A, the greater the likelihood that target nation B will respond with defiance.

Each of these hypotheses can be modified to take into account the more restrictive proposition that, whereas the realist prescription may work tolerably well in asymmetric disputes, the countermodel is more appropriate when the adversaries are evenly matched in power.

> *Hypothesis 6.* If adversaries A and B are evenly matched, then the greater the *degree* of negative inducement used by nation A, the greater the likelihood that target nation B will respond with defiance.
>
> *Hypothesis 7.* If adversaries A and B are evenly matched, then the greater the *credibility* of negative inducements used by A, the greater the likelihood that target nation B will respond with defiance.

The exploratory analysis undertaken in this study will not permit a direct test of the proposition that the discrete action-response sequences stated in Hypotheses 4 and 5 predict to a pattern of escalation that is associated with the onset of war.[7] Some purely suggestive findings, however, are reported at the conclusion of the analysis section of the study.

Generating the Data

Having stated the hypotheses to be tested, the next step is to describe how the behavioral data to be utilized in testing them will be generated.

The Universe of Analysis

The association between different types of influence attempts and the degree of compliance with them will be examined in 14 serious dyadic disputes occurring between 1850 and 1965. A stratified random sample has been employed in the selection of cases to obtain a representative set of disputes according to (1) the historical era in which they occurred, (2) the relative power of the adversaries, and (3) the outcome of the dispute. The methodological assumption behind the choice of a *stratified*, as opposed to a simple random sample, is that, in terms of the variables being studied, the differences which obtain among cases in different strata are greater than those among cases *within* each stratum (Blalock, 1972, pp. 516-551).

The time interval has been stratified into three periods to correspond to observed changes in the structure and functioning of the international system that could affect internation behavior. The first period, from 1850 to 1918, is within the diplomatic era when the rules of rational diplomacy, as prescribed by political realists, are said to have worked most successfully (Morgenthau, 1973, p. 525).[8] The second period, 1919 to 1945, extends from the end of World War I and the creation of the League of Nations through World War II. It marks the flowering of many of the changes that are alleged to have contributed to the decline of rational diplomacy: postwar disenchantment with secret diplomacy, democratization, the growth of ideologies, and "parliamentary diplomacy" in the form of the League of Nations (Morgenthau, 1973, pp. 528-529). The last period, 1946 to 1965, is considered a separate epoch because of the birth and growth of nuclear weapons. This is of particular importance if we are to consider the continuation of the realist tradition in the prescriptions of the conflict strategists, with their strong emphasis on nuclear risk taking or "brinksmanship" in conflict bargaining (Schelling, 1966).

At least two of the conflicts selected in each of these periods have resulted in war, and at least two have not. Morgenthau contends (1973) that diplomacy that results in war has failed in its purpose; therefore one measure of the success of a nation's conflict behavior is whether it has been able to attain its objectives *without* paying the price of war.

A final stratification has established a dichotomy between conflict adversaries of relatively equal and relatively unequal capabilities. For each time period and for each war and nonwar class, we have chosen at least one conflict in which diplomatic historians have considered the adversaries to be roughly equal in power and one conflict in which there was a clear-cut difference between the two. The distinction permits tests of Hypotheses 6 and 7 stemming from the arguments of some critics of the realist approach who contend that the "exploitation of potential force" is most likely to lead to defiance, as opposed to compliance, in situations of relative symmetry in the potential power of the adversaries.

In sum, we have sampled at least one serious dyadic dispute from each of 12 strata, based on three time periods and two distinctions based on the type of dispute. The 14 selected cases appear in Table 5-1.

Table 5-1. Stratified Sample of Serious Dyadic Disputes

Dispute and Adversaries	Dates	War or Nonwar	Power Relationship
Second Schleswig-Holstein (Prussia-Denmark)	3/30/1863– 2/01/1864	War	Uneven
British-Portuguese Colonial Dispute (Britain-Portugal)	8/15/1889– 1/10/1890	Nonwar	Uneven
Spanish-American War (United States-Spain)	1/15/1898– 4/21/1898	War	Uneven
First Balkan War (Serbia-Turkey)	3/13/1912– 10/17/1912	War	Even
Second Moroccan Crisis (France-Germany)	5/21/1911– 11/04/1911	Nonwar	Even
Teschen Dispute (Poland-Czechoslovakia)	12/17/1918– 7/28/1920	Nonwar	Even
Chaco War (Bolivia-Paraguay)	9/01/1928– 6/15/1932	War	Even
Italo-Ethiopian War (Italy-Ethiopia)	12/05/1934– 10/03/1935	War	Uneven
The Anschluss (Germany-Austria)	1/07/1938– 3/12/1938	Nonwar	Uneven
Polish-Lithuanian Crisis (Poland-Lithuania)	3/12/1938– 3/18/1938	Nonwar	Uneven
Sinai War (Britain-Egypt)	7/26/1956– 11/02/1956	War	Uneven
Cuban Missile Crisis (United-States-Soviet Union)	8/22/1962– 11/20/1962	Nonwar	Even
Second Kashmir War (India-Pakistan)	3/—/1964– 8/05/1965	War	Even
Cyprus Dispute (Turkey-Greece)	11/30/1963– 8/30/1964	Nonwar	Uneven

Defining a Serious Dispute

Selection of the stratified sample requires an operationally defined population of serious disputes. That half of the sample that consists of disputes that resulted in war has been chosen from the Singer and Small (1973) list of interstate wars occurring between

1850 and 1965. To obtain a population of serious nonwar disputes occurring within the same time interval, however, it has been necessary to compile an additional list of cases.

We have defined a nonwar dispute as serious if there is an abnormal amount of conflictive behavior and one of the adversaries either uses or threatens to use military force. The first criterion is intended to eliminate those sporadic international incidents that are resolved quickly through an apology or by clarifying a misunderstanding. The second criterion is consistent with an earlier investigation by the author of those types of behavior that predict to conflict escalation (Leng and Goodsell, 1974), as well as being consistent with the conceptual frameworks developed by other students of internation conflict behavior (see Bloomfield and Leiss, 1969; Young, 1968; K. Holsti, 1966). Utilizing these criteria, we have compiled a tentative list of serious disputes occurring between 1815 and 1965. Procedures for determining the beginning and ending dates of the cases selected are described in Leng and Goodsell (1974, pp. 11-12).

Data Sources

The impossibility of directly observing the multifarious actions of nations and other international actors condemns the student of international behavior to rely upon the written accounts of participants, journalists, and diplomatic historians. In this investigation, *The New York Times* (the daily microfilm edition) has been used as a constant source for each dispute, along with other press sources and the accounts of diplomatic historians. The addition of diplomatic histories has been especially helpful in adding a record of those secret consultations, threats, and promises that were not available to the contemporary press (see Leng, 1975b). The multiple sources, totaling 45, also help to eliminate some of the bias and distortion that one might expect in the media of a given nation.

Verbal chronologies of international acts undertaken by the participants in each conflict were constructed from each source. Then the chronologies for each case were merged into a single master chronology, to be converted into machine readable data according to the coding scheme described in the following paragraphs.

The Coding Scheme

The coding scheme categorizes the actions of the disputants according to types and assigns each action a numerical code to facilitate quick access on a digital computer. The coding scheme that was used to generate data for this investigation is the Behavioral Correlates of War Typology, which was designed by Leng and Singer (1977) for a general investigation of the behavioral events associated with war.

Construction of the coding scheme has been described in detail elsewhere (Leng, 1975a; Leng and Singer, 1977); the discussion here will be directed toward features most relevant to the investigation at hand. Each act is described according to the date, actor, target, location, and *tempo of action*. The last category offers a useful description of physical acts which continue for some time, by describing their movement, or tempo, as starting, increasing, decreasing, or stopping.[9]

From this point on, the scheme is in the form of a hierarchical "choice tree." Each act is described according to the "medium of action" used—people, places, things, or information—to communicate to the target the type of resource brought to bear—military, economic, diplomatic, or official—and, finally, a rather specific description of the action, such as consult, negotiate, declare neutrality, attack, blockade, assassinate, grant economic things, assist economically, and so on. There are 123 of these "specific descriptors" in the scheme (see Leng, 1975a).

The coding of acts where the medium is people, places, or things is straightforward enough, but a brief description of the "double-coding" of verbal, or information, acts is necessary to give the reader some understanding of how the scheme enables us to "observe" internation influence attempt-response sequences. There are three major subcategories of information acts: comment on action, request action, and intend action. The last two are the basis for our coding of influence attempts and inducements in the form of "requests" and "threats" or "promises." The descriptive categories of request action specify *what* the actor is asking the target to do in a particular influence attempt and *how* he makes the request. First, the "how" of the request is described according to any conditions which the actor might attach to the request, with regard to compensatory action by the actor or some other nation, whether there is a deadline for compliance, as in the case of an ultimatum, and whether or not there is a full specification of the action requested. Then, *what* is requested is described by "doubling back" to code a full description of the action requested of the target. This allows us to determine, by reading ahead in the data file, whether or not the target complies with the request. If the target nation has complied, we should find a subsequent act describing the target nation as undertaking, or promising to undertake, the requested action.

Verbal inducements, in the form of "threats" or "promises" accompanying requests, may be extracted from the coded data as particular types of *intend action*. The *intend action* category is used to describe statements by the actor indicating that it intends to undertake some future action. As in the case of requests, there is a coded description of *how* the intentions are stated. That is, a nation may state that it intends to take the action unconditionally, conditional on some action by the target, or dependent on some other set of circumstances. The coded description indicates whether or not the actor has stated *when* it intends to act, and if it has specified the action it intends to take. Then, *what* the actor intends to do is described according to the "double-coding" procedure described earlier.

In sum, the coding scheme allows us to obtain a relatively full description of each influence attempt, including *what* is requested of the target and *how*, as well as any inducements accompanying the request. It also contains the essential property of allowing a check to see if and when the target complies with the request.

Constructing the Indicators

The next step is to combine the appropriate coded action types into indicators which represent the variables appearing in the realist and counterrealist hypotheses. These hypotheses include three independent variables—*cost of compliance, degree of inducement,* and *credibility of inducement*—and a single dependent variable, *degree of compliance*. In the case of the counterrealist model, degree of compliance is dichotomized into responses of "defy" and "other" responses. Operational definitions for each of the variables are discussed in turn.

Cost of Compliance

Given the realist prescription that the prudent statesman must be concerned primarily with maintaining, demonstrating, or increasing his nation's power, the cost to the target of complying with an influence attempt is measured in terms of power. There are two indicators of power cost. The first, *tangible power cost*, refers to the loss of relatively tangible elements of power, such as territory, population, natural resources, industrial capability, and military strength or preparedness (Morgenthau, 1973, pp. 112-148). The second, and less tangible—*cost in reputation*, refers to the cost in a nation's reputation for successful diplomacy or conflict bargaining power. This notion assumes its greatest significance in the works of the conflict strategists, given their strong emphasis on credibility.

Each indicator presents measurement problems. Although the realists argue that it is the responsibility of a statesman to make accurate calculations of his adversary's power, they are most convincing in describing the near impossibility of ever doing so (see Morgenthau, 1973, p. 154). Consequently, no attempt has been made to measure degrees of tangible power cost beyond deciding whether or not there is any. Influence attempts are classified simply according to whether or not they request that the target nation undertake action or refrain from undertaking action, which would result in some direct cost to the domain, scope, or range of its power.[10] Specifically, an influence attempt is scored as incurring a tangible power cost to the target either (1) if it is asked to start, increase, or continue one of the following types of action from the coding scheme

pay reparations	evacuate territory
pay ransom	return military materiel
grant territorial concession	return strategic weapons
	surrender militarily
grant economic concession	grant independence
	withdraw military forces

or (2) if the target is asked to decrease, stop, or refrain from one of the following action types:

trade relations	alert
confiscate or nationalize	mobilization
maintain overseas base	show of strength

seizure (things)   blockade
seizure (territory)   change military force level
establish protectorate   attack
annex   continuous military action
antiguerrilla action   change in combat force level
intelligence intrusion   occupation
guerrilla action

What sorts of demands a nation is willing to accept from an adversary also will have an effect on its *reputation* for bargaining power. A nation that can be bullied into surrendering part of its domain does so at a cost in reputation as well as in real estate. But there is another dimension to the relative cost in reputation that may not be so obvious: the relationship between the action demanded and the state's current behavior. First, it can be argued that a nation's power reputation is likely to suffer less from complying with a request to refrain from acting than from complying with a request to undertake some new action. We use Singer's (1963) "dissuasion" and "persuasion" to distinguish between these two conditions, but a similar distinction is made by Schelling (1966) in a discussion of "deterrence" and "compellence." A related hypothesis would be that a request to continue existing action (reinforce) may be complied with at less cost than one that requires some change in behavior (modify). Distinctions between persuade and dissuade, and modify and reinforce, are identified in the coded data according to the combination of the tempo score and the requested action. If, for example, nation A asks nation B to *start* a blockade, the request would be classified as *persuade-modify*. If A asks B to *continue* the blockade, it is classified as *persuade-reinforce*. But, if A asks B to *stop* the blockade, it would be classified as *dissuade-modify*. And, if A asks a compliant B to *refrain from* any more blockades in the future, the request would be coded as *dissuade-reinforce*.

A final indicator of cost in reputation is based on whether the demand and accompanying inducements are communicated publicly or privately. The assumption is that it is more costly to give in to a demand backed up by a threat when it is delivered publicly than when the influence attempt is made in private. Of course, if a *promise* is used as an inducement, one would expect the opposite to be the case.

The *public-private* distinction raises an interesting problem which will be considered more fully in the section on analysis. Presumably, one increases the commitment to act and, consequently, the credibility of a threat by stating it publicly, as in the oft-cited use of a television speech by President Kennedy to communicate his threat to the Soviet Union during the Cuban missile crisis (see Schelling, 1966). But public communication also has the less desirable effect of making it more difficult for the adversary to comply without a high cost in its power reputation.

Degree of Inducement

Hypotheses 2, 4, and 6 posit associations between the degree of inducement accompanying requests and the target's response. We have classified inducements into three general types: threats, promises, and a combination of each, that is, "carrot and stick" inducements. In keeping with the earlier discussion of Schelling's (1966) emphasis on the "diplomacy of violence," threats of military violence are distinguished from other types of threats. A similar distinction is made between those threats and promises that are accompanied by demonstrations of the intent, in the form of overt punishments or rewards, and those that are not. Therefore, each of the three broad types of inducement—carrot and stick, threat, and promise—is subdivided according to whether there is a threat of military violence, an accompanying punishment, and/or an accompanying reward. The possibilities are exhibited in the choice tree of inducement types appearing as Figure 5-1.

Verbal threats and promises are extracted from acts that have been coded according to the BCOW coding scheme. The determination of whether a particular *intend action* should be identified as a threat or a promise is similarly dependent on the *tempo* and *specific descriptor* coded for whatever action is intended.[11] To intend to *start* a blockade, for example, would be a threat; to intend to *stop* a blockade would be a promise.

Credibility of Inducements

The third predictor variable presumed to be associated with the degree of compliance on the part of target nation B is the *credibility* of any inducements employed by nation A. Two types of credibility indicators are used in this study. The first is the relative power of the

Figure 5-1. Choice Tree: Inducement Types

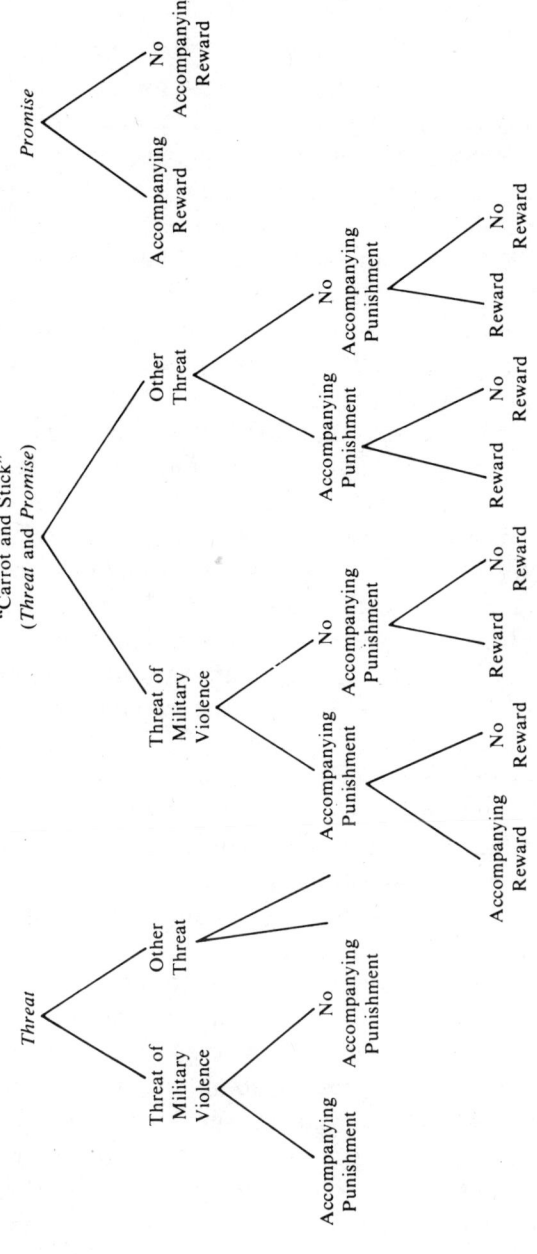

would-be influencer to carry out its threats and promises. If nation A possesses a significant power advantage over nation B, B presumably is more likely to find nation A's threat more credible than it would if the power relationship were the reverse. Because of the present difficulty of attaining an operational index of power that would satisfy the realist model (as noted earlier) and hold up across cases, the opinions of diplomatic historians have been used to obtain a simple distinction among cases where the adversaries are considered relatively even or uneven in power. This yields three gross categories of influence attempts in terms of power: strong to weak, evenly matched, and weak to strong.

As this is being written, efforts by researchers on the *Correlates of War* project at the University of Michigan to develop an operational index of national capability for each member of the interstate system between 1816 and 1965 are nearing completion.[12] When that work is completed, it will be possible to replicate the results of this study with a more objective measure of relative capability.

Most prominent among the other components of credibility posited by the conflict strategists are the quality of communication, the "art of commitment," and the reputation of the actor for carrying out its threats and promises. The quality of communication can be affected by a host of variables, including the attributes of nations and statesmen, which are beyond the scope of this investigation. Nevertheless, a reasonable behavioral measure of the quality of communication for an influence attempt may be the specificity both of what the target is asked to do, and of any inducements accompanying the request. Only requests that are quite specific are included in the study, but, with regard to inducements, the sample of coded threats and promises covers a wide range of specificity, from vague warnings to outright ultimatums. The "art of commitment" appears to be so closely tied to communication that the two may be considered together. After all, the greater the clarity and specificity of a nation's threats, the more it is committed to carrying them out. If an Arab statesman promises to end an oil embargo within one week after the beginning of an Israeli troop withdrawal, for example, he is more committed to take this action than if he made a vague promise to "respond positively" when the Israelis "demonstrated their good faith."

The specificity of threats and promises is scored according to (1) whether or not nation A's promised or threatened inducement is specified fully, (2) whether or not the time when the action would be taken is specified, and (3) whether A's decision to carry out the inducement is conditional on target nation B's behavior or some other eventuality. Descriptions fitting each of these indicators are included in the coding of each *intend action* statement.

We have mentioned reputation as another important component in determining the credibility of inducements. The best *behavioral* measure of reputation might be obtained by establishing a "conflict performance record" (McClelland, 1968; Forward, 1971) based on the actor's behavior in previous conflicts, especially in any conflicts that involved the same adversary. This is a measure that we hope to be able to obtain when we have coded a larger percentage of the full population of conflicts, but we do not have sufficient data to conduct such an analysis for the purposes of this investigation.

Finally, there is the problem of determining which inducements are appropriately linked with which requests. Our rule is that an inducement must occur *on the same date as a request* to be linked with that request, as part of one influence attempt.[13] Acts by nation A that *precede* A's attempt to influence B may well have an effect on the likelihood of compliance by B, but it does not seem logical to assume that they are necessarily inducements to obtain compliance with the subsequent request. A's request, in fact, may be prompted by B's reaction to the earlier acts. By the same token, actions that A takes subsequent to a request may be considered reactions to B's response to the influence attempt rather than inducements that are part of the initial influence attempt. No doubt this is not always the case. Our sample of influence attempts is likely to underestimate the degree of inducement in some cases, but this seems preferable to erring by overestimating inducements.[14]

Degree of Compliance

The dependent variable in all of the hypotheses is the degree to which B complies—or does not comply—with A's request. Once a specific request for action has been made by A, subsequent acts by B are checked to determine if it has complied with the request. If a request appears only once during the course of a conflict, compliance can come at any time during the remainder of the conflict. If a request is repeated, *any* instance of subsequent compliance is assumed to pertain only to the most recent request. If a target nation states that it *unconditionally* intends to take the requested action, that too is scored as compliance.

The dichotomous distinction presents few problems, but what of various alternatives to outright compliance? Besides outright compliance with the request, we have four other categories that describe the degree of compliance: *placate, ignore, defy,* and *mixed.* The response is classified as *placate* whenever the target offers alternative promises or rewards as its response to the influence attempt. *Ignore* indicates that the target responds to the influence attempt with nothing more than an evaluative comment. The response is described as *defy* if the target reacts to the request with a threat or punishment. And *mixed* represents a combination of *placate* and *defy.*

Given the variety of exchanges that can occur between the adversaries in a serious dispute, how can we possibly determine which of the target's acts are responses to any particular influence attempt? In one sense, we probably cannot, at least not with behavioral data alone; too many other variables can intervene. But this may not be the most realistic way to approach the problem at hand. What we are asking, in fact, is not "which acts are responses to a particular influence attempt?" but "what effect, if any, does the influence attempt have on the behavior of the target toward the influencer?" That is, does the target comply, seek compromise, ignore the attempt, or respond belligerently?

This still leaves the problem of establishing a proper time lag between the influence attempt and a set of responses. Previous research efforts by other scholars offer little help with this problem.[15] Response times may be expected to vary according to a wide variety of behavioral, organizational, personality, and cultural variables. A previous study by Leng and Goodsell (1974) did indicate, however, that, in the case of threats of military violence, an appreciable change in the behavior of the target could be observed within a period of 14 days.

Based on these results, which are certainly not conclusive, we tentatively decided to observe nation B's response to an influence attempt by nation A from the day of the influence attempt to either 14 days later or to the next influence attempt by A, whichever came first. We found that in 89% of the sample cases, target nation B had taken some action, directed at nation A, which went beyond a mere comment. It appears reasonable to assume that, if A's influence attempt had had any influence on B's behavior, it would be manifested in these actions.

Analyzing the Data

In keeping with the exploratory nature of this study, the analyses employ the simplest possible statistical techniques. The associations predicted by the realist and counterrealist hypotheses are examined via the presentation of contingency tables and tests of statistical significance, with the latter providing a convenient summary measure. Given the stratified nature of the sample, as well as some large variations in the number of influence attempts observed within different conflicts, these scores should not be read as reliable statements of the sample results with regard to the universe of all internation influence attempts in serious dyadic conflicts. (A total of 187 influence attempt-response combinations were coded from the sample conflicts.) Bearing this caveat in mind, the following tests, nevertheless, should provide a fruitful empirical reconnaissance of the realist prescription in practice.

The Realist Model

Hypothesis 1, which is based on the proposition that the statesmen in target nation B must calculate the costs of compliance with A's influence attempts in terms of power, states that the greater the cost of compliance to target nation B, the lower the degree of compliance by B. Cost of compliance is indicated by the *power cost* to the target and in the target nation's reputation for power. Percentage tables and significance tests[16] for each of the cost of compliance indicators appear in Table 5-2. The percentages in each row of the table indicate the proportion of responses, by type, associated with each of the cost of compliance indicators. For example, the figures in the first row indicate that, when a request represented a *tangible power cost* to the target, the target complied 22.4% of the time, placated the requester 7.9% of the time, and so on. The X^2 scores appearing in the last column represent the significance scores for the difference in percentage of responses for the pairs of rows.

There is no significant difference (NS) between the percentages for *tangible power cost* and *no tangible power cost*, for example.

The percentage differences between each of the dichotomous cost of compliance indicators are in the direction predicted by the realist model, but none is significant at the $p < .05$ level. Nonetheless, a closer look does suggest support for the realist position, if not for Hypothesis 1 as stated. In the case of responses to influence attempts containing some *tangible power cost* to the target, the high percentage (30.3%) of *defy* responses associated with the *tangible power cost* cases is consistent with the realist's emphasis on the importance of maintaining power. Moreover, the likelihood of threats appearing as accompanying inducements in the sample cases doubles when an influence attempt includes a request resulting in some *tangible power cost* to the target. If, as the realist model suggests, the use of threats as inducements increases the likelihood of compliance, this would reduce the impact of the cost of compliance on the likelihood of compliance. As we shall see shortly, Tables 5-4 and 5-5 support this proposition.

Any interpretation of the first two cost-in-reputation indicators, attempts to *persuade, dissuade, modify,* or *reinforce,* must be made with caution because of the low number of observations of either *dissuade* or *reinforce*. The high percentage (31.8%) of *defy* responses to attempts to *dissuade* the target, for example, probably effects the fact that five of the seven instances were cases of weak nations attempting to dissuade stronger adversaries.

As we mentioned earlier, the third indicator of cost in reputation, that is, whether an influence attempt is communicated *publicly* or *privately*, contains its own ambiguity. On the one hand, Hypothesis 1 implies that a nation's power reputation suffers most when it "knuckles under" to publicly stated demands in the course of a serious conflict, particularly if such demands are backed up by threats. On the other hand, Hypothesis 3 states that the credibility and, consequently, the likelihood of compliance increases when the commitment to carry out inducements is made publicly. The results of tests of the *public-private* indicator, with controls for the use of threats or promises as inducements, support the notion that the cost to the target's power reputation (Hypothesis 1) overrides the increased credibility that comes from making inducements public (Hypothesis 3). The percentages in Table 5-3 indicate that publicly stated threats are more likely to be met with defiance than compliance, whereas just the opposite is the case with regard to privately

Table 5-2. Cost of Compliance and Degree of Compliance

	Cost of Compliance	Comply	Placate	Mixed	Ignore	Defy	X^2
Cost in tangible power	Yes/	22.4% (17)[a]	7.9% (6)	17.1% (13)	22.4% (17)	30.3% (23)	—[b]
	No	24.3 (27)	17.1 (19)	12.6 (14)	27.9 (31)	18.0 (20)	NS
Type of Attempt	Persuade/	22.4 (37)	14.5 (24)	15.8 (26)	25.5 (42)	21.8 (36)	—
	Dissuade	31.8 (7)	4.5 (1)	4.5 (1)	27.3 (6)	31.8 (7)	NS
	Modify/	22.4 (38)	13.5 (23)	15.3 (26)	25.9 (44)	22.9 (39)	—
	Reinforce	35.3 (6)	11.8 (2)	5.9 (1)	23.5 (4)	23.5 (4)	NS
Cost in reputation	Public/	21.3 (19)	9.0 (8)	15.7 (14)	31.5 (28)	22.5 (20)	—
	Private	25.5 (25)	17.3 (17)	13.3 (13)	20.4 (20)	23.5 (23)	NS

[a]Percentages (across rows) are followed by raw scores in parentheses.
[b]Significance scores are reported only if $p < .05$.
NS – not significant.

communicated threats. On the other hand, the percentage of compliance and defiance in responses to promises remains fairly constant regardless of the mode of communication.

Overall, the cost of compliance indicators do not provide a dramatic demonstration of the power imperatives of the realist prescription at work, but the results are in no way inconsistent with the model.

The results of tests of Hypothesis 2, which states the greater the degree of inducement by A the higher the degree of compliance by B, appear in Table 5-4. Each of the three types of inducement—*threats, promises,* and *carrot and stick*—have been categorized according to the degree of inducement employed. Although the categories are ranked from strongest to weakest in the listing in Table 5-4, the analysis continues to be at a nominal level.

None of the tests is significant at the $p < .05$ level, but the percentage scores for threats and promises are in the direction predicted by the hypothesis. The low number of observations of carrot and stick inducements makes it difficult to draw any conclusions for that type.

The results for inducements based on the use of threats are of particular interest, given the strong emphasis placed on the threat and use of military power by the realists and conflict strategists. The most striking results in Table 5-4 are the high percentages for *each* of the most extreme responses—*comply* and *defy*—with *threats of military violence*, especially when these threats are backed up by a demonstration in the form of punishment. These results appear to support *both* the realist's emphasis on the "diplomacy of violence"

Table 5-3. Types of Responses to Publicly or Privately Communicated Threats and Promises

Degree of Compliance	Public			Private		
	All	Threat	Promise	All	Threat	Promise
Comply	21.3%	22.2%	28.0%	25.5%	38.7%	31.2%
Placate	9.0	15.6	24.0	17.3	19.4	31.2
Mixed	15.7	15.6	20.0	13.3	12.9	6.2
Ignore	31.5	17.8	12.0	20.4	9.7	15.6
Defy	22.5	28.9	16.0	23.5	19.4	15.6

NOTE: Read percentages down the columns for differences among response types.

Table 5-4. Type of Inducement and Degree of Compliance

Inducement Indicators	Comply		Placate		Mixed		Ignore		Defy		X²
Threat											
Military violence and punish	35.7%	(5)	14.3%	(2)	0.0%	(0)	14.3%	(2)	35.7%	(5)	NS
Military violence	26.8	(15)	19.6	(11)	16.1	(9)	14.3	(8)	23.2	(13)	
Other threat	20.0	(3)	6.7	(1)	13.2	(2)	33.3	(5)	26.7	(4)	
No threat	20.6	(21)	10.8	(11)	15.7	(16)	32.4	(33)	20.6	(21)	
Promise											
With reward	25.0	(4)	18.7	(3)	18.7	(3)	12.5	(2)	25.0	(4)	NS
Other promise	19.7	(12)	26.2	(16)	13.1	(8)	21.3	(13)	19.7	(12)	
No promise	25.5	(28)	5.5	(6)	14.5	(16)	30.0	(33)	24.5	(27)	
Carrot and stick											
With threat of military violence	16.0	(4)	36.0	(9)	20.0	(5)	8.0	(2)	20.0	(5)	NS
Other carrot and stick	33.3	(2)	16.7	(1)	16.7	(1)	16.7	(1)	16.7	(1)	
No carrot and stick	24.4	(38)	9.6	(15)	13.5	(21)	28.8	(4)	23.7	(37)	

NOTE: Read percentages across the rows. (Raw scores are in parentheses).
NS – not significant.

and the counterrealist argument that such techniques are more likely to lead to an escalation of the conflict.

This pattern does not change significantly if we control for power; very few of the threats of military violence observed in the sample, in fact, were directed by weaker powers at stronger adversaries. That much, at least, can be said for prudence! The diplomatic era in which the inducements are used, however, does make a difference. If the cases occurring in the post-World War II era are removed from the sample, the percentage of threats of military violence resulting in compliance increases, whereas the percentage of cases resulting in defiance decreases, with the difference in response outcomes associated with different degrees of threat significant at the $p < .05$ level. This is consistent with the contention that rationality in internation relations has declined in the modern era. But it also points to the increasing dangers of using the "diplomacy of violence" to force compliance in present and future internation disputes.

As one would expect, the responses to promises are less likely than threats to be at either end of the degree of compliance range. Not surprisingly, the percentage of *placate* responses is higher with promises than it is with threats, whereas the percentage of *defy* responses is lower with promises than with threats.

The results, in sum, provide some modest support for the validity of Hypothesis 2, at least where threats are concerned, but at the same time they suggest support for the validity of Hypothesis 4 of the counterrealist model.

Hypothesis 3, which states the greater the *credibility* of A's inducements, the higher the degree of compliance by B, reflects the conflict strategists' emphasis on the role of credibility in achieving compliance with threats and promises. That emphasis receives strong support in the results appearing in Table 5-5. The significance scores for the association between indicators of credibility, based on the relative power of the adversaries, and degree of compliance are significant at the $p < .05$ level and the measure of credibility based on the specificity of threats and promises is significant at the $p < .001$ level.

The relative power of the adversaries to carry out their threats and promises, based on the judgments of diplomatic historians of the conflicts considered, provides the most basic measure of the credibility of inducements. The results appearing in Table 5-5 provide support of the realist axiom that "power counts."

Table 5-5. Credibility of Inducements and Degree of Compliance

Type of Inducement		Degree of Compliance				
	Indicator	Comply	Placate	Mixed	Ignore	Defy	X^2
Relative Power	Large-small	29.7% (19)	17.2% (11)	9.4% (6)	26.6% (17)	17.2% (11)	6.66 $p<.05$
	Even	23.6 (21)	12.4 (11)	11.2 (10)	31.5 (28)	21.3 (19)	
	Small-large	11.8 (4)	8.8 (3)	32.4 (11)	8.8 (3)	38.2 (13)	
Specificity of Inducement	Threat specificity						
	Fully specified	45.8 (11)	29.2 (7)	4.2 (1)	0.0 (0)	20.8 (5)	15.42 $p<.001$
	Act specified	20.0 (6)	10.0 (3)	16.7 (5)	13.3 (4)	40.0 (12)	
	Unspecified	22.7 (5)	13.6 (3)	22.7 (5)	31.8 (7)	9.1 (2)	
	No threat	20.2 (22)	11.0 (12)	13.8 (15)	33.9 (37)	21.1 (23)	
	Promise specificity						
	Fully specified	— (1)	— (1)	— (0)	— (0)	— (2)	17.02 $p<.001$
	Act specified	29.8 (17)	28.1 (16)	12.3 (7)	14.0 (8)	15.8 (9)	
	Unspecified	16.7 (2)	8.3 (1)	25.0 (3)	33.3 (4)	16.7 (2)	
	No threat	21.6 (24)	6.3 (7)	12.6 (14)	32.4 (36)	27.0 (30)	

NOTE: Read percentages across the rows. (Each is followed by raw scores in parentheses).

The second category of indicators of credibility was based on the actor's commitment to act to carry out inducements, as communicated in the specificity of threats and promises. Again the results support the hypothesis, but with some revealing deviations. The scores for the first two categories of threat specificity provide an interesting variation on the pattern that was emerging with regard to responses to degrees of threat based on the types of inducements employed. The most striking percentage scores are those for *fully specified threats*, that is, ultimatums. Such inducements were credible enough to receive positive responses from the target 75% of the time and outright compliance 46% of the time. This success rate can be ascribed partly to the fact that 19 of the 24 ultimatums observed in the sample were directed by strong nations at relatively weaker adversaries and that these accounted for 16 of the 18 positive responses. On the other hand, threats that fell short of an outright ultimatum fared far less well. Those where the action to be taken was *specified* produced a negative response rate of 70%, with 40% resulting in defiance. *Unspecified* threats (warnings) have a similar success rate, but the negative responses were more often merely *ignore*, rather than *defy*.

In short, the percentages of defiant responses to threats suggest that they have been dangerous diplomatic tools unless they have been used by nations that were enjoying a decided power advantage and were willing to make very specific commitments (time, action, conditions) to carry out their threats. The results support Hypothesis 3, but they also suggest support for the escalatory pattern posited by the counterrealists.

The specificity of promises also produces a difference which is statistically significant at $p < .001$, but the high positive relationship between specificity and *defiance*, which obtained with threats, is missing. This is not unexpected. Unlike the threat, in which the risk to the target nation's power reputation encourages it to respond more defiantly as threats become more credible, the promise encourages a milder response, as in the relatively even balance of negative responses to action specific responses appearing in Table 5-5.

The Counterrealist Model

Taken together, the preceding tests provide support for the realist approach, but what of the dangers associated with following the realist prescription? Some early hints of risks accompanying threats to the adversary's power base and its reputation for power can be seen in the relatively high percentages of defiant responses associated with demands which would entail a tangible power cost to the adversary (Table 5-2), those which are publicly communicated (Table 5-3), and those which employ the use of the "diplomacy of violence," that is, threats accompanied by demonstrations in the form of punishment (Table 5-4).

A fuller picture emerges with an examination of the hypotheses associated with the counterrealist model. Hypothesis 4 states that there is a positive association between the *degree* of inducement employed by nation A and defiant responses by nation B, whereas Hypothesis 5 states that there is a positive association between the specificity of negative inducements and defiant responses. We noted earlier that there does appear to be some association between the degree of negative inducement, as indicated either by the type of threat (Hypothesis 4) or the specificity of commitment (Hypothesis 5) to carry out the threat and defy responses when these influence attempts do not obtain outright compliance. This is most evident in the percentages of *ignore* responses for *threats* in Tables 5-4 and 5-5.

But, taken by themselves, these results are not impressive. After all, no one would deny that there is *some* greater risk in threatening or employing force. Hypotheses 6 and 7 add an important additional variable to the counterrealist model—the relative strength of the adversaries. The argument is that a weaker power may be bullied into compliance or appeasement in the face of overwhelming strength, and a stronger power simply may choose to ignore the threats of a puny adversary, but, when the powers are evenly matched, the situation becomes more dangerous. And so it does, if our sample is at all representative. Tables 5-6 and 5-7 summarize the likelihood of defiant responses to threats, types of threats, and specificity of threats, first in Table 5-6 for all the conflicts (Hypotheses 4 and 5) and then in Table 5-7 for conflicts between evenly matched adversaries only (Hypotheses 6 and 7).

With one exception, when we consider only evenly matched powers, the percentage of defiant responses associated with threats increases regardless of the indicator, whereas the likelihood of a defiant response to other forms of inducements decreases slightly. Compare the first two columns of Table 5-6 with the first two columns of Table 5-7. The difference in the likelihood of a defiant response to a threat, as opposed to any other inducement, is now

Table 5-6. Threats, Types of Threats, and Specificity of Threats and Defiant Responses

	Threat		Type of Threat			Specificity of Threat		
Response Type	Threat	No Threat	Military Violence and Punishment	Military Violence	Other	Full	Act	Not Specified
Defiance	25.0% (21)	20.6% (21)	37.7% (5)	23.2% (13)	26.7% (81)	20.8% (5)	40.0% (12)	9.1% (2)
Other	75.0 (63)	79.4 (81)	64.3 (9)	76.8 (43)	73.3 (11)	79.2 (10)	60.0 (18)	90.9 (20)

NOTE: Read percentages down. (Raw scores appear in parentheses).

Table 5-7. Threats, Types of Threats, and Specificity of Threats when Adversaries are Evenly Matched and Defiant Responses

	Threat		Type of Threat			Specificity of Threat		
Response Type	Threat	No Threat	Military Violence and Punishment	Military Violence	Other	Full	Act	Not Specified
Defiance	35.3% (12)	12.7% (7)	27.3% (3)	42.9% (6)	33.3% (3)	60.0% (3)	43.8% (7)	9.1% (1)
Other	64.7 (22)	87.3 (48)	72.7 (8)	57.1 (8)	66.7 (6)	40.0 (2)	56.3 (9)	90.9 (10)

NOTE: Read percentages down (Raw scores appear in parentheses).

significant at the $p < .01$ ($\chi^2 = 6.373$), when the adversaries are evenly matched (Table 5-7).

Hypotheses 6 and 7 parallel Hypotheses 4 and 5 in demonstrating a pattern of increased likelihood of defiance, as threats become more violent and more specific. With one exception, the association is markedly stronger. The exception is the instance of those threats of military violence that are accompanied by demonstrations in the form of punishing coercive acts. But the number of observations of threats of this type is small for all conflicts taken together, and 11 of those 14 observations were from conflicts between adversaries classified as evenly matched in power. Consequently, there is little real change in this indicator. The number of observations for evenly matched adversaries is small for several of the other indicators too, but these all are subsets of indicators for which there are a reasonable large number of observations when all conflicts are included.

Overall, the consistency in the change across the different threat indicators is remarkable. It is reasonable to conclude that the tests of Hypotheses 4 and 5 support the notion that the negative inducements prescribed by the realists and conflict strategists increase the probability of defiant responses. And, as the percentages in Table 5-7 indicate, this is even more so in conflicts between evenly matched powers (Hypotheses 6 and 7).

War Outcomes

Critics of the realist approach contend that the pattern that we have been observing tends to set off a chain of threats and counter-threats that increases the likelihood of the conflict ending in war. If this is true, then the gain in the probability of compliance that comes with the use of higher degrees of negative inducement may be achieved only at the cost of an increased likelihood that the conflict will escalate to war. Studies of the conflict process by Leng and Goodsell (1975), North, Brody, and Holsti (1964), and North (1967) suggest that this "fight" (Rapoport, 1960) pattern of escalation may be common in serious conflicts.

The nature of this study allows us to approach the proposition very indirectly only, by asking whether those conflicts in the sample that did result in war exhibited higher percentages of threats, defiant responses, and, more specifically, defiant responses to threats. The results in Table 5-8 are interesting, if not altogether revealing.

Certainly, there is no positive association between the frequency of the use of threats per se and the outbreak of war, whereas such an association does exist with regard to defiant responses. These results are consistent with earlier indications that it is not the use of threats which predicts to war, but *unsuccessful* threats, that is, those which result in defiant counterthreats. That impression is supported by the percentages in Table 5-9. Whether we consider all the sample conflicts, or just those between evenly matched powers, those conflicts that ended in war exhibited a rate of defiance (punishment or counterthreat) to threats which was about 10% higher than in nonwar conflicts. Among even powers, the percentage of defiant responses to threats is also about 10% higher, whether or not the conflict ended in war, than in asymmetrical conflicts.

Table 5-8. Negative Inducements and Defiant Responses in Prewar and Nonwar Disputes

	War	Nonwar	X^2
Threat	35.5% (33)	47.6% (43)	NS
Other Inducement	65.5 (60)	53.3 (49)	
Defy	30.5 (29)	15.2 (14)	6.186
Other Responses	69.5 (66)	84.8 (78)	$p < .05$

NOTE: Read percentages down. (Raw scores in parentheses.)
NS — not significant.

Table 5-9. Responses to Threats in Prewar and Nonwar Disputes

Cases	Response Type	War	Nonwar	X^2
All disputes	Defy threat	15.1% (14)	5.4% (5)	4.643
	All other responses	84.9 (79)	94.6 (87)	$p < .05$
Even adversaries	Defy threat	21.2 (7)	10.3 (4)	NS
	All other responses	78.8 (26)	89.7 (35)	

NOTE: Read percentages down. (Raw scores are in parentheses.)
NS — not significant.

Conclusions

Exploratory analysis suggests that there is some validity to the realist prescription, with threats moderately more successful than promises in achieving outright compliance with influence attempts. As the level of negative inducements increases, there does appear to be a resultant increase in the likelihood of compliance, particularly with regard to the credibility of inducements, indicated either by the relative capability of the threatener vis-à-vis the target or by the threatener's commitment to act.

On the other hand, there appears to be something to the counterrealist argument that the tactics of the realists and conflict strategists are highly risky. The actions taken to increase the degree of negative inducement and credibility tend to be associated with extreme responses—either outright compliance or defiance in the form of counterthreats and punishments. Moreover, as the counterrealists predict, defiant responses occur most often in our sample when the adversaries are relatively evenly matched in power. Finally, there is some indirect evidence to suggest that defiant responses to negative inducements are associated with war.

Because this is the first empirical cross-conflict analysis of internation influence attempts over an extended historical interval, it is difficult to draw comparisons with other investigations. Perhaps the closest substantive approximation is in the work in experimental games undertaken largely by social psychologists. Tedeschi conducted experiments dealing with the responses of subjects to influence attempts accompanied by threats of varying degrees of severity and credibility (Horai and Tedeschi, 1969; Faley and Tedeschi, 1971). With credibility measured according to the likelihood that the threat would be carried out, he obtained results consistent with the support found for Hypotheses 2 and 3 in this investigation.

Kaplowitz (1973) investigated a "power credibility" model of interperson influence attempts which is quite similar to our realist model. He placed strong emphasis on the assigned relative power of the subjects and obtained results that, at first glance, are at variance with ours. He found that, although the subjects themselves predicted that they would play the game according to the dictates of power politics, that is, that they would be more defiant against weaker opponents than those who were more powerful than they, their actual play indicated a variety of less clearly rational responses. Kaplowitz hypothesized that the players' behavior often reflected an "equity principle." One may be willing to tolerate efforts by an adversary to assert himself, for example, if one is secure in his own power, but, against a stronger opponent, one may decide it is necessary to respond assertively to a bully. Questions of prestige, honor, or even principle compete with a calculation of gains and losses.

In politics among nations it is more dangerous to base policy on principle than on the secure setting of an academic experiment, although history certainly affords examples of nations that have done so. Our study obtained a ranking of the rate of compliance with influence attempts in the expected order of power relationships: (1) large nation to small nation (30%), (2) evenly matched (24%), and (3) small to large (12%). On the other hand, the rates of defiant responses to threats were (1) evenly matched (35%), (2) small to large (25%), and (3) large to small (18%). Modifying Kaplowitz's reasoning slightly, we could argue that government may decide that it can afford to tolerate a threat from a weaker power, that it must submit to the harsh realities of "a world where power counts" in the face of a credible threat from a stronger adversary, but that it must stand up for its "rights" among relative equals. Actually, it is hard to find an approach that does not posit mutual defiance in threat situations between equals. The conflict strategists prescribe an assertion of credibility; the counterrealists predict an escalating "fight" pattern of self-aggravating feedback from mutual attempts to deter. And, there is the folklore of international politics which historically has encouraged and rewarded the belligerent assertion of power by national leaders in conflict situations.[17]

None of these findings is counterintuitive. The relatively low association found between cost of compliance and negative responses to influence attempts is a minor deviation from what appeared to be a commonsensical Hypothesis 1. It may be that, once nations have reached the serious conflict stage, their mutual behavior is taken so seriously that *what* is requested becomes less important than *how* it is requested. This seems plausible when we consider that more costly requests are more likely to be backed by stronger inducements.

Finally, we found some evidence that, at least in cases of threats of military violence directed by strong powers at weaker adversaries, the rate of complete compliance has declined and the rate of outright defiance has grown in the post-World War II era. Unfortunately, only a few conflicts fit these categories, so the results are suggestive at best. But the possible difference raises the all-important question of whether or not those tests that provide positive support for the realist prescription in our "historical experiments" may support a theory of internation influence that is becoming more dangerous as it approaches obsolescence.

Future Research

The substantive results of this investigation are no more than suggestive, but the findings, coupled with our earlier study of the conflict process (Leng and Goodsell, 1975) and ongoing research on the learning behavior of nations (Leng, 1974), provide us with increased confidence in the expanding data base and the validity of the operational indicators.

These studies have served as pretests of the structure of a model of the conflict process, including its phases and turning points, that the author has designed as a working computer simulation (Leng, 1976). The simulation, in turn, will serve as the basis for the comparative examination of the dynamics of operational versions of extant verbal theories of conflict behavior, such as the realist and counterrealist models appearing in this study. The next step will be to compare the conflict behavior patterns and outcomes generated by simulated adversaries behaving according to the decision rules prescribed by different behavioral models with those obtained from events data utilizing an expanded set of the real world cases examined in this study. This should provide a comparative test of the validity of these models of internation conflict behavior that will do justice to the dynamic richness of their verbal conceptualizations. Ultimately, as the other studies appearing in this volume will attest, the findings from this extended investigation of the conflict process must be reexamined in a variety of ecological contexts. Only then will we be able to make confident generalizations about the war proneness of nations involved in serious conflicts.

III

Accounting for the Expansion of War

6

Interstate Alliances: Their Reliability and the Expansion of War

Alan Ned Sabrosky
Catholic University

There are many perspectives on the formal alliance, and practitioners as well as scholars differ widely as to what this type of interstate bond *should* achieve and what it *does* achieve. The alliance has been praised as a deterrent to war and as an essential part of the balance-of-power mechanism. Conversely, it has been criticized on the grounds that it not only inhibits a nation's freedom of action in peacetime but that it increases the likelihood of its being dragged into war and, thus, contributes to the expansion of ongoing war.

Whereas most would agree that alliances are *intended* to provide their signatories with greater security and more diplomatic maneuverability than each would have alone (Bueno de Mesquita and Singer, 1973; Friedman, 1970; Gulick, 1967; K. J. Holsti, 1972, pp. 111-121; Liska, 1962; and Morgenthau, 1972, pp. 181-193), the extent to which they actually *have* that effect is less certain. Simply being part of an alliance system does not guarantee any state either assistance from or forebearance on the part of an ally in the event of war. Some states have obviously failed to assist, or have even attacked, their nominal allies. Some alliances have been semipermanent associations, whereas others have been only temporary pacts of convenience (Aron, 1968, p. 28). One-time allies have even become adversaries and vice versa, as the "diplomatic revolutions" preceding the Seven Years' War (1756-1763) and up through the Soviet-American Cold War can attest. Moreover, although the folklore is replete with anecdotes about "special relationships" that allegedly bound two or more nations to one another, there are also enough tales of "perfidious allies" to suggest a more cautious appraisal of the reliability of interstate alliances.

Still, there is some empirical evidence currently available, and it does indicate that alliance partners seem to be more likely to assist, and less likely to attack, one another than is true for nations that are not allied to each other (Singer and Small, 1966a, p. 19). On the other hand, even alliance partners are more likely to remain neutral than to fight either alongside *or* against one another when one of their number is already involved in a war, regardless of either the nominal strength of the alliance commitment or the power status of the signatories. But of the states that *do* enter a war involving one of their alliance partners, those in defense pacts are more likely to assist one another militarily than are states with less demanding formal alliance commitments. Further, major powers are more likely both to assist *and* to attack their nominal allies than is the case with non-major powers (Singer and Small, 1966a, pp. 17-19). In addition, a more recent study (Holsti, Hopmann, and Sullivan, 1973, pp. 48-87), using a set of coding rules different from those of Singer and Small, found that alliances tend to be honored in a majority of those cases in which their specific *casus foederis* is invoked. And no significant differences appeared in the relative frequency with which alliances are or are not honored by their signatories, controlling for (1) the size of the alliance or the number and specificity of its goals; (2) the geographical distance between, or the ideological similarity of, the signatories or the stability of their regimes, and (3) the time period within which an alliance's *casus foederis* is invoked.

These findings are certainly suggestive, providing some baseline data on the war performance of alliance partners as well as some thoughtful insights into the larger question of alliance behavior. Still, it *is* possible—and, given the current state of our knowledge about the phenomenon of interstate alliances, *essential*—to go beyond these initial studies.

First, both studies employed what Singer and Small (1966a, pp. 17-18) acknowledged to be fairly elementary measures of alliance performance. Given the "brush-clearing" nature of these studies, each of which also dealt with issues other than alliance performance, this was quite understandable. But there exists a second, more compelling reason for proceeding with a further analysis of alliance performance, namely, a reconsideration of the coding rules used in both the Singer and Small (1966a) and the Holsti, Hopmann, and Sullivan (1973) studies that raises the possibility that each might have included inadvertently some systematic measurement error.

In the case of the initial Singer and Small study, the problem seems to lie with their assumption that all members of an alliance have the same opportunity to take part in any war involving one of their number. Such an assumption may well hold for *some major* powers, of course, but it seems unlikely to hold for the general population of nations. The constraints on most minor powers, plus the special problems that they face in the international arena (Rothstein, 1968; Singer, 1972) are usually too formidable to permit them that "freedom of choice." Thus, applying to *all* nations a set of performance criteria that may be applicable only to a very few states would tend to inflate the proportion of actions in the "neutral" category and thus understate the proportions of states that fight either alongside or against their alliance partners. On the other hand, the more recent work by Holsti, Hopmann, and Sullivan seems to err in the opposite direction, by *overstating* the extent to which alliances are "honored" by their signatories. This difficulty stems largely from their linking the honoring of alliance commitments too closely to the contingencies specified in a formal class of alliance. That is, because many alliances require only neutrality or consultation from their signatories if the *casus foederis* is invoked, a state in such an alliance could be coded as "honoring" its commitment without fighting alongside its alliance partner.

In sum, there is good reason to regard the reliability of interstate alliances as an open question, and the present paper undertakes to measure that reliability more validly. To do so, we shall first redefine the more general concepts of "reliability" and "war performance" to give greater weight to the behavior of those states that actually fight alongside (or against) their alliance partners than has been done in either of the previous studies. Next, whereas those studies both dealt with the 1815-1939 period, we shall extend our analysis up through 1965, in addition to examining any interepoch differences that appear. Third, we shall construct a set of indices of alliance performance intended to provide us with more sensitive measures of alliance reliability than exist at present. And, finally, we shall use those indices of alliance performance to examine the reliability of different types of alliance in greater detail than was done in the previous work, controlling both for alliance class and for the power status of the signatories.

To pursue this inquiry, certain operational and analytical steps are necessary. After providing operational definitions of *reliability* and *war performance*, we shall articulate the hypotheses to be tested in this study. The empirical domain of the study will then be delineated, and the interstate wars and alliances within that domain will be identified and classified. After that, the resulting war and alliance data sets will be used to identify those wars that included states with formal alliance commitments, as well as the actions taken by each belligerent's alliance partners. Finally, the war-performance data and the scores obtained from the indices of alliance reliability will be examined to ascertain the existence of any patterns that tend to confirm or disconfirm the basic hypotheses.

Alliance Reliability

A fundamental element in the appraisal of alliance reliability is the evaluation of that reliability in terms of what the signatories *hoped* to accomplish, as compared with what they *actually* achieved by joining an alliance. But what *do* states seek from an alliance? In general, although a nation may enter an alliance for a variety of reasons (Fedder, 1968, p. 67; Osgood, 1968, pp. 21-22), consensus has it that alliances are intended to accomplish two basic objectives. These are (1) to help deter a potential adversary from waging war against one or more of the signatories and (2) to commit the alliance partners to assist one another, or at least stand aside, if deterrence fails. Some alliances, of course, do have (or ultimately acquire) an offensive character as well, either in addition to, or in place of, their war-deterring and war-performance functions. Still, explicitly offensive alliances constitute only a small fraction of the entire population of interstate alliances. Governments seldom seem to enter an alliance for the express purpose of waging war against another state, unless a war involving one of them is already in progress. And, in fact, most alliances *are* couched in terms of (1) mutually pledged assistance, (2) neutrality, or (3) at least consultation or conversations in the event that one of the signatories becomes involved in hostilities.

It is clear that the closer an alliance comes to fulfilling its members' expectations, the higher its overall reliability. It is equally clear, however, that there are two distinct aspects of alliance reliability, paralleling the two objectives that alliances are intended to accomplish. That is, a reliable alliance is one that not only serves its usual war-deterring purpose but that also serves a win-the-war function if deterrence fails. If alliances accomplish their war-deterring objective without fail, none of their signatories will be victims of an attack so long as the alliances are in force. Thus, the prewar reliability of these admirable alliances would be perfect, whereas their potential wartime reliability would not have been tested. On the other hand, if alliances successfully accomplish their war-performance objective each time that a signatory becomes involved in a war, then all the belligerent's allies will come to its assistance or at least (and, from its usual perspective, less desirably) remain neutral through the war. But, whereas the successful war performance of these alliances would reflect favorably on their wartime reliability, the fact that they were invoked at all would necessarily detract from their prewar reliability.

On balance, it is likely that alliance partners would prefer not having to test the wartime reliability of their alliances. Despite the unfortunate incidence of *some* war in *some* parts of the world at different times, most states are at peace most of the time (Singer and Small, 1972, pp. 286- 287), and most of their decision makers would probably want to avoid war in most instances. Nevertheless, governments cannot overlook the possibility that they might become embroiled in a war despite any efforts on their part to avert it. In such a "worst case" outcome, a nation's principal concern is with the *wartime reliability* of its alliances: that is, whether its allies will fight alongside, against, or merely remain neutral during the war. In this sense, the ultimate reliability of an alliance can best be measured in terms of its relative success in accomplishing its war-performance objective when confronted with a war-performance opportunity.

It is this *fight*-the-war aspect of alliance reliability that we will examine, reserving an assessment of the *deter*-the-war reliability of alliances for a later study. From this perspective, an alliance would be given the highest possible wartime reliability score if all of a state's alliance partners come to its assistance in a given war performance opportunity and the lowest possible score if all of them fight against it. But, if all of a state's alliance partners remain neutral during a war-performance opportunity, the alliance would be given an intermediate score between the extremes. This scoring, in turn, rests upon highly operational criteria for defining (1) that class of contingency that constitutes a war-performance opportunity and (2) the war performance of interstate alliance members in a war-performance opportunity.

War-Performance Opportunities

The first of these definitional decisions is relatively straightforward, as the principal options have already been identified in the two previous studies of alliance performance. Essentially, we could define a war-performance opportunity as either (1) the involvement of an alliance partner in *any* interstate war under *any* circumstances during the time that its alliance was in force (Singer and Small, 1966a) or (2) only those cases in which the specific *casus feoderis* was invoked, regardless of any additional—and more demanding— obligations that the alliance might have gradually acquired (Holsti, Hopmann, and Sullivan, 1973). And, although good arguments can be made for the more restrictive second option, we are still persuaded that the initial Singer and Small decision more accurately reflects the war-performance opportunities open to alliance partners over time. Thus, we shall retain their definition of a war-performance opportunity in our study.

Coding the War Performance of Interstate Alliances

The second, and perhaps more important, definitional issue concerns the coding of the war performance of interstate alliances when war-performance opportunities arose. The first step entails the selection of the unit of analysis that will be employed. The decision taken here will have a significant influence on both the number of war-performance opportunities that an alliance would have in any single contingency and the relative performance and reliability scores that would be assigned to it. That is, alliances may be thought of as (1) a single entity, regardless of the number of signatories involved, (2) an aggregation of single states, or (3) an aggregation of dyadic bonds. If a member of a ten-nation alliance became involved in a war, then the number of alliance war-performance opportunities would range from 1 through 45, depending on which of the preceding conceptions of an alliance were used, with obvious effects on the war-performance score of the alliance.

After a careful evaluation of the theoretical and empirical implications of each of these operational definitions of an alliance for our analysis, we decided to use the *alliance-as-entity* definition employed by Holsti, Hopmann, and Sullivan. Our unit of analysis is therefore the alliance itself, not the number of individual states or dyadic bonds within it. Some, of course, might quarrel with this decision, and thus we shall treat this as an empirical question in a subsequent study, where we shall replicate our analytical steps but treat an alliance as an aggregation of (1) single states and (2) dyadic bonds to ascertain what effect, if any, that may have on our findings. For the present, however, it was our judgment that treating an alliance as a single entity provided a parsimonious way of examining the reliability of interstate alliances in greater detail than had been done to date.

With the unit of analysis selected, we turned to the definition of war performance itself. Our procedure here generally parallels that used earlier by Singer and Small (1966a), defining war performance simply in terms of whether formal allies (1) fought as partners, (2) fought as adversaries, or (3) remained neutral during their war-performance opportunities. Some modifications were necessitated, however, by our decision to treat an alliance as a single entity. That is, whereas Singer and Small assigned to each alliance as many war-performance opportunities as there were nations in the alliance, our formulation means that each alliance has only *one* war-performance opportunity per war, regardless of the number of states in that pact. Our alliance war-performance opportunity scores, as well as the measures of alliance reliability derived from them, therefore represent an assessment of the *net* performance of an alliance (or set of alliances) within a given time period. They are not simply an aggregation or an arithmetic mean of the individual scores of all of the alliance partners.

This has two immediate implications for our study. First, it is necessary to explicate the criteria for coding the war performance of an alliance as entity in greater detail than would be required if the alliance were defined as an aggregation of individual states or dyadic bonds. And, second, because we are dealing here at a higher level of generalization than Singer and Small, it seemed advisable to use a different set of labels of alliance performance as well, to (1) provide a summary statement of the net war performance of a particular alliance or set of alliances and (2) facilitate our subsequent discussion of that performance. To aid the reader in comparing our findings with those obtained by Singer and Small, each of our labels will be cross-referenced to its closest analog in their study when it is initially used.

The following criteria were used in coding and labeling alliance performance during a war-performance opportunity. First, there is the definitional equivalent of the "fight alongside" category used by Singer and Small: the *honoring* of an alliance commitment. For an alliance to be classed as honored during a war-performance opportunity, two conditions must be met: (1) at least two of the alliance partners must fight alongside one another against a third party, and (2) none of the signatories may fight against any of their alliance partners. If either of these conditions is not met, then the alliance has not been honored in that war-performance opportunity. This is a restricted use of the label "honored," because nearly half (45%) of the entire population of alliances required only neutrality or conversations from their signatories in the event of war. Even the nominally strongest defense pacts were usually applicable only if a specific *casus foederis* was invoked; "blank checks" were rare (and usually informal) adjuncts to the actual alliances. Thus, if we held closely to the formal terms of each alliance, we might well find that most alliance partners could have remained neutral during many (if not all) of their war-performance opportunities without repudiating the specific obligations that they had undertaken to fulfill. But such an approach, it seems to us, is unwarranted here, particularly as we have not defined a war-performance opportunity *itself* in such a strictly legalistic manner. Moreover, it is obvious that a number of nominally weak alliances did acquire a stronger and more assertive character over time—the pre-1914 Anglo-French (1904) and Anglo-Russian (1907) ententes being among the most notable of them. Taken together, it seems clear that fighting alongside an alliance partner reflects at least the honoring, and frequently the surpassing, of whatever formal alliance commitments a state might have incurred. We are therefore satisfied that the label "honored" can be applied to that type of war performance. Nevertheless, the reader should be alert to the fact that we are *not* using it to signify adherence to a specific treaty commitment.

Yet just as some allied states have fought as partners, others, as we have mentioned earlier, have fought as adversaries. And, when allied states "fight against" one another, their alliance commitment is coded as having been *violated*. Specifically, an alliance is *violated* during a war-performance opportunity if (1) any of the signatories fight against one another or (2) one of the signatories is forcibly annexed by a putative alliance "partner."[1] When these coding rules are applied to a *bi*lateral alliance, no difficulty arises. For one of the two alliance partners to attack—or forcibly annex—the other obviously means that the alliance has been violated. But some question could be raised when these coding rules are applied to a *multi*lateral alliance. For example, if only one member of a six-nation alliance "turns traitor" and attacks one or more of its nominal allies, has the alliance really failed? Whether one views an alliance as a seamless web, an aggregation of states or an aggregation of dyadic bonds could certainly influence one's response to that query. But a more productive approach, it seems to us, is to forgo speculation on hypothetical situations and instead to look ahead at the data. Doing so, we find that only one of the four multilateral alliances that we would code as having been violated did not have its signatories divided evenly (or nearly so) between the opposing sides. That single outlier was the ten-nation German Confederation, which had only a single "traitor." But, since that "traitor" (Prussia, during the Seven Weeks' War in 1866) was one of the two major powers in the alliance, its "treason" (or that of Austria, depending on one's interpretation of the origins of that war) evenly divided the alliance's primary major-power bond. The extent of this pact's failure therefore seems sufficient to warrant its being coded as a "violated" alliance.

Finally, there is the category made up of those alliances whose other members remained neutral, or *abstained*, during a war-performance opportunity. An alliance is placed into this category only if *none* of the warring state's alliance partners fight alongside *or* against it during a given war-performance opportunity. In some respects, this is a residual category. For, if a single signatory fights alongside its alliance partner, then the alliance commitment has been honored; and, if a single signatory fights against its erstwhile ally, then the alliance would have been "violated." Only if neither of these events occurs, and all of a belligerent's alliance partners abstain from participating in the war, would an alliance's war performance be placed into the neutral category. Thus, for example, if two of the members of a six-nation alliance fought alongside one another and the other four members abstained, the alliance would have been honored—even though a majority of the alliance partners remained neutral.

The Hypotheses

Having provided operational definitions of (1) the wartime reliability of alliances and (2) war performance, we are now in a position to articulate the hypotheses that are to be tested in this study. In formulating them, we are drawing on those findings from Singer and Small (1966a) and Holsti, Hopmann, and Sullivan (1973) that have been summarized in the introduction. The first hypothesis, reflecting the most general concern with the war performance of alliances, is simply: *(H-1) Alliances reliably accomplish their wartime objectives.* If this hypothesis is supported, alliance partners would be most likely to honor, and least likely to violate, their commitments. Regardless of how reliable alliances prove to be in the aggregate, of course, interepoch differences in their wartime reliability may still appear. Therefore, our second hypothesis is: *(H-2) The wartime reliability of interstate alliances is constant over time.* Even if the wartime reliability of all interstate alliances is constant over time, however, the wartime reliability of different *types* of alliance may still vary. Thus, our third and fourth hypotheses are: *(H-3) The higher the formal class of an alliance commitment, the greater its wartime reliability,* and *(H-4) The wartime reliability of major-power alliances is greater than that of nonmajor-power alliances.*

Data Collection and Management

The Empirical Domain

The empirical domain employed in this analysis is the interstate system from 1816 through 1965, as defined in *The Wages of War* (Singer and Small, 1972, ch. 2). Unlike the earlier *Correlates of War* study of alliance performance (Singer and Small, 1966a), no differentiation is made here in the pre-1920 period between the European-oriented "central system" and the largely extra-European "peripheral system." Instead, all political entities that qualify as members of the "total (interstate) system" are included and classified as either "major" or "minor" states.[2]

After defining the spatial-temporal domain of the study, we examined data for those wars in which at least one sovereign state had participated militarily on each side. The list of interstate wars presented in Table 4.2 of *The Wages of War* is the source of the war data, providing an N of 50 interstate wars for the 150 years of the study.

Our next step was to examine data for all alliances involving at least two members of the interstate system. Our list of interstate alliances is an extension of that presented in a previous study (Small and Singer, 1969), which had an original N of 173 alliances. The initial list did not include certain alliances that were consummated during, or within three months prior to, the onset of a war. We have since been persuaded, however, that excluding an alliance from our list because one or more of its signatories became involved in a war less than three months later is an unnecessarily conservative criterion. There may be some circumstances (e.g., focusing on the relationship between alliance aggregation and war *initiation*) in which one should exclude such alliances, but there would also be other times (e.g., looking at the relationship between alliance aggregation and war *duration*) when the inclusion of these wartime alliances would be merited. Accordingly, the revised list now includes all interstate alliances (18 of which appeared recently in Holsti, Hopmann, and Sullivan, 1973, pp. 234-235) that were consummated either prior to or during a war in addition to those on the original Singer and Small alliance list. Some corrections were also made in that original list of 173 alliances on the basis of information uncovered in our continuing research effort, with the result that the number of alliances in it was reduced by one. Thus, the corrected original list plus the new "wartime" alliances give us a total of 190 interstate alliances active in the period 1816-1965.

These alliances were first classified according to the strength of the commitment. Because a full discussion of the considerations involved in this process appears elsewhere (Singer and Small, 1966a, 1966b, 1968; Small and Singer, 1969), a brief description will suffice here. The strongest alliance commitment is a *defense* pact (class I), in which the signatories agree to intervene militarily in the event of an attack on one of their number. Next, insofar as the *formal* strength of the alliance is concerned, is the *neutrality* or *nonagression* pact (class II), which obligates the signatories to remain militarily neutral should one of them become involved in a war. (The "nonaggression" variant of the class II alliance, which was popular between the two world wars, was an agreement that the "allies" would not attack one another. Some, such as the Nazi-Soviet pact of 1939, also included a "neutrality" provision.) Finally, the *entente* (class III) merely required consultations or conversations if one of the signatories was attacked.

In addition, the interstate alliances were further classified according to the power status of the participating states (Singer and Small, 1968, p. 267). In this typology, *Major-Major* (M-M) denotes an alliance including at least two major powers, with or without any minor states; *Major-minor* (M-m) identifies an alliance involving only one major power, along with one or more minor states; and a *minor-minor* alliance is one in which all of the participants are minor states.

Finally, because of our inclusion of the wartime alliances, it was decided to identify those that were clearly *offensive* alliances. These offensive alliances fall into two groups: (1) those concluded between two states that were already fighting alongside one another against a third party and were intended to reinforce an existing commitment and (2) those that explicitly included an offensive provision, usually with the object of bringing a still-neutral state into the war on the side of the other signatories. These 16 offensive alliances are associated with 5 interstate wars: The Crimean War (4), the Seven Weeks' War (1), World War I (4), World War II (5), and the Korean War (2). The alliance data that have been compiled using these coding rules are available through the Inter-University Consortium for Political and Social Research at the University of Michigan. And in Table 6-1 we summarize the distribution for the entire period, by alliance class and participant status.

War-Performance Opportunities

In sum, then, our study focused on all 50 interstate wars and 190 formal alliances from 1816 through 1965. To identify the alliance war-performance opportunities within that period, we first examined the lists of interstate wars and alliances to determine which wars had

Table 6-1. Number of Interstate Alliances by Alliance Class and Status of Participants, 1816–1965

	Status of Participants							
	Major-Major		Major-minor		minor-minor		Total	
Class of Alliance	N	%	N	%	N	%	N	%
I. Defense	28	15%	38	20%	38	20%	104	55%
II. Neutrality/nonaggression	10	5	25	13	12	6	47	24
III. Entente	22	12	10	5	7	4	39	21
Total	60	32%	73	38%	57	30%	190	100%

formal allies that were (1) fighting as adversaries, (2) fighting as partners, or (3) remaining neutral when one of their alliance partners became involved in a war. Only those alliances that were active when a war began and included at least one of the belligerents and those that were not explicitly offensive pacts are included. The identification alliances that were actually involved in a war-performance opportunity also required deciding whether or not to allow a time lag between the termination of an alliance commitment and the onset of a war involving at least one of the formal allies. There is some evidence (Singer and Small, 1966a, p. 18) that the likelihood of a state's becoming involved in a war either alongside of, or against, a (former) ally increases when a time lag is included. After considering the merits of this point, however, we decided *against* including a time lag, as it is generally recognized that entering into an alliance essentially formalizes a relationship that has been developing over time. Similarly, the termination of an alliance commitment normally occurs after that bond has ceased to have any substantive meaning. This is certainly most apparent in the case of states that are attacked by their nominal allies, but it also applies to a less violent termination of an alliance. The participation of a state on either side of a war that is in progress undoubtedly reflects a number of considerations, but there is no sound theoretical reason to assume that a defunct alliance commitment is of sufficient importance to warrant its being included in our analysis.

Using these coding rules, we identified 177 alliance war-performance opportunities in 32 of the 50 interstate wars, with each alliance counting for a single war-performance opportunity in each war when it was in force and subject to being honored or violated by its signatories. In the remaining 18 interstate wars, none of the participants had any formal alliance commitments. However, alliances that were violated during a war, after initially having been honored by their signatories, are coded twice: once as having been honored and then a second time as having been violated when one or more of the signatories changed sides near the end of the war and attacked an erstwhile alliance partner. This coding decision was necessitated by the realignments of Italy, Bulgaria, and Rumania during the latter years of World War II. The distribution of the population of alliance war-performance opportunities in the entire 1816–1965 period, by alliance class and participant status, appears in Table 6-2.

Table 6-2. War Performance Opportunities for Interstate Alliances by Alliance Class and Status of Participants, 1816–1965

	Status of Participants								
	Major-Major		Major-minor		minor-minor		Total	
Class of Alliance	N	%	N	%	N	%	N	%
I. Defense	39	22%	34	19%	12	7%	85	48%
II. Neutrality/nonagression	15	8	43	24	4	2	62	35
III. Entente	24	14	2	1	4	2	30	17
Total	78	44%	79	45%	20	11%	177	100%

Analyzing the Data

The War Performance of Interstate Alliances

The initial step in our analysis is to assess the war performance of interstate alliances in the aggregate over time, putting aside for the moment a consideration of the differentiation among alliance types. To make that assessment we first used the conventional dichotomization of 1816-1899 and 1900-1965 to differentiate between the two centuries[3] and then made a further distinction and compared the *three* periods 1816-1899, 1900-1945, and 1946-1965. This decision was prompted in part by the relatively large number of alliance commitments that have been undertaken since the end of World War II. In many respects, that 20-year span may well deserve to be called the "Age of Alliances." Although it comprises only 13% of the entire 150-year period, more than one-third of *all* alliances were formed during that epoch—including nearly half the nominally strongest (class I, defense) pacts. Because it is recognized, however, that not all will find this additional temporal distinction appropriate, all the analyses will be done twice: first treating the 65 years in the twentieth century as a single period and then again after subdividing that period into the two segments just indicated. In addition, alliances that overlapped the 1899-1900 and (when appropriate) the 1945-1946 breaks are included in *both* relevant periods, on the assumption that it more accurately reflects the war-performance opportunities open to alliances over time. The aggregate distributions of the war performance of interstate alliances during their war-performance opportunities, 1816-1965, by time period, are summarized in Table 6-3.

When we examine the data in Table 6-3, it is apparent that alliance partners are more likely to abstain than to fight alongside of, or against, one another during their war-performance opportunities throughout the 150 years of the study, as well as in each of its subperiods. Neutrality was slightly more pronounced in the nineteenth century (66% of the war-performance opportunities) than in the twentieth century as a whole (60% of the war-performance opportunities). But, when the latter century is partitioned into its pre- and post-World II subperiods, then neutrality was *most* likely in the 1946-1965 epoch (76% of the cases) and *least* common in the 1900-1945 era (56% of the war-performance opportunities), with

Table 6-3. Summary of the War Performance of Interstate Alliances by Time Periods, 1816-1965

Time Period	War Performance							
	Fights Alongside (Honors)		Remains Neutral (Abstains)		Fights Against (Violates)		Total	
	N	%	N	%	N	%	N	%
1816-1899	12	32%[a] (7)[b]	25	66% (14)	1	3% (1)	38	100% (22)
1900-1965	36	26 (20)	83	60 (47)	20	14 (11)	139	100 (78)
1900-1945	31	27 (18)	64	56 (36)	19	17 (11)	114	100 (65)
1946-1965	5	20 (3)	19	76 (11)	1	4 (1)	25	100 (15)
1816-1965	48	(27)%	108	(61)%	21	(12)%	177	(100)%

[a] Percentage of row (time period) total.
[b] Percentage of all war-performance opportunities ($N = 177$).

the nineteenth century falling between them. Further, alliances were somewhat more likely to be honored in the nineteenth century (32% of the cases) than in the 1900-1965 period (26% of the cases). And when the twentieth century is again partitioned into its two subperiods, we find that alliances were honored more frequently in the pre-World War II era (27% of the war-performance opportunities) than in the "atomic age" (20% of the cases), although the nineteenth century continues to lead in this category. The largest differences, however, appear in the relative frequency with which alliances are *violated* during their war-performance opportunities. In this category, the twentieth century in general, and the 1900-1945 subperiod in particular, lead the nineteenth century and the 1946-1965 subperiod in infamy. Specifically, alliances were nearly five times as likely to be violated in the entire twentieth century (14% of the cases) as in the 1816-1899 period (3% of the war-performance opportunities) and almost six times as likely to meet a similar fate in the 1900-1945 subperiod (17% of its cases) as in the preceding century.

Taken together, we do find some support here for some of the findings in both of the earlier studies of alliance performance (Singer and Small, 1966a; Holsti, Hopmann, and Sullivan, 1973); that is, alliances *are* more likely to be honored than violated in each of the epochs examined. Moreover, while the differences in the *relative* frequency with which alliances are violated over time are sometimes substantial, the *absolute* incidence of "treason" is comparatively low in even the most perfidy-prone era. Still, when we partition the 150-year period into its three principal epochs, each does seem to have certain distinctive characteristics. First, although neutrality was least likely in the 1900-1945 subperiod, the apparently greater willingness of states in alliances to take sides in a war was not necessarily beneficial to their alliance partners. Alliances *were* violated far more often in those years than in any other epoch, and the fact that such incidents constitute a minority of all war-performance opportunities in that era should not obscure that finding. Second, it seems that allied states have been markedly *unwilling* to get involved either alongside of *or* against their allies during the post-1945 war-performance opportunities. Whatever value alliances had in earlier times would seem, at first, to have lessened somewhat in recent years. And, finally, in contrast to the anarchy of 1900-1945 and the numerous abstentions of 1946-1965, the nineteenth century appears to have been a period of "law and order" insofar as the war performance of interstate alliances is concerned. Alliance partners did remain neutral in two-thirds of their war-performance opportunities between 1816 and 1899. Yet, if they entered the war, the alliance was almost certain to be honored; in only one case did a signatory fight against its alliance partner.

One important question remains at this point, however: Given that these observed interepoch differences in the war performance of alliances exist, what is the probability that they are larger than might be expected by chance alone? To address this question, we have used a test of significance that entails the computation of z scores based on the difference between the proportions of two groups that performed a specified action (Blalock, 1960, pp. 149-152, 176-178). Two principal criteria are usually given for the use of this test. These are that the data be (1) mutually exclusive and dichotomous and (2) made up of responses or actions in which those in each group are independent of the ones in the other. To satisfy the first criterion, given that we have *tri*chotomized the war performance of alliances, the following procedure has been used. When we test for the significance of interepoch differences in the proportions of alliances that have been honored during their war-performance opportunities, the total number of war-performance opportunities within each time period is dichotomized into (1) honored alliances and (2) all others. A similar procedure is used to test for the significance of the interepoch differences in the proportions of alliances that were violated, or whose signatories abstained, during their respective war-performance opportunities.

To meet the second criterion, it was necessary to use two different, yet related, tests of significance. When the nineteenth and twentieth centuries are compared with each other, or when the 1900-1945 and 1946-1965 segments are compared either with the nineteenth century or with one another, then a *two*-sample test (Blalock, 1960, pp. 176-178) is employed. The formula for this test is

$$z = \frac{P_1 - P_2}{\hat{\sigma} P_1 - P_2}, \quad \text{with}$$

$$\hat{\sigma} P_1 - P_2 = \sqrt{\hat{P}_u (1 - \hat{P}_u)} \sqrt{\frac{N_1 + N_2}{N_1 N_2}} \quad \text{and}$$

$$\hat{P}_u = \frac{N_1 P_1 + N_2 P_2}{N_1 + N_2},$$

where P_1, P_2 are the proportions of the two groups that perform the specified action, N_1, N_2 are the number of cases in each group, Pu is the pooled estimate of the joint probability of the action being performed in both groups, and $\sigma P_1 - P_2$ is the pooled estimate of the standard error of the two proportions.

When *any* segment is compared with the entire 1816-1965 period, however, or when either segment of the 1900-1965 period is compared with the longer segment, then the actions in the shorter period are obviously in the longer one as well. In such a situation, the cases in the shorter time segment are not independent of those in the longer period. Thus, in these instances we have used a *single*-sample test (Blalock, 1960, pp. 149-152). The formula for this test is

$$z = \frac{P_s - P_u}{\sqrt{\frac{P_u(1 - P_u)}{N}}}$$

where P_s, P_u are, respectively, the proportions of the shorter time segment (e.g., 1816-1899) and the population from which it is

Table 6-4. A Test of the Significance of Interepoch Differences in the War Performance of Interstate Alliances by Different Time Periods, 1816–1965; An Extension of Table 6-3.

A. Interepoch differences in the proportion of alliances that were *honored* in these time periods

	1816–1965 (.27)	1816–1899 (.32)	1900–1965 (.26)	1900–1945 (.27)
1816–1899 (.32)	.69†			
1900–1965 (.26)	.26	.73		
1900–1945 (.27)	.00	.59	.24	
1946–1965 (.20)	.79	1.05	.68	.72

B. Interepoch differences in the proportion of alliances whose signatories *abstained* in these time periods

	1816–1965 (.61)	1816–1899 (.66)	1900–1965 (.60)	1900–1945 (.56)
1816–1899 (.66)	.63			
1900–1965 (.60)	.24	.67		

	1816–1965 (.12)	1816–1899 (.03)	1900–1965 (.14)	1900–1945 (.17)
1900–1945 (.56)	1.09	1.08	.87	
1946–1965 (.76)	1.54	.85	1.64*	1.85*

C. Interepoch differences in the proportion of alliances that were *violated* in these time periods

	1816–1965 (.12)	1816–1899 (.03)	1900–1965 (.14)	1900–1945 (.17)
1816–1899 (.03)	1.71*			
1900–1965 (.14)	.73	1.87*		
1900–1945 (.17)	1.65*	2.19*	.92	
1946–1965 (.04)	1.23	.21	1.44	1.66*

NOTE: The values in the matrices are scores obtained from testing the significance of differences in the war performance of interstate alliances in each pair of time periods. They are *not* correlation coefficients. Thus, for example, we find in section C above that interstate alliances were violated in 12% (.12) of the cases in the entire 1816–1965 time period but suffered a similar fate in only 3% (.03) of the cases in the 1816–1899 epoch. When we test for the significance of that difference, we obtain a score of 1.71. This is significant at the .05 level, indicating that this difference had only a low probability of occurring by chance alone.

†Significance levels of scores: *.05 ($z \geq 1.64$), **.01 ($z \geq 2.33$).

drawn (e.g., 1816-1965) that perform the specified action, and N is the number of cases in the shorter time segment. The three matrices of z scores, one for each of the three possible categories of alliance performance, obtained from the application of these tests of significance are in Table 6-4.

When we examine these matrices of z scores, we find that there are no significant interepoch differences (at the .05 level or better) in the proportions of alliances that are honored during their war-performance opportunities. Thus, we must conclude that there is an unacceptably high probability that what differences exist here could have occurred by chance alone. On the other hand, some significant interepoch differences *do* appear at the .05 level in the proportions of alliances that are violated, or whose signatories abstain, during their respective war-performance opportunities. First, alliances are significantly *less* likely to be violated in the nineteenth century than in either the entire 1816-1965 time period or in the twentieth century. Further, when the twentieth century is partitioned into its pre- and post-World War II segments, we find that alliances are significantly *more* likely to be violated in the 1900-1945 subperiod than in (1) the nineteenth century, (2) the entire 1816-1965 period, or (3) the 1946-1965 segment. Finally, the possibility that the post-World War II period may well merit separate analysis, rather than being subsumed into a single twentieth century period, receives some support when we examine the interepoch differences in the proportions of alliances whose signatories abstained during their war-performance opportunities. Here we do not find any significant differences between the nineteenth and the twentieth centuries or between either of them and the entire 150-year period of the study. But alliances *are* significantly more likely to be plagued with abstentions during their war-performance opportunities in the 1946-1965 subperiod than in either the 1900-1945 subperiod or the 1816-1965 period.

Indices of the Wartime Reliability of Interstate Alliances

Now that we have assessed the aggregate war performance of alliances over time, we turn to the central concern of our study. This is the evaluation of the wartime reliability of different types of interstate alliances, as well as the reliability of all alliances over time. To undertake this assessment, two separate indices are employed, utilizing the data presented earlier in Table 6-3 and reflecting a different theoretical perspective on how the wartime reliability of alliances can best be measured.

Before continuing, however, an explanatory note is required on the scoring procedure that we have employed here. A single alliance that was *honored* in a war-performance opportunity receives a score of +1.0, whereas an alliance that was *violated* is given a score of -1.0. However, as noted in our discussion of alliance performance, the fact that alliances are not violated does not necessarily mean that they have been honored, as we are using that term. And, in fact, the assumption of a *neutral* stance (an abstention) by alliance partners during a war-performance opportunity is an intermediate category between the honoring and the violating of an alliance. Thus, an alliance in which all of the signatories (except the one member whose involvement in a war precipitated the war-performance opportunity in the first place) *abstained* receives a score of 0.0. Both indices therefore produce scores ranging from +1.0 to -1.0, inclusive. The former value would mean that all alliances within that particular cell or marginal had been honored during their war-performance opportunities, whereas the latter value would signify that all such alliances had been violated. Most scores, of course, fall between the two extremes. And except for a few instances in which there were fewer than two war-performance opportunities, perfect scores do not appear.

Alliance Reliability: A Preliminary Index

The first index we shall present is essentially a preliminary measure of the wartime reliability of interstate alliances. It puts aside for the moment those war-performance opportunities in which the alliance partners abstained and focuses instead solely on those alliances that were honored or violated when the opportunity appeared. It is, then, a rather restricted measure of the relative reliability of those alliances whose signatories decided to fight alongside, or against, their alliance partners. This index, which we shall label the "fighting reliability" index, or FIGHT, is defined as

$$\text{FIGHT} = \frac{\text{Honored alliances} - \text{violated alliances}}{\text{Honored alliances} + \text{violated alliances}}$$

where each term reflects the number of alliances that were honored or violated, as appropriate, in their war-performance opportunities in a given time period; abstentions are not included. The scores obtained with this index, both for each type of alliance and for all alliances over time, are in Table 6-5.

When we examine the scores in these tables for all alliances, we find that the nineteenth century pacts had a substantially higher "fighting reliability" value than those in the twentieth century (+.85 versus a markedly lower +.29). Moreover, when the latter century was partitioned into its pre- and post-World War II segments, an interesting difference appeared between them. Here, the FIGHT score for the 1900–1945 period fell to a relatively low +.24, whereas that of the 1946–1965 period rose to a respectable +.67. For the entire 1816–1965 period, however, the FIGHT index value was a far from impressive +.39. In general, it appears that the wartime reliability of alliances varies widely over time, at least on our preliminary measure of reliability.

Moving, then, to the FIGHT reliability scores for the different types of alliance, we find that there is only mixed support for the hypothesized ordering of alliance reliability. The Major-Major alliances do have (with a single exception) the greatest reliability, with a solid +.56 for the entire 150-year period and with scores for the four subperiods ranging from a close +.45 upward. Yet the nominally weakest level of alliance—the minor-minor pact—ran a close second, sometimes equaling or even surpassing the reliability scores of the Major-Major pacts. But the Major-minor alliances had (except for 1816–1899) a rather mediocre record, with FIGHT scores twice taking on negative values—indicating that more alliances were violated than honored during those periods.

A similar pattern appears when we look at the FIGHT reliability scores for the different classes of alliance. The class I (defense) pacts do have a relatively high overall reliability of +.68, with scores ranging from a strong +.60 in 1946–1965 to a very high +.83 in the nineteenth century. But the nominally weakest class III ententes consistently do *better* than the class I alliances, having a high overall FIGHT score of +.80 and other scores ranging from an almost equally high of +.75 upward. The intermediate class II (neutrality/nonaggression) pact, on the other hand, is little better than an albatross among alliances. *All* its scores are *negative*, giving it an extremely poor net wartime reliability of −.73 using this index. That is, there seems here to be a curvilinear relationship between the

Table 6-5. The "Fighting Reliability" (FIGHT) Index: A Preliminary Measure of the Wartime Reliability of Interstate Alliances 1816–1965

A. By Participant Status or Alliance Class in Different Time Periods

	Wartime Reliability						
	Participant Status			Alliance Class			All Alliances
Time Period	M-M	M-m	m-m	I	II	III	
1816–1965	.56	.17	.38	.68	−.73	.80	.39
1816–1899	.75	1.00	1.00	.83	**	1.00	.85
1900–1965	.50	.00	.33	.63	−.73	.78	.29
1900–1945	.45	.00	.20	.63	−.73	.75	.24
1946–1965	1.00	.00	1.00	.60	**	1.00	.67

(Continued on page 186)

Table 6-5. The "Fighting Reliability" (FIGHT) Index: A Preliminary Measure of the Wartime Reliability of Interstate Alliances 1816–1965 (Cont)

B. By Participant Status *and* Alliance Class in Different Time Periods

	Wartime Reliability									All Alliances
	Major-Major			Major-minor			minor-minor			
Time Period	I	II	III	I	II	III	I	II	III	
1816–1965	.71	-.50	.71	.71	-.78	1.00	.56	-1.00	1.00	.39
1816–1899	.71	**	1.00	1.00	**	**	1.00	**	**	.85
1900–1965	.71	-.50	.67	.60	-.78	1.00	.50	-1.00	1.00	.29
1900–1945	.67	-.50	.67	.75	-.78	1.00	.43	-1.00	1.00	.24
1946–1965	1.00	**	**	.00	**	**	1.00	**	1.00	.67

** = No war-performance opportunities in cell.
NOTE: Each time period has the following *N* of war-performance opportunities:

1816–1965: 177
1816–1899: 38
1900–1965: 139
1900–1945: 114
1946–1965: 25

nominal strength of a class of alliance and its actual FIGHT reliability, with the highest and lowest classes doing well and the middle class running a very poor third. These patterns generally hold when we combine categories, looking at the reliability of alliances both by signatory status and alliance class, with the class II alliances doing poorly regardless of the power status of the signatories.

Alliance Reliability: A Revised Index

Although FIGHT provides a useful "first cut" at the measurement of the wartime reliability of interstate alliances, it makes one assumption that needs additional scrutiny. That assumption is that the reliability of alliances is not affected by the number of *abstentions* that occur during their war-performance opportunities. If the rate of abstentions remained essentially unchanged over time, then this assumption might hold. But, as we have seen, the incidence of neutrality ranges from 56% (in 1900-1945) up to 78% (in 1946-1965), with possible implications for the wartime reliability scores. That is, the FIGHT index measures only the difference between the numbers of alliances that are honored and violated, respectively, in a given period, regardless of the total number of alliance war-performance opportunities. Thus, if one period had *ten* honored alliances and *five* violated pacts, whereas another period had *two* honored alliances and a *single* violated pact, each period would receive a FIGHT index value of +.33. Yet, if there had been a *total* of only *fifteen* war-performance opportunities in each period, could we be certain that the fact that the first period had *no* abstentions, whereas the second period had an abstention rate of 80%, was unrelated to the reliability of alliances in that period? Perhaps—but, again, this is an empirical question, and one that merited attention here.

To deal with this potential problem, we constructed an index to measure the reliability of interstate alliances which would take into consideration the effect of different abstention rates. This index, which we shall label the "adjusted fighting or abstention" reliability index, or FIGHT/ABSTAIN, is defined as

$$\text{FIGHT/ABSTAIN} = \frac{\text{Honored alliances - violated alliances.}}{\text{Total war performance opportunities}}$$

where (besides the terms used earlier in the FIGHT index), the denominator includes those alliances whose signatories *abstained* during their war-performance opportunities, in addition to those that were honored or violated by their signatories. Thus, FIGHT/ABSTAIN measures the wartime reliability of each type of alliance and of all alliances over time, *whether or not* any of a warring state's alliance partners became militarily involved on either side of the war. The FIGHT/ABSTAIN scores appear in Table 6-6.

With the inclusion of those war-performance opportunities in which alliance partners abstained from entering a war alongside or against one of their number, the absolute values of all the reliability scores decrease markedly. In addition, the relative wartime reliability of all alliances over time alters somewhat. As before, alliances did better in the nineteenth century (+.29) than in the entire twentieth century (+.12), although neither century's FIGHT/ABSTAIN score is particularly impressive. As before, differences appeared between the pre- and post-World War II segments of the twentieth century when the period was partitioned, with the 1946-1965 segment doing better (+.16) than the 1900-1945 years (+.11).

Looking now at the reliability of the different types of alliance as measured by the FIGHT/ABSTAIN index, we find both similarities and differences when compared with the scores obtained with the preliminary index. As before, the Major-minor alliances do less well than either of the other levels of alliance. Their overall reliability score was only a very low +.05, although they *did* attain a respectable +.44 in the relatively "law-abiding" nineteenth century. On this revised index, however, the minor-minor pacts do as well or better than the Major-Major alliances in all periods except for the 1900-1945 segment. Neither alliance's overall reliability is very high, but that of the minor-minor alliance (+.25) is slightly above the Major-Major pact's +.23.

A similar pattern appears when we examine the FIGHT/ABSTAIN reliability of the different classes of alliance. The relatively ill-fated class II alliances continue to do poorly; their *best* score is a .00! Moreover, in the aggregate they fell to a poor -.18, slipping somewhat further in the 1900-1945 period to -.21. As with the FIGHT index, both the class I and class III alliances do better than the class II pacts. But, with the FIGHT/ABSTAIN index, we find that their relative positions are reversed. That is, with this revised index, the class I (defense) pacts are now strongest in actual, as well as formal, terms in all eras except for the 1946-1965 period.

Table 6-6. The "Adjusted Fighting or Abstention Reliability" (FIGHT/ABSTAIN) Index: A Revised Measure of the Wartime Reliability of Interstate Alliances 1816-1965

A. By Participant Status *and* Alliance Class in Different Time Periods

	Wartime Reliability						
	Participant Status			Alliance Class			
Time Period	M-M	M-m	m-m	I	II	III	All Alliances
1816-1965	.23	.05	.25	.35	-.18	.27	.15
1816-1899	.21	.44	1.00	.36	.00	.14	.29
1900-1965	.23	-.02	.24	.35	-.19	.32	.12
1900-1945	.22	.00	.14	.41	-.21	.32	.11
1946-1965	.40	.00	.40	.20	.00	.25	.16

(Continued on page 190)

Table 6-6. The "Adjusted Fighting or Abstention Reliability" (FIGHT/ABSTAIN) Index: A Revised Measure of the Wartime Reliability of Interstate Alliances 1816–1965 (Cont)

B. By Participant Status *and* Alliance Class in Different Time Periods

	Wartime Reliability										
	Major-Major			Major-minor			minor-minor			All Alliances
Time Period	I	II	III	I	II	III	I	II	III	
1816–1965	.38	−.13	.21	.29	−.16	.50	.42	−.50	.50	.15
1816–1899	.28	.00	.14	.44	**	**	1.00	**	**	.29
1900–1965	.48	−.17	.24	.24	−.17	.50	.36	−.50	.50	.12
1900–1945	.47	−.17	.25	.38	−.18	1.00	.33	−.67	.50	.11
1946–1965	.50	**	.00	.00	.00	.00	.50	**	.50	.16

** = No war-performance opportunities in cell.
NOTE: Each time period has the following *N* of war performance opportunities:

```
1816–1965:  177
1816–1899:   38
1900–1965:  139
1900–1945:  114
1946–1965:   25
```

190

Except for the latter epoch, where the class I alliances reliability of +.20 is slightly below that of the class III pact (+.25), the class I alliance's reliability scores of +.35 to +.41 led the class III's +.14 to +.32. And, as before, these patterns generally hold when we look at the reliability of alliances both by class and by signatory status.

Taken together, these findings suggest that the rate of abstentions during war-performance opportunities does have some impact on the relative reliability of alliances, both in the aggregate and by each type of alliance. Both the class II (neutrality/nonaggression) and Major-minor alliances are in the last place in their respective categories, of course, whether or not one controls for the rate of abstentions. But differences appear with regard to the rank ordering of the other types of alliance, depending on whether one uses the FIGHT or the FIGHT/ABSTAIN index of wartime reliability. That is, if one does *not* take into consideration the possible impact of different abstention rates during war-performance opportunities, then the Major-Major and the class III (entente) pacts have the highest reliability. But, if one *does* include those abstentions in the measure of alliance reliability (as in the FIGHT/ABSTAIN index), then the minor-minor and class I (defense) pacts have that distinction.

Accounting for Alliance Reliability

From the preceding analyses, it is apparent that differences in (1) alliance class, (2) signatory status, and (3) time period can produce variations in the wartime reliability scores of interstate alliances. Further, an inspection of the data suggests that the convergence of certain combinations of these three predictors seems to accentuate the relative reliability (or *un*reliability) of alliances in the aggregate. That is, whatever net reliability alliances possess in the entire 1816-1965 time period is certainly enhanced by the high reliability of all alliances (and particularly major-power defense pacts) in the 1816-1899 era. On the other hand, the marked unreliability of alliances (and particularly the Major-minor neutrality/nonaggression pacts) in the 1900-1945 time segment clearly detracts from the overall reliability of alliances in the entire 150-year period.

Having said this, however, still leaves one issue unresolved: the relative explanatory power of each of the three predictors. To address this issue, we have employed a data analysis program known as THAID (Morgan and Messenger, 1973). This is a searching procedure that, with nominal-level predictor variables and a dichotomous outcome variable (honor/violate), sequentially partitions the data into two groups with maximally different probability distributions. The relative explanatory power of each predictor variable is expressed by a DELTA-statistic (δ'), whose values range from .000 to 1.000 and whose formula is

$$\delta'_{y/x} = \frac{\delta_{y/x}}{2N[1 - \Sigma (\frac{N}{N}j)^2]}, \text{ where}$$

$$\delta_{y/x} = \sum_{i=1}^{2} \sum_{j=1}^{G} |fe_{ij} - f_{ij}|, \text{ and}$$

where fe_{ij} and f_{ij} are, respectively, the expected and the observed frequencies in each cell of a G-dimensional space, N is the total number of cases in the data set, and N_j is the total number of observed cases in a given group.

The delta measures of the explanatory power of the alternative predictors of alliance performance are presented in Table 6-7. The "THAID tree," which depicts the actual partition of the data at each interation, appears in Figure 6-1. The group of *all* alliances provides the N of alliances that were honored ($N = 48$) and violated ($N = 21$) during the 177 war-performance opportunities from 1816 to 1965. Each subgroup indicates (1) the modal category in that subgroup, based on the best predictor, (2) the ratio of honored to violated alliances in that subgroup, and (3) the proportion of *all* alliances in that subgroup that were honored.

When we examine these findings, it appears that *alliance class* has the greatest explanatory power ($y_i y/x = .577$) in the initial partition of the data, followed by *signatory status* ($y_i y/x = .280$) and *time period* ($y_i y_j x = .259$) in that order. Partitioning the data into two subgroups (honored/violated alliances) using the best predictor—alliance class—also increases the theta (modal predictive) power from *.696* for all alliances, to *.851* after this initial split. No additional increases in modal predictive power occur, however, following the subsequent partition of the first two subgroups. This suggests that one can best account for variations in the net reliability of alliances by looking for variations in the distribution of different classes of alliance commitment over time.

Table 6-7. Delta Measures of the Explanatory Power of Alternative Predictors of Alliance Performance, 1816–1965

	Initial Condition	Predictor (Initial Condition)		
		Alliance Class	Signatory Status	Time Period
1.	All alliances	.577	.280	.259
2.	Class I, class III	.071	.054	.136
4.	1816–1899	.083	.417	—
8.	Major-Major	.143	—	—
9.	Major-minor, minor-minor	—	1.000	—
5.	1900–1965	.092	.071	.004
10.	Class I	—	.128	.013
11.	Class III	—	.375	.125
3.	Class II	—	.269	—
6.	Major-minor	—	—	—
7.	Major-Major	—	—	—

NOTE: The majority (.85) of the alliances in subgroup 2 were honored; the majority (.87) of the alliances in subgroup 3 were violated.

To elaborate on this, as well as to take into consideration the role of the other predictors in the subsequent partitions, we find that only one additional split is possible with the violated alliances. This partitions the class II alliances by signatory status ($\delta'_{y/x}$ = .269) into Major-minor and Major-Major alliances. More extensive partitioning is possible, however, with the set of class I and class III alliances that were largely honored in their war-performance opportunities. The first partition of this set of alliances is accomplished using time period ($\delta'_{y/x}$ = .136), dividing the alliances into the 1816–1899 and 1900–1965 eras. The alliances in the former epoch were then partitioned in their turn by signatory status ($\delta'_{y/x}$ = .417), whereas the twentieth century alliances were split by alliance class ($\delta'_{y/x}$ = .092).

Examining the consequences of these partitions as they are presented in Figure 6-1 raises an important question. If we wished to select those alliances that were *most* likely to be honored, where would we turn? On this point, it appears that alliances were most likely to be honored if they were (1) class I or class III pacts, (2) active in the nineteenth century, and (3) included no more than *one*

Figure 6-1. Partition of the Alliance Performance Data Using the Best Predictor at Each Iteration

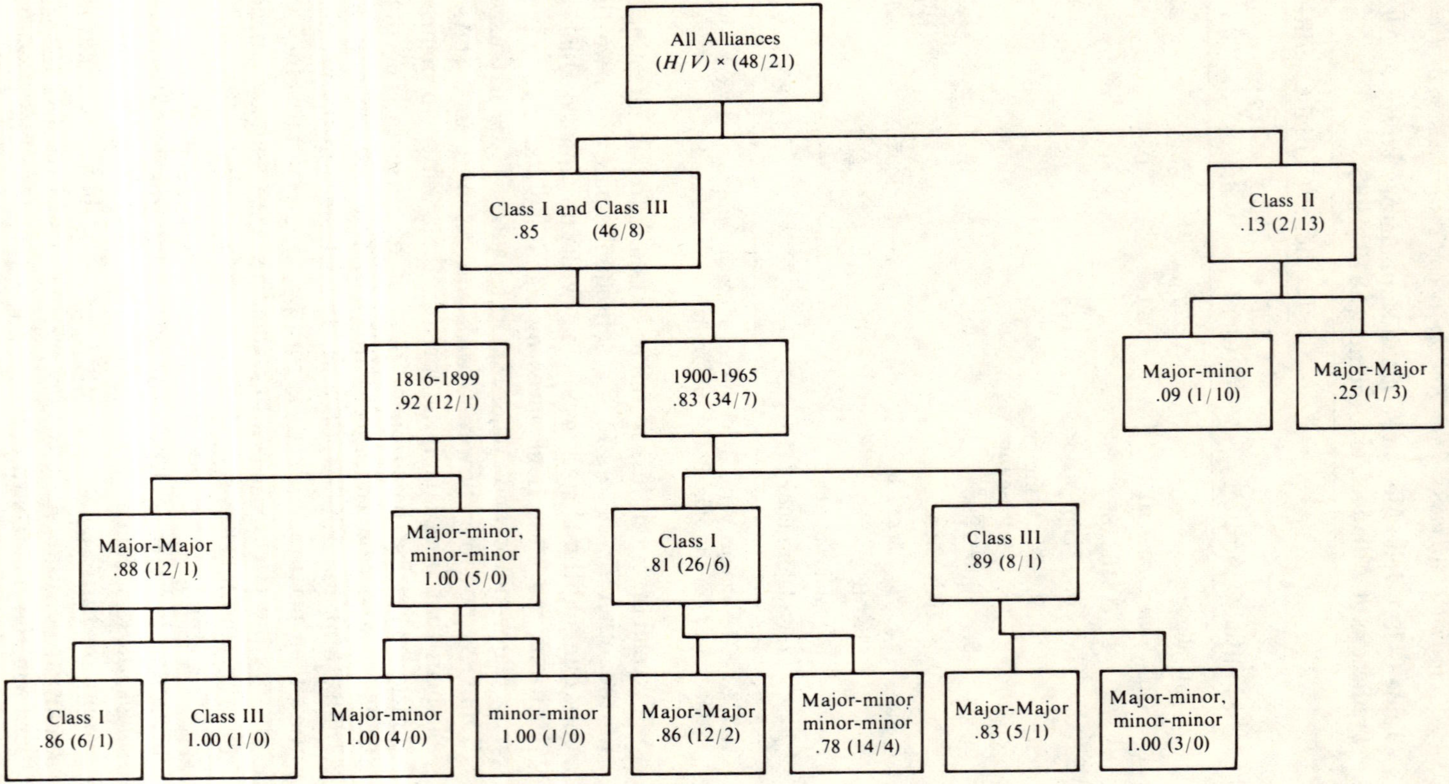

- All Alliances (H/V) × (48/21)
  - Class I and Class III (46/8) .85
    - 1816–1899 .92 (12/1)
      - Major-Major .88 (12/1)
        - Class I .86 (6/1)
        - Class III 1.00 (1/0)
      - Major-minor, minor-minor 1.00 (5/0)
        - Major-minor 1.00 (4/0)
        - minor-minor 1.00 (1/0)
    - 1900–1965 .83 (34/7)
      - Class I .81 (26/6)
        - Major-Major .86 (12/2)
        - Major-minor, minor-minor .78 (14/4)
      - Class III .89 (8/1)
        - Major-Major .83 (5/1)
        - Major-minor, minor-minor 1.00 (3/0)
  - Class II .13 (2/13)
    - Major-minor .09 (1/10)
    - Major-Major .25 (1/3)

major power. Yet, because we *are* in the twentieth century, the fact that alliances performed their wartime roles better in the nineteenth century than in the twentieth century leads us to a more restricted query. That is, even if we grant that the war performance of alliances *is* less impressive in the twentieth century than in the earlier era, what combination of attributes seems best in the more recent epoch? And, here, our findings seem to favor the less demanding formal ties of the class III alliance, although the more numerous class I alliances do nearly as well. Yet there is a further distinction to be made there. For, if one opts for the class III alliances, then alliances encompassing two or more major powers do less well than pacts with only a single major power signatory. But, when the stronger class I pacts are selected, then Major-Major alliances seem to be preferable.

Conclusion

"The universe of historical alliances," it has been suggested, "consists of two classes: those that were put to the test and those that were not" (Pfaltzgraff, 1969, p. 1). In our analysis, we focused our attention on those alliances that *were* "put to the test" in 177 war-performance opportunities from 1816 to 1965. Having done this, we must now ask how well our four basic hypotheses have stood their own test.

The first hypothesis, it will be recalled, was that *alliances reliably accomplish their wartime objectives*. When we examine the data, however, we find that this hypothesis receives relatively little support. Alliance partners are more likely to honor their commitments than they are to violate them, but they are *most* likely simply to stand aside when one of their number becomes involved in a war. In general, it seems that the common faith in the reliability of alliances has been somewhat misplaced. Being part of an extensive alliance network may provide some *subjective* comfort to various political leaders in different nations, but the *objective* wartime reliability of alliances, as we have measured it, is remarkably low. Alliances simply do not accomplish their principal war-performance objective with any marked success.

Yet even if the wartime reliability of all alliances is relatively low, are there any variations in that reliability over time? This question was addressed in the second hypothesis, which was that *the wartime reliability of interstate alliances is constant over time.* This hypothesis, however, receives only mixed support. Although there is some variation insofar as the reliability of certain types of alliance is concerned, a type of alliance that is relatively reliable (or *un*reliable) in one period is usually in the same rank in the remaining periods with respect to the other types of alliance. In the aggregate, however, there is a considerable degree of variation over time. Alliances have the highest overall reliability on both indices in the nineteenth century and the lowest reliability in segments of the twentieth century. Thus, we *could* modify our preceding judgment on alliance reliability to some extent. That is, alliances may once have been reliable enough to provide their signatories with some objective support in addition to whatever subjective comfort the decision makers received from their pacts. In the twentieth century, however, confidence in the reliability of alliances is sustained more by faith than by fact.

Turning now to the third hypothesis, which states that *the higher the formal class of an alliance commitment, the greater its wartime reliability,* we again find only mixed support for it in the data. The nominally strongest class I (defense) pacts usually do have a relatively impressive wartime reliability. Yet the nominally *weakest* alliance—class III (entente)—also does well, and on one index of alliance reliability (FIGHT) it does *better* than the class I alliance. The intermediate class II (neutrality/nonaggression) pacts, however, consistently have the lowest wartime reliability scores of all classes of alliance. Many of the signatories to this class of alliance may well adhere to the formal terms of the pact and forgo participating in a war involving their alliance partner. But it is clear that, if the signatories to a neutrality/nonaggression pact *do* participate in a war, they tend to fight *against* their nominal allies more often than they fight alongside them.

Finally, *is the wartime reliability of major-power alliances greater than that of nonmajor-power alliances?* If true, this would mean that Major-Major alliances would have the greatest reliability, followed by Major-minor and minor-minor alliances in that order. Our findings, however, are mixed here as well. The Major-Major alliances generally do well, but the minor-minor alliances often do as well or better in the aggregate. But the Major-minor alliances—which might have been expected to rank second in overall reliability—almost invariably had the lowest reliability scores of the three alliance types. In some instances, these Major-minor alliances even had highly *negative* scores, with alliances being violated more frequently than they were honored. When combined with our previous findings, it is clear that the class II/Major-minor alliance offers very little security to the weaker partner.

Three inferences may be drawn from these findings. First, there seems to be a direct relationship between the level of power similarity in the membership of an alliance and its wartime reliability. That is, alliances made up solely of major powers *or* of minor powers consistently tended to have greater reliability than alliances that included one major power and one or more minor powers. Minor powers would do well to reflect on this pattern before entering (or remaining within) such an arrangement, particularly given the prevalence of such alliances in the present era.

Second, the marked decrease in the wartime reliability of alliances in the twentieth century coincides with the degeneration of the balance-of-power system in that same period.[4] Because alliances are one of the primary means by which such a balance is maintained (Gulick, 1967, p. 61), it is not surprising that the fortunes of alliances and of the balance-of-power system should go hand in hand. Whether the decreasing reliability of alliances *contributes* to the decline of the balance-of-power system, or simply *reflects* that decline, remains an empirical question to be addressed in later research.

This brings us to the third and final point. Should the post-World War II period be treated separately from the 1900-1945 segment of the twentieth century or not? One recent study (Singer, Bremer, and Stuckey, 1972, pp. 47-48) argued strongly against making such a distinction, and the present paper certainly does not allow us to make a definitive judgment on this issue. But our findings *do* suggest that the 1946-1965 period *is* different from the earlier part of this century, at least with regard to the reliability of interstate alliances. Specifically, the post-World War II period has (1) a significantly sharp *increase* in the rate of abstentions during war-performance opportunities (78%, the highest of any period) and (2) an equally sharp *decrease* in the number of alliances that were active in that period's war-performance opportunities (23%, the lowest of any period).[5] What cannot be ascertained at this time, however, is whether the 1946-1965 period is similar to the nineteenth century (as the FIGHT index suggests), or whether it represents some other pattern without an analog in an earlier period.

What are we to make of these findings? Taken together, the general implications of the present analysis are perhaps best reflected in a brief analogy. In it, the war performance of alliances corresponds to the success or failure of investors in securities on the stock exchange. In the nineteenth century, most of the trading was done by a few large investors. They chose to concentrate their investments in "blue-chip" stocks—the *defense* pacts—rather than in less valuable securities, although a few of the latter were acquired. The market was generally favorable during that time, with the investors receiving substantial dividends and incurring very few losses. Between 1900 and 1945, smaller investors began to enter the market in greater numbers. Moreover, all the participants began to expand and to diversify their holdings. Throughout those years, the market fluctuated wildly. Many investments prospered, but many others failed. This did not deter the traders, however. In the 20 years following World War II, even more of the smaller investors entered the market. After the many disappointments of the early twentieth century, however, they once again concentrated their investments in the "blue-chip" stocks. Unfortunately, the 1946-1965 period was marked by a severe recession, combined with massive inflation. Consequently, the market value of those securities was reduced, even though a run on the market was forestalled and most of the investors chose not to liquidate their holdings. But it was apparent that never before had so many states contracted so many alliances of such theoretical strength and received so little in return for their efforts.

7

Wider Wars and Restless Nights: Major Power Intervention in Ongoing War

Yoshinobu Yamamoto
Saitama University
AND
Stuart A. Bremer
Science Center, Berlin

After consuming too much exotic cuisine at a state dinner or imbibing too much champagne at a diplomatic reception, statesmen, like other mortals, may be prone, upon retiring, to experience a peculiar and bothersome neurological phenomenon known as the nightmare. On some occasions, the gist of the nightmare may be as follows.

Nation A, a minor power, launches a surprise attack against another minor power, nation B. After some initial success by nation A, the tide of battle turns as nation B's counterattack threatens to rout the forces of nation A. Nation X, the major power ally of nation A, fearing that an ignominious defeat of its ally is at hand, sends large amounts of aid to nation A. Once again the tide of battle turns, and nation B's major power ally, nation Y, becomes concerned over the fate of nation B, and it too begins to assist its ally. As the conflict escalates and intensifies, the major powers, nations X and Y, perceive that more and more is at stake in the outcome of the conflict. Consequently, both move toward greater and more direct participation in the war, and finally they begin to draw their other major and minor power allies into the fray. World War III has begun.

At this point the statesman may awaken abruptly, wipe the perspiration from his brow, roll over on his side, and hope that peaceful sleep will soon come so that he will be ready for the following day's reception and dinner.

What makes this particular scenario so nightmarish is the large number of potential nation A's and nation B's that exist today. Israel and Egypt, North and South Korea, India and Pakistan, East and West Germany are only a few of the candidates for the roles of nations A and B during the 1970s. And the record of this century alone reminds us that this sequence of events is by no means mere fantasy. Similar deadly progressions began in 1914, in 1939, and again in 1950 and produced results that few have forgotten. Perhaps more forgettable, but equally deserving of attention, are those wars that might have followed this pattern, but did not. What, for example, would have happened if Russia had chosen to enter the Franco-Prussian War in 1870? Or, what if England had intervened in the Russo-Turkish War of 1877, as it repeatedly threatened to do?

Ultimately, of course, we hope to be able to answer such specific questions, but this paper has a more general, and at the same time, more modest, focus. We are concerned here with developing and testing probability models of the decision processes that underlie the historical and hypothetical examples of major power intervention in ongoing interstate wars given above. More specifically, we will postulate three models of war expansion by major power entry and examine the wars that occurred between 1816 and 1965 to assess their relative merits. It should be stated at the outset that all these models are relatively simple, but simple they must be, if we are to deduce their consequences. Let us first turn to an articulation of these models.

Three Probability Models of War Entry

All these models take as their initial condition the onset of an interstate war, and they all posit that all major powers, with their far-reaching concerns and capabilities, make decisions as to whether they should or should not enter the fray. The models also share an assumption that the reactions of the major powers are governed by the same decision process. Furthermore, all three assume that initially each major power has a certain probability of entering the ongoing war, but the models differ with respect to how this probability is altered by subsequent decisions of other major powers.

In this section we will discuss each of these models in detail, giving emphasis to their differences rather than to their similarities. Each model will be described in two ways. First, we will use the metaphoric language that probability theorists frequently employ and portray the war-entry decision *as if* it depended on the draw of a ball from an urn containing a certain number of black and white balls. If a black ball is drawn, the major power enters the war, whereas, if a white ball is drawn, it does not. A description of this sort will be followed by a formal, mathematical specification of the particular model under discussion. We will begin with the simplest model which rests upon the assumption of independent choices.

Independent Choice

If each major power is assumed to have the same constant probability of entering any particular war, and if this probability is not affected by whether or not other major powers enter the war, then we may say that each power's decision is *independent* of other powers' decisions. One way of exemplifying this process is to imagine that each major power makes its war-entry decision by drawing a ball from an urn containing B black balls and W white balls. If a black ball is drawn, the power enters the war, but, if a white ball is drawn, it does not. The powers make their selections sequentially, and, after each draw the ball is replaced, thus restoring the urn to its original composition.

If we designate the original proportion of balls in the urn that are black, $B/(B + W)$, as p and the corresponding proportion of white balls, $W/(B + W)$, as q, we can say that the probability that the first power will enter the war is p and the probability that it will abstain is q. Because the process we have outlined above constitutes sampling *with replacement*, the probabilities that the second power will enter or abstain are also p and q, respectively. These same probabilities apply, of course, to all subsequent powers as well. We can portray a sequence of such choices as a decision tree, and Figure 7-1 shows in diagrammatic form the possible decisional permutations for three hypothetical major powers. The probabilities associated with each fork in the decision tree are included in this diagram, as well as the joint outcomes and their probabilities.

Because the decision process we have outlined corresponds to a sequence of independent Bernoulli trials, we know that the probability that exactly k out of N major powers will enter a war is simply

$$P(k \text{ will enter}) = \binom{N}{k} p^k q^{N-k}$$

where p and q have the meanings discussed earlier. This is, of course, the familiar binomial distribution.

This simple model of the decision process may strike some as trivial and uninteresting, yet some thoughtful consideration reveals that it is a good deal more profound than it appears at first blush. One justification that can be put forth is as follows. The decision as to whether or not to enter an ongoing war is based on a very large number of factors, each of which has only a small influence on the final outcome. Hence, the decision to enter a war stems from the confluence of many factors, only one of which is the action that

Figure 7-1. Decision Tree for the Independent Choice Model

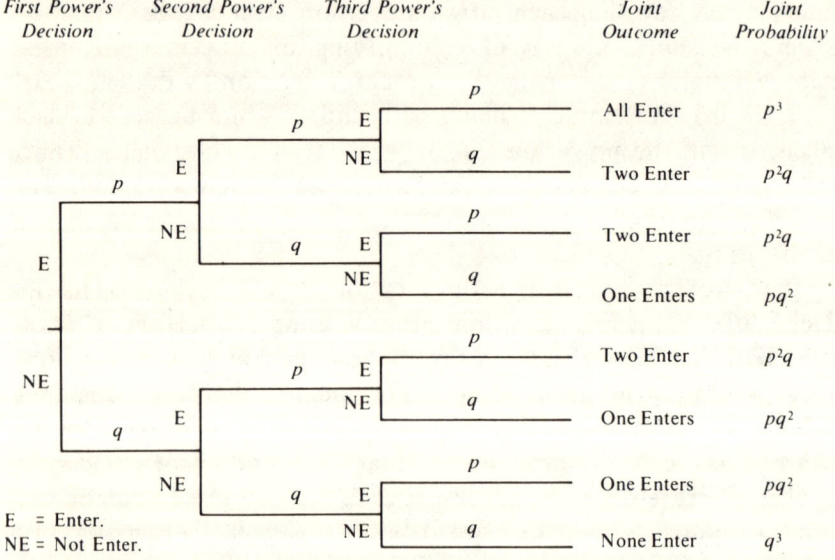

other major powers have taken. If these war entrance promoting factors are relatively equal in strength and essentially randomly distributed across wars, then this model may be applicable.

Nevertheless, the assumption that major powers, when making their own war-entry decisions, assign little or no weight to the prior decisions of other major powers may strike some as lacking face validity. Diplomatic historians, for example, frequently express the opinion that one major power's decision to enter a war was heavily influenced by another major power's earlier decision, and we will refer to this generally as *conditional choice*. In the remainder of this section, we will develop two models that incorporate decisional dependence of this sort. Before doing so, however, we need to examine the concept of conditional choice a little more closely.

For the most part, foreign affairs analysts have suggested that the decision of one major power to enter an ongoing war stimulated another power to do the same, rather than deterring it from doing so. Expressed as a probabilistic generalization, we would say that a decision by one major power to enter an ongoing war leads to an increase in the probability that other major powers will also enter the war. Before we can construct a model of this process, however, we must specify how the probabilities change if the decision of the first major power is *not* to enter the war, and on this point the scholarly literature is ambiguous. It may be, on the one hand, that a decision by the first major power to abstain from the war leaves the second major power's probabilities *unchanged*. Or, on the other hand, abstention by the first major power may lead to an *increase* in the probability that the second will also abstain and, necessarily, a *decrease* in the probability that it will enter.

We will call the first version *one-way conditional choice* because, as we shall see shortly, the probability that a major power will enter a war can increase or remain the same as a result of other powers' decisions, but *not decrease*. In the second version, however, the war-entry probability can increase *or* decrease, depending on the decisions of other powers, and it will, therefore, be referred to as *two-way conditional choice*. Or, to draw the distinction in a somewhat different way, under two-way conditional choice, the decision of the first major power leads to an increase in the probability that the second power will select the same option, regardless of the option chosen, but, with a one-way conditional choice process, this emulation effect occurs only if the first power decides to enter the war.

Before turning to a detailed specification of these two models, we should hasten to point out that the two particular versions we have selected are by no means the only ones available to us. On the contrary, there are many probability models that have been, or can be, postulated that include decisional dependence of the sort just discussed. We have selected two of the simpler and more widely applied members of this family for investigation here.

One-Way Conditional Choice

Suppose for a moment that the war-entry decision process were as follows. As in our first model, each power in turn draws a ball from an urn containing B black and W white balls, and, if a white ball is drawn, denoting noninvolvement, it is returned to the urn and the deadly lottery continues. If, however, a black ball is selected, signifying participation, then the ball is returned to the urn and a certain number of black balls, b, is added to the urn and an equal number of white balls, w, is taken out, thus keeping the number of balls in the urn constant. In this way the composition of the urn may change, but only in the direction of a higher proportion of black balls, as under no circumstances are white balls added to the urn. This decision process incorporates what we have called one-way conditional choice.

Before we can consider the decision tree that this model implies, we need to establish some notation. The initial proportion of black and white balls in the urn, corresponding to the probabilities that the first major power will enter or abstain from the war respectively, are designated p and q as before, and these are simply equal to $B/(B + W)$ and $W/(B + W)$. We stated that, if a black ball were drawn on the first draw, b black balls would be added to the urn and w white balls would be removed. If this were done, then the probability of drawing a black ball on the second trial would be $(B + b)/(B + W + b - w)$. Earlier we stated that the number of black balls added, b, was the same as the number of white balls removed, w, so the probability $(B + b)/(B + W + b - w)$ is simply $(B + b)/(B + W)$. If we designate $b/(B + W)$ as r, then the probability of drawing a black ball on the second trial, given that a black ball was selected on the first, is simply $p + r$, and the probability of drawing a white is $q - r$. With this in mind, let us examine the decision tree that would apply to a situation involving three hypothetical major powers that is portrayed in Figure 7-2.

As we can see, a decision to enter the war by the first power increases the probability that the second will enter to $p + r$, and, should the second select this option, the probability that the third will do the same rises to $(p + r) + r$ or $p + 2r$. In general, we can state that the probability that a major power will intervene is $p + ir$, where i is the number of major powers that have already decided to enter, and the probability that it will not enter is simply $q - ir$.

Mathematically, it can be shown that the probability of exactly k out of N total major powers entering an ongoing war under these conditions is

$$P(k \text{ will enter}) = \frac{\prod_{i=0}^{k-1}\left(\frac{p}{r}+r\right) \sum_{i=0}^{k}\left[(-1)^i \binom{k}{i}(q-ir)^N\right]}{k!}$$

where p, q, and r are the parameters already discussed. This model was developed by Rutherford (1954), and we should note one limitation to its applicability. If r is assigned a value greater that

Figure 7-2. Decision Tree for the One-Way Conditional Choice Model

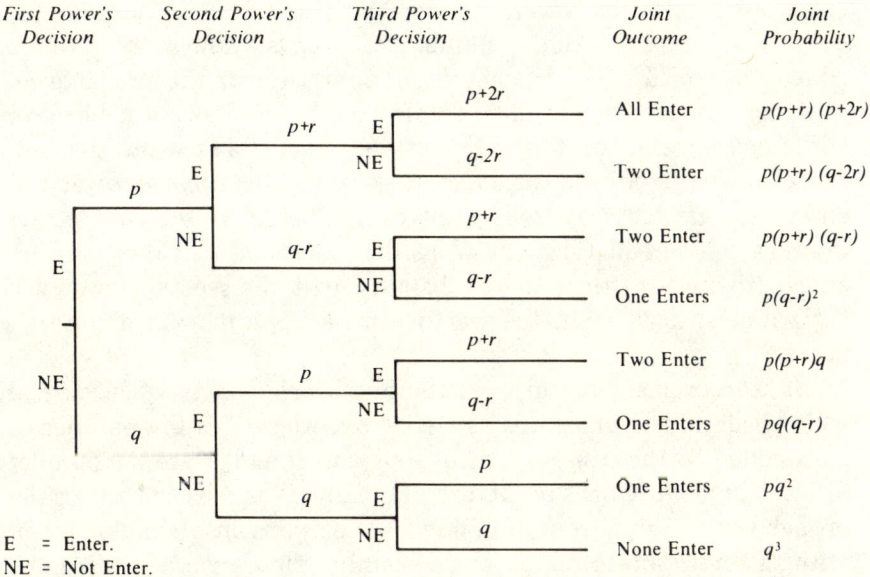

$(1 - p)/(N - 1)$, then probabilities greater than 1.0 and less than 0 are generated, and this is, of course, by definition impossible. This would correspond to the situation where there were no more white balls to be removed from the urn because all had been removed as a result of earlier outcomes. In this case the sampling would simply stop and the outcome remain undefined. The bounded nature of this model suggests that it is most appropriate when only a small to moderate degree of decisional dependence is present.

The last model we will examine is not limited in this way and allows the war-entry probability to decrease as well as increase.

Two-Way Conditional Choice

We stated earlier that under two-way conditional choice a decision to enter a war by a major power would lead to an increase in the probability that other powers would also enter and a decision to abstain would lead to a reduction in the probability that others would enter. Let us construct a decision-by-sampling scheme that incorporates this process.

Assume, as before, that the powers each draw a ball from an urn containing B black balls and W white balls and that, if the ball drawn is black, it enters the war, whereas, if the ball is white, it abstains. After each draw, however, the ball is replaced and, whatever the color of the ball, a specified number, c, of balls of the same color are added to the urn. Obviously, the composition of the urn changes over consecutive draws, and the probability of drawing a black or white ball depends on the outcomes of earlier draws. Note that this model differs from the former, as the probability that a power will enter may *decrease* as well as increase. That is, if the first power draws a white ball (abstains from the war), and c white balls are added to the urn, then the probability that the second power will draw a black ball (enter the war) is smaller than it was for the first power.

If we designate p and q as the initial proportions of black and white balls in the urn and s as $c/(B + W)$, where c is the number of balls added to the urn after each draw and B and W are the number of black and white balls in the urn originally, then we can express the probabilities that govern the powers' decisions in a simpler form. With this notation in mind, let us examine the decision tree for our hypothetical three-power situation.

Figure 7-3 lays out in diagrammatic form the possible decisions that could be reached by three major powers and the probabilities associated with the individual choices and joint outcomes. As we can see, the probabilities that the first major power will enter or abstain are p and q, respectively, the same as stipulated by the first two models.

The second major power's decision, however, is based in part on the first major power's decision. If that decision was to enter the war, then the probability that the second major power will also enter is $(p+s)/(1+s)$, and the probability that it will abstain is $q/(1+s)$. If, on the other hand, the first major power's decision was to stay out of the war, then the second major power's probabilities of entering or abstaining would be $p/(1+s)$ and $(q+s)/(1+s)$, respectively. If the constant, s, is positive in value, we can see that, whatever the decision of the first major power, the model predicts that the second major power will experience an increase in the probability of selecting the same option that the first power chose.

Turning to the decision of the third major power in our example, we can see that, if both the first and second powers decided to enter the war, the probability that the third will do likewise is

Figure 7-3. Decision Tree for the Two-Way Conditional Choice Model

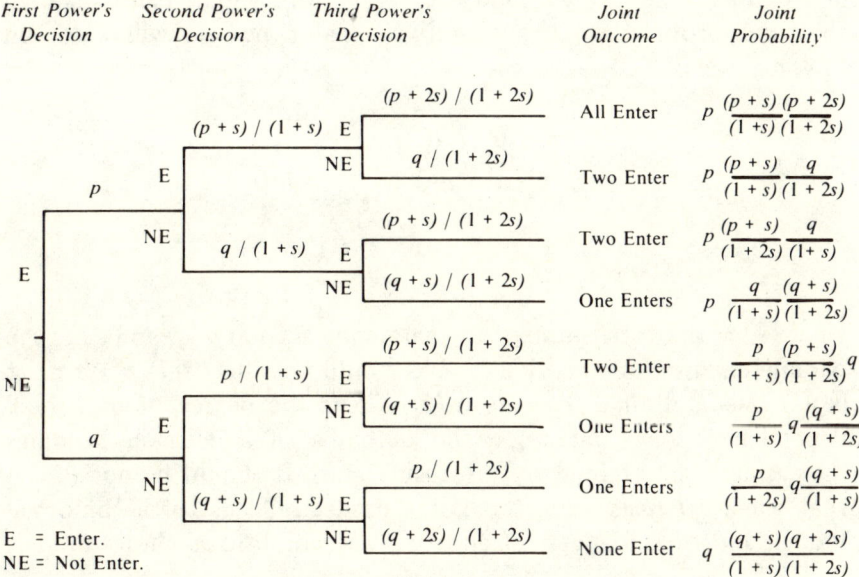

$(p + 2s)/(1 + 2s)$, whereas a decision to abstain has a probability of $q/(1 + 2s)$. If either, but not both, of the two major powers opt for intervention, then the third's probabilities of intervening or abstaining are $(p + s)/(1 + 2s)$ and $(q + s)/(1 + 2s)$, respectively. Finally, if both of the prior decisions were to abstain from involvement in the war, then the third power would intervene with a probability $p/(1 + 2s)$ and abstain with a probability $(q + 2s)/(1 + 2s)$.

In general we can state that the probability that the $k + 1$th major power will intervene is

$$\frac{(p + is)}{(1 + ks)}$$

where i is the number of major powers that have already decided to enter and k is the total number of major powers that have made decisions. Similarly, the probability that the $k + 1$th state will abstain from war involvement is

$$\frac{(q + js)}{(1 + ks)}$$

where j is the number of major powers that have already opted for abstention and k is the number of powers that have previously rendered decisions. Obviously, $i + j$ must equal k.

The decision process that we have been discussing corresponds to a probability model developed by Polya (Feller, 1968, pp. 119-121; and Johnson and Kotz, 1969, pp. 229-232), and it can be shown that the probability that exactly k major powers will enter an ongoing war is

$$p(k \text{ will enter}) = \frac{\binom{N}{k} \prod_{i=0}^{k-1} (p + is) \prod_{i=0}^{n-k-1} (q + is)}{\prod_{i=0}^{N-1} (1 + is)}$$

where N is the total number of major powers and p, q, and s are the parameters discussed previously. We should note here that $p + q$ must equal one and that the size of s reflects the degree of decisional dependence. As s increases, the outcome of a decision becomes increasingly determined by prior outcomes. It should be noted also that when s equals zero, the Polya model reduces to the binomial model, and the independent and two-way conditional choice models thus make the same predictions. The one-way conditional choice model also reduces to the binomial if its decisional dependence parameter, r, is given a value of zero.

Before turning to parameter estimation and model testing, let us consider how the models might differ in their predictions in a given situation. Table 7-1 shows some hypothetical probabilities that various numbers of major powers in a three-power system will decide to enter an ongoing war, according to the independent and conditional choice models. The values of p and q have been arbitrarily set at .10 and .90, respectively, and r and s were assigned the value of .30 in computing the probabilities of the conditional choice models.

As we can see from this table, the models differ chiefly with respect to the probability that all powers will enter the war. Under the independent choice model, the probability that all three join is one in a thousand, whereas this development is considerably more likely if the conditional choice models are employed. In contrast, the outcomes that lie in the middle of the distribution, reflecting one or two powers joining, are more likely if independent choices are assumed than if choices are viewed as conditional.

Before shifting to the topic of parameter estimation, we need to identify one important aspect of the war expansion process that is not dealt with by any of the models. Although all three enable us to make predictions about the likelihood that different numbers of major powers will enter an ongoing war, they neither predict whether one or both sides of the conflict will be joined nor do they specify, in the eventuality that both sides are joined, how many powers will be on each side. Thus the models do not differentiate between what might be called "collective security" wars, in which all the major powers join one side, and "world" wars, in which the powers are

Table 7-1. Hypothetical Predictions of the Decision Models

Number of Powers Entering	Model		
	Independent Choice	One-Way Conditional Choice	Two-Way Conditional Choice
0	.73	.73	.78
1	.17	.17	.16
2	.10	.07	.05
3	.001	.03	.01

arrayed against one another. We will consider this omission in the concluding section.

Research Design and Parameter Estimation

Having laid out three probability models of war entry, we can now turn to the tasks of specifying the spatial and temporal domains that will be used to test the models and the procedures that will be employed to estimate their parameters.

Spatial and Temporal Domain

The data we will be using are drawn from Singer and Small's *The Wages of War* (1972), which covers the period 1816-1965. We will be concerned only with those 50 wars that are interstate in nature, that is, wars in which at least one political entity on each side is a member of the interstate system. We will not repeat here the definitions of, and rationale for, what constitutes a war or participation in a war, since all of this is adequately defined in Singer and Small (1972, ch. 2).

Because we are interested in the question of major power entry into wars after their onset, we need first to specify the set of major power actors and then to operationally define post-onset entry. Our definition of the major power set is the same as that used by Singer and Small (1972, p. 23).

England	1816-1965
France	1816-1940, 1945-1965
Germany	1816-1918, 1925-1945
Austria-Hungary	1816-1918
Italy	1860-1943
Russia	1816-1917, 1922-1965
United States	1899-1965
Japan	1895-1945
China	1950-1965

As to our definition of post-onset war entry by a major power, it is simply a war entry by a major power that occurs *after* the first day of the war. Because the dates of entry are given in Singer and Small

Table 7-2. Major Power Entry into Ongoing Wars, 1816–1965

Number of Powers Entering	Number of Wars
0	42
1	3
2	2
3	0
4	1
5	0
6 or more	2

NOTE: With one exception, our decisions as to when major powers entered wars accord with those of Singer and Small (1972). That exception is the entrance of Italy into the Seven Weeks' War on the side of Prussia. They consider Italy to be a participant from June 15, 1866, whereas other sources (Dupuy and Dupuy, 1970, p. 842) give June 20, 1866 as the entry date. We have thus coded the war in accordance with the latter date as a post-onset war entry.

(1972, pp. 60–69), we can easily determine for each war the number of major powers that entered after the first day of the war. Classifying the 50 wars in this manner produces the distribution presented in Table 7-2. As we can see, in 42 of the 50 interstate wars, there was no subsequent major power war entry, making the phenomenom we are concerned with—war expansion by major powers—a relatively rare event.

Parameter Estimates

In the course of describing each of the probability models, we presented distribution functions that stated the probabilities that exactly k out of N major powers would join an ongoing war, and once we have computed these probabilities we can easily obtain the expected *number* of such wars by multiplying each probability by the number of interstate wars that occurred during the 1816–1965 period. To obtain these probabilities, however, we must first assign values to the parameters that each distribution function contains. For the most part we will do this by using what is sometimes called the "method of moments" (Hayes and Winkler, 1971, pp. 322–324). This is a standard estimation procedure that involves calculating the mean and variance of the *observed* distribution and substituting these values into the equations that specify the *expected* values of the mean and variance of the probability distribution under consideration. The solution of these equations yields estimates for the model's parameters. The name of this procedure stems from the fact that the mean and variance of a probability distribution are often called the first and second central moments of the distribution, respectively.

A list of the models' parameters is given in Table 7-3, along with a substantive interpretation of the meaning of each. Because all the models share a common parameter, N, the number of major powers making war entry decisions, we will begin with that parameter.

Specifying the number of major powers making war-entry decisions poses two problems: (1) the number of major powers has not been constant over the century and a half, but instead has fluctuated between 5 and 8, and (2) major powers were original participants in some wars. Surveying all the interstate wars, we find that there were from 4 to 7 major powers who initially abstained from war involvement, with 5 or 6 as the most frequent. Thus, for testing purposes we will assume that, in any given war, there were 6 initially nonparticipating powers.

To estimate the remaining parameters, we will assume that the major powers are more or less homogeneous with respect to their propensity to join ongoing wars, and we will further assume that this propensity has not changed over the century and a half under consideration. For the independent choice model, this means that

Table 7-3. Parameters of the Models

Model	Parameter	Interpretation
Independent choice	N	Number of decision-making powers
	p	Probability that each power will enter an ongoing war
One-way conditional choice	N	Number of decision-making powers
	p	Probability that first power will enter an ongoing war
	r	Impact of a decision to enter on subsequent decisions
Two-way conditional choice	N	Number of decision-making powers
	p	Probability that first power will enter an ongoing war
	s	Impact of a decision to enter or abstain on subsequent decisions

the values of p and q are constant across major powers and time. This is also assumed to be true for the conditional choice models, but we need to assume also that the decisional dependence parameters, r and s, do not vary over time or across major powers. In later sections we will consider some evidence pertaining to the validity of these assumptions.

Turning first to the independent choice model, it can be shown that the mean and variance of a binomially distributed random variable are given by the following equations.

$$u = Np \qquad (1)$$

$$\sigma^2 = Npq \qquad (2)$$

The mean and variance of the observed distribution of major power war entries presented in Table 7-2 are .46 and 1.80, respectively. Substituting the value for the mean into eq. 1 gives a value of .08 for p, and, because q is equal to 1 - p, our estimate of q is .92. Equation 2, however, cannot be solved in such a way that p and q have values between 0 and 1.0 and sum to 1.0 with the observed variance. As a comparison of eq. 1 and 2 reveals, the variance of a binomial distribution should always be less than the mean. Because we have found that the observed variance is considerably larger than the observed mean, it seems unlikely that the independent choice model will fit the data well. We will, nevertheless, examine its predictions using the values discussed above.

Rutherford (1954, p. 705) has shown that the mean and variance of the distribution corresponding to what we have called the one-way conditional choice model are as follows:

$$u = \left(\frac{p}{r}\right)\left|(1+r)^N - 1\right| \qquad (3)$$

$$\sigma^2 = \left(\frac{p}{r}\right)\left(\frac{p}{r}+1\right)\left|(1+2r)^N - 2(1+r)^N + 1\right| \qquad (4)$$

Substituting the observed values for the mean and variance into these equations, one obtains the values of .02 for p and .48 for r. This is not a satisfactory estimate for r, for, we noted earlier, the maximum value for r was $(1-p)/(N-1)$, which, with p equal to .02 and N equal to 6, would be .196. Our estimate of the value for r exceeds its theoretical maximum because the amount of variance in the observed distribution is much larger than we would expect to find if the underlying process was similar to that posited by our one-way conditional choice model. We could merely omit the model from further consideration, as we already know that it will probably not produce predictions that accord well with the observed values, but instead we will set r at its theoretical maximum and carry through our comparison of the three models. To obtain a value for p and r, then, we set r equal to $(1 - p)/5$ and solve eq. 3 using the value of .46 as the mean. The solution yields values of .0475 and .1905 for p and r, respectively.

Turning our attention to the last of our three models, it can be shown that the mean and variance of the Polya distribution, which corresponds to our two-way conditional choice model, is

$$u = Np \tag{5}$$

$$\sigma^2 = Npq \, \frac{1 + Ns}{1 + s} \tag{6}$$

Substituting the observed values for the mean and variance into these equations yields values of p and s of .08 and 1.86, respectively. Let us now see how well these three models account for the war-entry decisions of the major powers between 1816 and 1965.

Empirical Results

Before discussing the empirical results, we need to say something about the way we will assess the goodness-of-fit between the observed and predicted frequencies. As one will recall from Table 7-2, we are dealing with the distribution of 50 wars over 7 categories of war, each category corresponding to a specific number of major power entrants. When we are dividing N objects among k mutually exclusive classes, where p_i is the probability that an object will fall into the ith class, then the probability that exactly n_1 will fall in class 1, n_2 in class 2, ... and n_k in class k is given by the multinomial distribution.

$$P(n_1, n_2, \ldots n_k) = \frac{N!}{n_1! \, n_2! \, \ldots \, n_k!} \, (p_1)^{n_1} (p_2)^{n_2} \ldots (p_k)^{n_k}$$

In the present situation, the p_i's correspond to the *predicted relative frequencies*, and the n_i's correspond to the *observed absolute frequencies*. Ordinarily, of course, we are not interested in the probability of obtaining a particular observed distribution, but rather the probability that we would obtain one as deviant, or more so, than the one we have if the model was correct. If this probability turns out to be large, indicating that the deviations between the expected and observed values are, in a probabilistic sense, small, then we would conclude that there is a good fit between the model and the data. Unfortunately, for all but the simplest situations, it is virtually impossible to calculate the cumulative multinomial probability that is needed, due to the number of combinations possible. Thus, we must turn to some other procedure.

The most common practice in situations like this is to use the familiar χ^2 statistic, and it is generally conceded that, if the number of cases is large and the number of categories is small, then the χ^2 value provides a good approximation. Unfortunately, however, our application must be considered a borderline case, as the number of wars is relatively small and the expected frequencies in some categories are also small. We will use it here, nevertheless, because it is widely known and understood, but caution must be exercised when interpreting the results.

The χ^2 statistic is an absolute measure of goodness-of-fit in that all three models' predictions could deviate markedly from the observed values. Because we are also interested in determining how the models compare with each other, we will employ a second goodness-of-fit measure that assesses in a relative sense how the predictions of the models compare against the data.

The measure we will use rests on Bayesian inferential logic and is derived in the following way. In Bayesian analysis one begins with some a priori probabilities, which indicate one's initial assessment of the credibility of the alternative models, and, after an empirical observation is made, these probabilities are revised to obtain posterior credibility measures. These revisions are based on the relative likelihood of obtaining the observed distribution if each of the alternative models is in turn assumed to be true.

Our adaptation of this procedure is as follows. We have three models each generating a set of predicted values, and we will assume that all three are equally credible alternative explanations. Using the mathematical formula given earlier, we compute the likelihood of obtaining the observed distribution if each model is in turn assumed to be correct. Let us take, for example, the independent choice model and demonstrate the procedure. If we let n_0 through n_6 stand for the number of *observed* wars falling in each of the categories and

p_0 through p_6 as the *predicted* proportions of wars that should be found in these categories if the independent choice model is an accurate representation of reality, then the likelihood of obtaining the observed distribution is

$$\frac{N!}{\prod_{i=1}^{6}(n_1!)} \cdot \prod_{i=1}^{6}\left[(p_i)^{n_i}\right]$$

The corresponding likelihood values for the one-way and two-way conditional choice models are similarly obtained by using their predicted proportions in the above equation. Finally, if we divide each of these likelihood values by the sum of all three, we obtain a measure of the relative credibility of each model. From a Bayesian standpoint, these values constitute posterior probabilities when each model is assigned a prior probability of one-third. Because these posterior probabilities must sum to 1.0, it is obvious that they measure the fit of the models vis-à-vis one another. Having dealt with these methodological matters, let us now turn to the task of evaluating the models.

In Table 7-4 we reproduce the observed distribution from Table 7-2 and then include the predicted distributions that are obtained when the appropriate parameter values are introduced into the three distribution functions. It is readily apparent that the predictions of the independent choice model compare very poorly with the empirical data. In fact, this model predicts that the odds are only about 1 in 5 million that all six major powers would join a war. The χ^2 value is practically infinite in size and, therefore, not reported, and its relative credibility is virtually zero.

The one-way conditional choice model fares better than the independent choice model, but, as the χ^2 and relative credibility measures indicate, it is decidedly inferior to the two-way conditional choice model. The latter model yields predictions that are clearly excellent, and these results suggest rather strongly that decisional dependence of the double nature posited by the two-way conditional choice model was operative in the war-entry decision-making procedures of the major powers during the period under consideration.

Before sketching out the implications of this finding, it would be prudent to pause and evaluate the plausibility of some of the assumptions that we have made. First, we will examine the assumption of

Table 7-4. Observed and Predicted Distributions of War Entry, 1816–1965

Number of Powers Entering	Observed Distribution	Predicted Distributions		
		Independent Choice Model	One-Way Conditional Choice Model	Two-Way Conditional Choice Model
0	42	31.0	37.3	42.7
1	3	15.5	6.9	2.0
2	2	3.0	3.0	1.2
3	0	0.5	1.5	0.9
4	1	0.0*	0.8	0.8
5	0	0.0*	0.3	0.9
6	2	0.0*	0.2	1.5
χ^2			21.18 $df = 4$, $p < .005$	3.06 $df = 4$, $p < .70$
Relative credibility		.000	.012	.988

*Numbers far too small to report.

overtime invariance in the key parameters and then the assumption of homogeneity with respect to the propensity of major powers to enter ongoing wars.

Assumption of Temporal Invariance

Fortunately, perhaps, from an humanistic point of view, but unfortunately from a statistical one, war expansion by major power entry is not a frequent event. This fact limits our ability to test the assumption of temporal invariance in the parameters, and we will confine ourselves to dividing the century and a half into two long subperiods. Table 7-5 presents a breakdown of the observed distribution by century, which gives us a roughly equal number of wars in each period, with 27 in the nineteenth century and 23 in the twentieth century.

A comparison of the figures in Table 7-5 suggests that the centuries are different with respect to war expansion and casts doubt on the assumption that the parameters are constant over time. These differences suggest further that a reestimation of the parameters of the models is called for.

If we recompute the parameters of the models for each century separately, we find that for the nineteenth century the estimated value for p in the independent choice model is .03, lower than the .08 value found to characterize the entire period. The parameters of the one-way conditional choice model, p and r, are .03 and .14, respectively. And p and s, the parameters of the two-way conditional choice model, are .03 and .06, respectively. The relatively small estimated values for r and s suggest immediately that decisional dependence of the sort we have been discussing was weak in the nineteenth century.

Table 7-5. Observed Distributions of War Entry by Century

Number of Powers Entering	Nineteenth Century	Twentieth Century
0	23	19
1	3	0
2	1	1
3 or more	0	3

This conclusion is reinforced by an examination of the predicted and observed values contained in Table 7-6. Due to the relatively small estimated values of r and s, all three models make similar predictions, and they reproduce the observed distribution fairly well. The χ^2 and relative credibility measures still give the edge to the two-way conditional choice model; however, our test is not really powerful enough to discriminate clearly between the three models. Suffice it to say that, in the nineteenth century, major powers seem to have been only marginally, if at all, attentive to other powers' decisions about war entry when making their own decisions on this matter.

If we reestimate the parameters for the twentieth century, we find that the independent choice model's parameter, p, is .13. We also find that, as was true when we examined the entire period, the estimated values of p and r, the one-way conditional choice model's parameters, do not satisfy the condition that r must not be greater than $(1 - p)/(N - 1)$. Hence, we will use the theoretical maximum values discussed above, setting p equal to .0475 and r equal to .1905. Turning finally to the two-way conditional choice model, the estimated values for p and s are .13 and 3.96, respectively, indicating that the degree of decisional dependence is quite high in this century. An examination of Table 7-7 reveals what we already suspect: the independent choice model produces a very poor approximation of the observed distribution, the one-way conditional choice model does somewhat better, and the two-way conditional choice model is easily the best of the three.

To summarize the evidence, then, it would appear that in the twentieth century major powers are (1) more likely to enter ongoing wars and (2) more likely to alter this propensity in accordance with what other major powers do. In the nineteenth century, on the other hand, major powers did not frequently join ongoing wars, and their decisions to do so were only weakly influenced by what other major powers did. We will leave for another time the question of why this difference between the centuries is present.

Assumption of Major Power Homogeneity

As we indicated earlier, our test of the models was based also on the assumption that the values of the various parameters are the same

Table 7-6. Observed and Predicted Distributions of Nineteenth Century War Entry

Number of Powers Entering	Observed Distribution	Predicted Distributions		
		Independent Choice Model	One-Way Conditional Choice Model	Two-Way Conditional Choice Model
0	23	22.5	22.5	23.0
1	3	4.2	2.9	3.3
2	1	0.3	1.0	0.6
3 or more	0	0.0	0.6	0.1
χ^2		1.99 $df = 2$ $.3 < p < .5$	0.61 $df = 1$ $.3 < p < .5$	0.39 $df = 1$ $.5 < p < .7$
Relative credibility		.281	.290	.429

Table 7-7. Observed and Predicted Distributions of Twentieth Century War Entry

Number of Powers Entering	Observed Distribution	Predicted Distributions		
		Independent Choice Model	One-Way Conditional Choice Model	Two-Way Conditional Choice Model
0	19	9.8	17.2	18.7
1	0	8.9	3.1	0.7
2	1	3.3	1.4	0.4
3 or more	3	1.0	1.3	3.2
χ^2		22.1 $df = 2$ $p < .001$	5.63 $df = 1$ $.01 < p < .05$	1.62 $df = 1$ $.2 < p < .3$
Relative credibility		.000	.042	.958

221

for each major power. At this point we will consider some evidence that bears on the question of whether this is a reasonable assumption. To do so, however, we must introduce another measure of decisional dependence.

Consider, for the moment, the situation in which two major powers are confronted by an ongoing war. According to the two-way conditional choice model, the first major power has a probability of p of entering and a probability q of abstaining. The likelihood of the second major power's entering depends on the decision of the first in the manner specified earlier, and the probabilities that both, only one, or neither will enter are equal to the products of their respective probabilities. Table 7-8 presents these relationships in contingency table form, and we can see that, for example, the probability that *both* will enter is equal to the product of p—the probability that the first power will enter—and $(p+s)/(1+s)$—the probability that the second will enter, *given* that the first enters. Similarly, the probability that neither will enter is the product of the probability that the first abstains, q, and the probability that the second abstains *given* that the first has abstained, $(q+s)/(1+s)$. The remaining two probabilities are derived in the same way.

From this contingency table, we can calculate a correlation coefficient, ϕ, that will reflect the degree of decisional dependence between these two powers. Substituting the appropriate values into the formula[1] for ϕ yields

$$\phi = \frac{p\left(\frac{p+s}{1+s}\right)q\left(\frac{q+s}{1+s}\right) - q\left(\frac{p}{1+s}\right)p\left(\frac{q}{1+s}\right)}{\sqrt{pqpq}}$$

Table 7-8. Hypothetical War Decision Probabilities of Two Major Powers

		Second Power's Decision		Sum
		Enter	Not Enter	
First Power's Decision	Enter	$p\dfrac{p+c}{1+c}$	$p\dfrac{q}{1+c}$	p
	Not Enter	$q\dfrac{p}{1+c}$	$q\dfrac{q+c}{1+c}$	q
	Sum	p	q	1.0

which reduces to

$$\phi = \frac{pq\frac{(p+s)(q+s)}{(1+s)^2} - pq\left[\frac{pq}{(1+s)^2}\right]}{\sqrt{p^2 q^2}}$$

As a matter of fact, this equation can be further reduced to the following simple formula:

$$\phi = \frac{s}{1+s}$$

Thus, ϕ can be computed directly from s, and we can see that if s equals zero, indicating no decisional dependence, ϕ will also equal zero. If s is positive, then ϕ will also take on a positive value. Earlier, we estimated the value of s as 1.86, which corresponds to a ϕ of +.64. This indicates that the level of decisional dependence is moderately high overall.

This relationship between ϕ and s can be used to examine the assumption of homogeneity among the major powers in the following way. Let us consider the war experience of two specific powers, England and France. Neither was an original participant in 43 of the 50 interstate wars, and their decisions in those wars are given in Table 7-9. A casual inspection of this table reveals some obvious covariation in their decisions, and the ϕ value corresponding to this table is a rather high +.82. This means that, if England entered a war, there was a significant increase in the probability that France would also enter and vice versa.

If we perform a similar tabulation and calculation for the nations that have had a long tenure in the major power system (England, France, and Russia), we obtain the results given in Table 7-10. As can

Table 7-9. War Decisions of England and France

		France's Decision		Total
		Enter	Not Enter	
England's Decision	Enter	5	0	5
	Not Enter	2	36	38
	Total	7	36	43

Table 7-10. War Decision Correlations

	England	France
France	.82 (43)	—
Russia	.59 (49)	.60 (35)

NOTE: As explained in the text, these are ϕ correlations, and the numbers in the parentheses indicate the number of wars on which the correlations are calculated.

be seen, the ϕ values that are obtained are quite similar in size, and all are positive in direction. This suggests that the decisional dependence we have found was generally shared by these major powers. Unfortunately, due to the limited tenure of the remaining major powers in the major power subsystem, we do not have enough observations to perform a similar analysis of their war experiences. Despite this limitation, the values contained in Table 7-10 are sufficiently similar to the overall +.64 value to suggest that the homogeneity assumption is not an unreasonable one with respect to one of the two parameters, s. Let us now consider the other parameter, p.

We assumed earlier that all nonparticipating major powers have a .08 probability of entering any war after its onset. If this assumption is valid, then the empirically derived relative frequency of war entry for each major power should not be significantly higher or lower than .08.

One can estimate the probability of entering a war from a third-party status for each major power in the following way. England, for example, entered 5 out of 48 wars after their onset and was an original participant in the remaining two. Thus, our estimate of England's entrance probability would be 5/48, or about .10. Is this significantly different from the .08 value that we assumed characterized all of the major powers? Although the binomial confidence limits are not strictly appropriate here, as we are assuming that the Polya distribution—which underlies the two-way conditional choice model—is the correct one, they may be sufficiently close to the true limits to serve as a guide here. If we place a 95% confidence interval around the .08 probability value, we find that England's .10 value is well within this bound. Following a similar procedure for each of the remaining major powers, we find that all lie within the range specified by this confidence interval.[2] Thus, we would conclude that the assumption that all major powers are equally likely, at least initially, to enter ongoing wars, is at least not contradicted by the available evidence.

In sum, then, our assumptions about major power homogeneity appear to be reasonable. Before spelling out the conclusions and implications of our results, one additional consideration merits attention.

Our overall findings, and particularly those for the twentieth century, suggest that the two-way conditional choice model, as represented by the Polya probability model, is a good predictor of the pattern of major power war entry, albeit with an apparent shift in the decisional dependence parameter. We would be remiss, however, if we did not mention an important characteristic of the Polya distribution. This distribution can emerge from a compound binomial distribution; that is, if the values of the parameter p vary over time and/or space and are distributed in accordance with the B distribution, the resulting aggregate distribution will be a Polya distribution (Ishii and Hayakawa, 1960). In substantive terms this would mean that major powers are following an independent choice model, but their probabilities of war entry differ from each other and/or vary from decade to decade. Our efforts to eliminate this rival model have been admittedly indirect and far from definitive. The evidence at hand does not, however, point in the direction of a compound binomial, and that evidence, together with the greater parsimony of the Polya model, leads us to favor it over more complex and, as yet, formally unspecified models.

Conclusions and Implications

We began this paper by sketching out what might be called the contemporary nightmare of power politics. We are, of course, concerned about the expansion of wars precisely because these wars tend to be so destructive of human life and well-being. We must, however, pause for a moment and evaluate this implicit assumption. It should be recalled that, although our analysis of the data demonstrates that one major power's decision to enter a war increases the probability that other powers will do likewise, the conditional choice model per se does not predict which of the sides the powers will join. Thus, an expanded war may stem from a collective security operation in

226   Accounting for the Expansion of War

which many major powers intervene against an aggressor nation, or it may be that they divide and join opposing sides. We would, of course, expect wars of the latter variety to be a good deal more destructive than wars of the first type.

An examination of the eight wars that expanded to include major powers after their onset reveals the following. In three of the eight wars, only one power joined, and in two of them two powers joined on the same side. With the exception of the Crimean War, all these wars were short (under three months), and battle deaths were under 40,000. The Crimean War, of course, lasted for more than two years and killed more than a quarter of a million military personnel, not to mention countless others.

The remaining three of the eight wars—World War I, World War II, and Korea—involved the entrance of one or more major powers on both sides of the war, and these are the most destructive wars that have occurred in the last century and a half. Hence, our conclusion is that, since the powers may join only one side of a war and bring it thereby to a rapid close, our model does not necessarily imply that Armageddon will occur if major powers enter ongoing wars. It is clear, however, that if the major powers end up on opposite sides, the danger to mankind is very great indeed, and the likelihood of this occurring once the war expansion process is triggered is by no means small.

With this caveat in mind, let us restate our findings and spell out some of the possible policy implications. First, we found that, for the whole century and a half, the model—which assumes that major powers predicate their decisions about war entry, in part, on the decisions of other major powers, whatever those decisions might be—enables us to deduce the observed distribution of war entries with far greater accuracy than does the model that assumes independent choices. In addition, we found that the degree of decisional dependence is substantially higher in the twentieth century than it is in the nineteenth century. As we shall see, this difference has some serious implications for our present situation.

Let us begin with the brighter side of the question. Using the two-way conditional choice model, we can calculate how likely it is that the kth major power will decide *not* to enter a war after $k - 1$ powers have previously decided *not* to enter. Table 7-11 presents these values for the nineteenth and twentieth centuries. By way of explanation, note that in the nineteenth century the probability that the first major power will abstain is .970 and that the probability that the second major power will abstain *given* that the first abstained is .972. We can see that each succeeding major power's decision *not* to enter the war slightly increases the probability that subsequent major powers will also abstain. The same is true, of course, for the twentieth century, although there is a greater shift in the probabilities as a consequence of the first major power's decision not to enter from (.87 to .97). We should note that, if the first major power decides to abstain from the war, the differences between the centuries for the likelihood of subsequent abstentions become quite small.

Table 7-12 presents information about the darker side of the question, that is, the likelihood that the kth power *will* enter an ongoing war after $k - 1$ powers have already decided to do so. Once again, we differentiate by century, and, contrary to what we found, the resulting differences are dramatic. In the nineteenth century, a major power's decision to enter an ongoing war produces a moderate increment in the likelihood that the remaining major powers will follow suit, but the overall probability that wars will expand to include *all* major powers remains low. In the twentieth century, however, if the first major power decides to enter, the rise in the probability that the second will also enter is very large (from .13 to .83). Thus, we can already see that the first major power's decision is vital in determining the probable outcome of the war expansion process in the twentieth century.

Focusing on the decision of the first major power and comparing the results in Tables 7-11 and 7-12, we can see that the twentieth century is a great deal more dangerous than the nineteenth. In the nineteenth century the first power's decision to enter or not to enter produces modest increments in the probabilities that other powers will do likewise. Similarly, in the twentieth century, if the first major

Table 7-11. Likelihood of Consecutive War Abstention Decisions

	Number of Consecutive Abstentions (k)				
	1	2	3	4	5
Nineteenth Century Probability	.970	.972	.973	.975	.976
Twentieth Century Probability	.870	.970	.985	.990	.992

NOTE: More specifically, these are the probabilities that the kth power will *not* enter after $k - 1$ powers have already decided not to enter.

Table 7-12. Likelihood of Consecutive War Entrance Decisions

	Number of Consecutive Entrances (k)				
	1	2	3	4	5
Nineteenth Century Probability	.03	.09	.13	.18	.22
Twentieth Century Probability	.13	.83	.90	.93	.95

NOTE: More specifically, these are the probabilities that the kth power will enter after $k - 1$ powers have already decided to enter.

power decides *not* to intervene, the resulting increments in the probability that other powers will follow suit are also modest. But, if the first major power should decide to enter, the expansion of a war to include all major powers becomes very likely. It is in this sense that the twentieth century appears to be a great deal more dangerous than the nineteenth.

The prospects for the remainder of the twentieth century would seem rather gloomy if the parameters p and s keep approximately the same values. There have been, however, recent developments in the major power system which might suggest that a degree of "decoupling" is taking place. It has been suggested, for example, that the international system is shifting from a bipolar to a multipolar structure, with a subsequent increase in the independence of the decision-making centers. Rather than speculating on the likelihood of such a shift's occurring, we would prefer to end this paper by spelling out, albeit in the abstract, what its implications might be for the process of war expansion.

We will assume that we are dealing exclusively with wars that do not involve major powers at their onset; thus, the current five major powers—the United States, England, France, Russia, and China—are assumed to be nonparticipants in the initial days of such a war. For illustrative purposes, we will assume that the initial probability of these powers entering is .10, this value being somewhat smaller than the value estimated for the twentieth century. Table 7-13 shows how the probabilities of various numbers of major powers entering a war change as decisional dependence changes. Note that in this table we measure the degree of decisional dependence by the ϕ value rather than s, but, as we pointed out above, one is a function of the other.

The ϕ value of .75 corresponds roughly to the estimated parameter values for the twentieth century, and we can see that, under

Table 7-13. Decisional Dependence and the Likelihood of War Expansion

Number of Powers Entering War	Probability of Occurrence by Degree of Decisional Dependence (ϕ)						
	.00	.33	.50	.67	.75	.83	1.00
0	.59	.74	.79	.83	.85	.87	.90
1	.33	.13	.08	.05	.03	.02	.00
2	.07	.06	.05	.03	.02	.01	.00
3	.01	.04	.03	.02	.02	.01	.00
4	.00	.02	.03	.03	.03	.02	.00
5	.00	.01	.02	.05	.06	.07	.10

our assumptions, wars will remain localized about 85% of the time and become world wars (i.e., involve all major powers) 6% of the time. If the degree of decisional dependence were to drop by slightly more than half, corresponding to a ϕ value of .33, we would expect the probability of a world war to decline from .06 to .01 and the probability of complete localization to decrease from .85 to .74. However, the probability that one or two major powers will become involved would increase from .05 to .19.

This suggests that if increasing multipolarity is the trend for the future *and* if multipolarity leads to decreased decisional dependence among the major powers, then the likelihood of world wars will decrease, but military intervention by one or two major powers will increase.

In closing we should point out that our prognostications about the future are based on a constant p and a varying ϕ. If, by some miracle, we could reduce the value of p, which reflects the autonomous propensity of major powers to enter wars, to something near zero, then the sleep of all, including diplomats, would certainly be more restful.

IV

Accounting for the Outcomes of War

8

The Costs of Combat: Death, Duration, and Defeat

Cynthia A. Cannizzo
Ohio State University

As we look at the history of interstate warfare since the Napoleonic wars, we are amazed by the diversity of these wars. Some last only a few weeks, whereas others rage for years; only a few thousand lives are lost in some wars, whereas millions are lost in others; sometimes the allegedly more powerful nation wins, but sometimes it loses. The obvious question is, why do these differences occur? This chapter represents initial efforts to answer that question by specifying and testing a simple model of two-state warfare. We begin by defining a four-variable model of this type of warfare that is based on military history; this model is then operationalized and tested using statistical analysis of the 30 dyadic wars that occurred in the interstate system between 1816 and 1965.

Model Specification

The two most common types of war discussed in the literature are the rout and the war of attrition. A rout is a war in which one side has a preponderance of capabilities and is able to bring this strength to bear so that (1) the war is short, (2) the stronger side incurs a lower loss rate than does the weaker side, and (3) the stronger side wins the war. At the opposite extreme is the war of attrition, in which the opposing sides are of roughly equal strength; this equivalence predicts to (1) a long war, (2) approximately equal loss rates, and (3) approximately equal chances of victory for the two sides. These two extreme types of wars can be combined into a single analytic model, shown in "path diagram" form in Figure 8-1 and hereinafter referred to as the "rout-attrition model." In the diagram, nation A is defined as the nation having the greater capabilities, as measured by the size of the prewar standing armies, and the greater the preponderance of A over B, the higher the ratio. Each of the relationships shown in Figure 8-1 is discussed more fully in the following paragraphs. The ratio "armed forces of A to armed forces of B" is hereinafter referred to as the capability or strength ratio, and the ratio "deaths/armed forces of A to deaths/armed forces of B" is referred to as the relative loss ratio.

We realize that this model is, perhaps, overly parsimonious. It does not include initiation of the war, any loss-of-strength gradient for troop forces, and any of a host of qualitative variables such as leadership and morale that might affect the course of a war. The model does not allow for reinforcement or change in troop levels over time, and it has no reciprocal paths. Many of these extensions *are*, however, included in the larger work to which this was a precursor (Cannizzo, 1976); others still remain for future research. The relationships shown in Figure 8-1 do, however, constitute a "core" model of warfare. Another weakness of the current work is the restriction of the data base to two-state wars; both coalitional wars (wars that began with more than two states involved) and

Figure 8-1. The Basic Four-Variable Model Reflecting the Rout and the War of Attrition

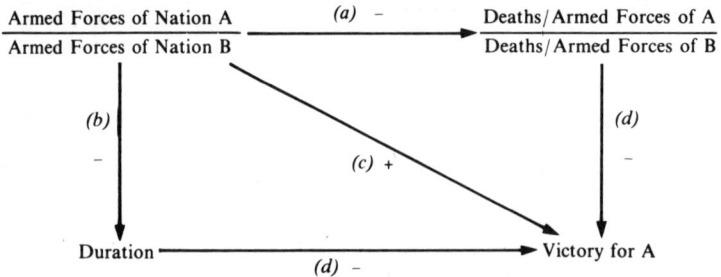

expanded wars (wars that began with two states but eventually had more than the number involved in the fighting) are investigated in Cannizzo (1976). Not the inclusion of additional variables, reciprocal linkages, nor the extension of the data base substantially alters the conclusions presented here; rather, they serve to refine, enrich, and expand the knowledge generated by this "core" model.

Capability Ratio to Relative Loss Ratio (a)

Capabilities, or strength, are measured by the size of the prewar standing armed forces and are expressed as a ratio, as a nation's military power with regard to war has meaning only when contrasted to that of its opponent. A relatively weak opponent can resist less effectively than can an opponent of equivalent strength and should, in principle, accept defeat more easily and rapidly (Calahan, 1944, p. 16). Thus, if one nation has overwhelming numbers of forces, the war could devolve into a rout, even into a massacre, with the weaker side suffering disproportionately heavy losses. Alternatively, wars between equivalent forces are apt to become wars of attrition with relatively equal casualty rates for both sides (Falls, 1961, p. 10; Coser, 1961, p. 347).

Capability Ratio to Duration (b)

Falls (1961, p. 10) argued that wars between forces of equal quality (i.e., morale, leadership) and that equal strength would most likely be stalemates until one side managed a strategic breakthrough. Similar arguments are advanced by Ropp (1962, p. 222), Coser (1961, p. 348), and Bird (1920, pp. 275-276). In effect, then, we could expect that a war between two nations of approximately equal capabilities to last a fairly long time. Wright (1965a, p. 652) found that major powers fought relatively short wars, typically fighting nations that were, by definition, weaker than themselves. Further, he found that a war "in which the belligerents are fairly equally balanced is likely to last for four or five years" (1965a, p. 226). Ferris (1973, p. 22) tested the hypothesis that the greater the disparity in power capabilities between antagonists, the shorter the war, but his analysis, using Richardson's wars with a battle-death threshold of 317 deaths plus the Singer and Small interstate wars, offered little support for this hypothesis. However, the theoretical argument favors this negative relationship between capability ratio and duration, and most prior evidence supports that contention; we thus retain it in the model.

Summarizing linkages (*a*) and (*b*), we propose to test the hypothesis that the relationships between the capability ratio, on the one hand, and relative loss ratio and war duration, on the other, will be negative; when preponderance is high, the loss rate of the larger nation relative to the loss rate of the smaller nation should be low, and the war should be short. Conversely, if the opposing armies are of roughly equal size, the loss rates should be approximately the same, and the war should be long.

Capability Ratio and the Probability of Victory (c)

Despite disagreement on the empirical components of power, or even of capabilities, a basic consensus would exist for the generalization that the more "powerful" antagonist is usually victorious in conflict. If this idea is carried to its logical extreme, one ends up defining power in terms of victory, and, indeed, this is sometimes the case. Organski's power transition hypothesis (1968, ch. 14) is partially based on the notion that, if a challenger can defeat the status quo power, the challenger will assume the top slot in the power hierarchy. Although the existence of a reciprocal relationship between capabilities and victory is certainly plausible, one can and must distinguish—both temporally and analytically—between the effects of power on victory and the effects of victory on power. The present model will only include the effect of capabilities on victory, assuming that the stronger nation has a higher probability of emerging victorious, and the greater the preponderance, the higher that probability.

To buttress this hypothesis, given our operationalization of capabilities in terms of the prewar standing armed forces, we must turn to the more speculative military literature, as few data-based analyses can be found. Hart (1960) computed defensive-offensive ratios for battles in several major wars of the last century, relating this ratio to the ability of the offense to break through the defensive line; this is not quite the same question as the one being addressed in the model. Military histories are replete with arguments as to the impact of numerical superiority, relative to other indicators of capability, on the chances of victory. Such arguments are usually made *ceteris paribus*; for example, Bird (1920, p. 28) noted that, "when moral qualities, discipline, training, and armament are approximately equal, superiority of numbers is likely to prove victorious even against superior leadership." On the other hand, Henderson (1916, p. 169) argued that an army inferior in numbers, but superior in leadership, is more often victorious than the army superior in numbers, but inferior in leadership. Reasoning anecdotally, Browning (1903, p. 281) stated that, with regard to the Russian defeat in the Battle of Inkerman in the Crimean War, "the English had not the numbers nor the French the desire to turn the defeat into a rout."

Despite such arguments, in several nonsystematic investigations, numerical superiority of approximately 3-5 to 1 on the battlefield is generally favored as being highly conducive to victory (Hart, 1960, pp. 92-93, 180; Clausewitz, Book III, ch. 8; Enthoven and Smith, 1972, p. 141; and Halperin, 1971, p. 106). Thus, in the absence of reproducible analyses, but with a good deal of anecdotal evidence to back up the theoretical argument, the positive influence of capabilities—measured by armed forces size, whether in the theater or not—is hypothesized to be operative: the greater the numerical preponderance, the greater the probability of victory for the stronger nation.

Relative Loss Ratio, Duration, and Probability of Victory (d)

We have set up the various relationships between relative loss ratio, duration, and victory as a "causal chain" that begins with the capability ratio. The capability ratio predicts to relative loss ratio and to duration, both of which, in turn, predict to the probability of victory. As well as mediating the effects of capability ratio on victory, we assume that relative loss ratio and duration have independent, negative effects on the probability of victory. Rosen's conceptualization of cost tolerance (1972) is useful in establishing these links, as are the ideas of Klingberg (1966), Richardson (1960), Calahan (1944), and Coser (1961).

According to Rosen, a nation can increase its cost tolerance in two ways: (1) increase the base amount of resources so that the same absolute loss is less, relatively speaking and/or (2) increase the willingness to suffer. In the model presented here, the stronger nation in a war presumably has a greater ability to follow option 1 and to keep putting men and material in the field. The opponent, to compensate and keep the war going, must however operate under option 2 and keep increasing its willingness to suffer. Strategically, then, the stronger nation should attempt to quickly inflict heavy losses at such a rate that the opponent cannot readily increase its willingness to suffer proportionately; thus, the war will be brought to a speedy and victorious conclusion for the stronger nation. In fact, this is the strategy recommended by many "classical" military theorists and commanders of the nineteenth and early twentieth centuries: Napoleon, Clausewitz, Jomini, and Foch come to mind as examples. Thus, the links from the relative battle-death ratio and from duration to victory, although based on the concept of relative strength, are assumed to be theoretically meaningful in and of themselves.

Prior empirical research on these two relationships has yielded mixed results. First, on the relationship between casualty rates and victory, Fuller (1961, p. 121), reasoning on the basis of his personal experience, noted that the "victor often lost more men than the vanquished." Somewhat more systematically, Rosen (1972, p. 175) found that the winning side suffered *fewer* absolute battle deaths than did the losing side in a majority of the wars in his data base. Singer and Small (1972, p. 349) also found that the majority of interstate wars from 1816–1965 (35 out of 49 wars) are characterized by the vanquished suffering more battle deaths than the victor; comparing battle deaths to total population, the vanquished nation(s) again had the greater relative losses in 36 out of 49 wars. Although the direction of this relationship is clear, Singer and Small found no threshold or constant ratio vis-à-vis either absolute losses or losses per capita.

Second, we turn to the empirical evidence for the link between duration and victory. In general agreement with the hypothesized negative association, Rosecrance (1973, p. 37) noted that, after the Franco-Prussian War of 1870, an "army which could mass and invade first could disrupt the opponent's mobilization and railway time tables, thus winning a relatively easy victory." Whitman (1941, p. 32) argued similarly: "The sooner the decisive battle can be won, the more likely is complete victory. Moreover, the enemy's plans have so much the less time to develop." To tie both these assertions to the increased probability of victory for the numerically stronger nation, we quote Bird (1920, p. 33), who stated that "in war the result of the first great battle is largely influenced by the number of efficient units that are available, and defeat in the first serious encounter is ... often followed by failure in the campaign." The lack of systematic inquiry on this relationship is regrettable, but the theoretical argument and ancedotal evidence are enough to formally posit as a working hypothesis: the longer the war, the lower the probability of victory for the nation with the larger prewar standing army.

In summary, then, the model includes negative relationships between both relative loss ratio and victory, and between duration and victory: (1) the higher the relative loss ratio (i.e., the greater the loss rate of the stronger side compared with that of the weaker side), the lower the probability of the stronger side's winning the war, and (2) the longer the war, the lower the probability of the stronger side's winning the war.

Variable Operationalization

As happens in most research, the operationalization of the variables depends to some extent on data availability, but a fairly plausible argument can be made for the indicator that was adopted. The discussion that follows is rather brief, as a fuller treatment may be found in Cannizzo (1976).

Capability Ratio

The strength or capability ratio of the antagonists in a war is defined as the ratio of the size of the military forces of the "stronger" nation to the size of the military force of the "weaker" nation. This is determined as the number of men in the prewar standing armed forces (army, navy, and airforce), excluding reserves, in the year the war began. Thus, the strength ratio is measured on an interval scale with 1.0 as its lower limit, and the higher the value, the greater the preponderance of the larger nation over the smaller.

Relative Loss Ratio

Although civilian casualties in war are an important cost, especially since the dawn of air power as the "fourth arm" (Klingberg, 1966; Richardson, 1960; Douhet, 1942; Dumas, 1923; Vedel-Pederson, 1923; Bodart, 1916), reliable figures on civilian casualties are extremely difficult to estimate or obtain. The most reliable casualty figure for military personnel are for combatants killed directly in battle or dying of wounds received in battle. This is the "battle deaths" variable in the *Correlates of War* data base (Singer and Small, 1972, pp. 47-48), and the one that will be used in this paper.

The relative loss ratio is defined, then, as

$$\frac{\text{Battle deaths of nation A}}{\text{Standing forces of nation A}} \div \frac{\text{Battle deaths of nation B}}{\text{Standing forces of nation B}}$$

where nation A is the nation having the greater number of persons in the prewar standing armed forces, as defined. As the formula makes clear, if the two antagonists lose equal fractions of their forces, the relative loss ratio will be 1.0; if nation A suffers relatively more, the ratio will be greater than 1.0; if A suffers relatively less, the ratio will be a fraction.

Duration

In specifying duration, a decision must be made on the coding of the beginning and ending dates of a war. Naturally, several options are open (see Carroll, 1969, pp. 297 ff. for a relatively comprehensive list), but we have chosen to use the *Correlates of War* version (Singer and Small, 1972, pp. 44-45). Rather than legal or formal declarations, the beginning of a war is termed as the opening date of active, sustained hostilities; likewise, the end of the war is defined by the cessation of hostilities. The length of truces, cease-fires, and other temporary halts of active fighting greater than 30 days is subtracted from the duration of the war. Once the beginning, ending, and interruption (if any) dates are established, the number of days of "war" are counted and converted into "standard" months by dividing the total number of days by 30.11 days. Duration is thus reported in months, rounded to tenths.

Victory for the Stronger Nation

As with the preceding variables, there are many criteria of victory (see Starr, 1972; O'Connor, 1969; Carroll, 1969; Young, 1966; Gordon, 1966; Coser, 1961; Speier, 1955). A victor may be defined as the nation that (1) dictated the terms of peace, (2) did not sue for peace if peace terms were negotiated, (3) received territory and/or reparations (if applicable), (4) suffered less, in either absolute or relative casualties—military and/or civilian or economic, (5) won the majority of, or the major, battle(s), and/or (6) achieved its war aims. Using any of these definitions, the coding would probably result in at least one anomaly; that is, a country that one intuitively feels "lost the war" might be classed as a victor. The *Correlates of War* victory variable combines all these variables in an intuitive way by accepting "consensus among the acknowledged specialists," as to which was the victorious side (Singer and Small, 1972, p. 348). Application of this decision rule results in no real anomalies and is the one used here. The coding is only a dichotomy—victor/vanquished—and as such neglects the theoretically important outcome of a tie or stalemate. Although all 30 wars in the current data base had a relatively discernible victor, there is no guarantee that such would always be the case. Our statistical procedure, however, will allow us to predict *probabilities* of victory, and thus incorporates the "missing" category of stalemate.

To summarize the variable operationalizations, Table 8-1 reviews the various measures and descriptive statistics for each of the four variables. These statistics are based on the 30 dyadic wars in the *Correlates of War* data set.

Spatial-Temporal Domain

The universe of cases with which we are dealing, as noted, consists of the two-state interstate wars that occurred between 1816 and 1965, as identified in *The Wages of War* (Singer and Small, 1972, pp. 38 ff.). An interstate war is a war in which at least one participant on each side was a member of the interstate system and in which a total of at least 1,000 battle deaths was sustained by all participants. Inclusion in the interstate system required diplomatic recognition from Britain and France prior to World War I, and membership in the League of Nations, the United Nations, or recognition by any two major powers after 1918; in addition to either of these qualifications, a nation must also have had a population of at least a half million.

To be classed as a participant in a given war, a nation had to

Table 8-1. Summary of Operationalization Procedures and Descriptive Statistics

Variable	Measure	Scale	Range	Mean	Standard Deviation
Capability ratio	Prewar standing army of larger nation divided by prewar standing army of smaller nation	Interval	1.33–200	14.68	36.24
Duration	Continuous months of combat	Interval	.5–57.7	12.47	15.21
Relative loss ratio	Deaths per armed forces of larger nation divided by deaths per armed forces of smaller nation	Interval	.002–1.75	.377	.444
Victor	Historical consensus—defined in terms of larger or smaller nation	Nominal	Larger side victories in 21 of the 30 wars		

commit at least 1,000 troops to active combat, or a minimum of 100 battledeaths had to be sustained by the troops that *were* committed. Fifty wars fit this definition of an interstate war; 30 of these 50 were confined to two participants, the latter group constituting the cases over which the model is tested.

Methods of Analysis

The summary in Table 8-1 indicates that we are dealing with two types of variables: three measured on interval scales, and one—victory—measured as a nominal dichotomy. The testing of the model has basically been set up in a form for which ordinary least squares regression (OLS) would be an appropriate technique. The assumptions of OLS are met for the equations predicting duration and relative loss ratio; however, note that these two outcome variables can only assume positive values in reality, whereas no such restriction is guaranteed for their *predicted* values. On the other hand, because victory for the stronger nation is treated as a dichotomy, it is not a suitable regressand for OLS. Logit regression is, however, quite appropriate and will be used to predict victory, but, because it is relatively new to the social sciences, a brief summary is required. The logit program at the University of Michigan (DREG within OSIRIS; DuMouchel, a and b) produces the following summary statistics:

1. Regression coefficients via maximum likelihood estimation procedures for predicting the log-odds of the dependent variable
2. Standard errors of the regression coefficients
3. Predictive power of the equation
4. A measure of the overall reduction in predictive error based on residuals, similar to the R^2 from an OLS regression
5. A measure of reduction in predictive error for each predictor in a multivariate logit, similar to partial r^2 in an OLS regression
6. A χ^2 statistic, similar to the analysis of variance F test for OLS to test the overall significance of the logit model
7. Predicted probabilities and confidence intervals for each case

These various statistics will be discussed more fully in the context of their first substantive application.

The analysis is done in three basic sections. First, bivariate relationships are examined via scatterplots, correlations, and regressions. The bivariate statistics provide the only test of the capability ratio to duration and the capability ratio to relative loss ratio relationships. For analyzing the probability of victory, they provide only a first look. Second, the multivariate logit analysis for predicting the probability of victory is examined. Last, a control for intercentury differences is introduced, and the results are reexamined.

Empirical Results: Bivariate Relationships

Capability Ratio and Relative Loss Ratio

We begin our empirical investigations by examining scatterplots, although these are not reproduced here in the interests of space. The scatterplot of the capability ratio versus the relative loss ratio indicated a negative, exponential relationship. This same relationship is more strongly evidenced if we delete the Ecuadorian-Colombian War, whose capability ratio score is 200 to 1; this deletion effectively stretches the lower end of the scale. Another way of stretching the scale without deleting this war is to take the natural log (hereinafter abbreviated ln) of both variables. This transformation does "linearize" the relationship, but we are now predicting proportional rather than absolute deviations from the mean. That is, correlation and regression algorithms are based on the quantity $(Y_i - \bar{Y})$; if performed on logged variables, that is, $(\ln Y_i - \ln \bar{Y})$, we are actually dealing with (Y_i/Y), because subtraction of logs is equivalent to dividing the antilogs. Thus, an exponential relationship is based on proportional deviations from the means.

The correlation coefficients on the raw and logged data confirm the inferences drawn from the scatterplot; the raw data correlation is $-.28$, and the ln data correlation is $-.98$. The estimated regression equation for predicting "ln relative loss ratio" from "ln capability ratio" is

$$\ln \text{Relative loss ratio} = .20 - 1.19 \ln \text{capability ratio}$$

Taking the antilog of this equation, we have

$$\text{Relative loss ratio} = (1.22) \left[\frac{1}{(\text{capability ratio})^{1.19}} \right]$$

In terms of this equation, if the two opponents have a capability ratio of 2 to 1, the larger's deaths/armed forces should be approximately 0.5 that of the smaller's deaths/armed forces. In other words, if the larger nation suffered a loss rate of 10%, the model would predict that the smaller nation suffered a loss rate of 20%.

Capability Ratio and Duration

With the capability ratio to relative loss ratio examined and found to be relatively strong in the hypothesized direction, we turn to the link between the capability ratio and duration, which is also hypothesized to be negative. The nature of the relationship between the strength ratio and duration also turns out to be exponential, and in the direction predicted by the model. In the bivariate scatterplot, a triangular pattern was evident, indicating that the strength ratio is not a symmetric predictor to duration. High preponderance predicts to low duration, but near equivalence does not necessarily predict to long duration. In other words, preponderance is seemingly sufficient for a short war, but at the attrition end of the scale our hypothesis is not confirmed. The regression equation for the logged data, accounting for only 14% of the variance in duration is

$$\ln \text{Duration} = 2.57 - .43 \ln \text{Capability ratio}$$

or, taking the antilog,

$$\text{Duration} = (13.07) \left[\frac{1}{\text{capability ratio}} \right]^{.43}$$

For example, a strength ratio score as high as 10 would predict a war length of approximately 4.9 months.

Capability Ratio and Victory

The final predicted effect of the strength ratio is on victory; the rout model predicts the larger nation to be the winner, whereas, in the war of attrition, neither opponent, *ceteris paribus*, should have a distinct advantage. The logit regression equation is

$$\text{Log-odds } \textit{defeat} \text{ of the stronger nation} = -.31 - .069 \text{ Strength ratio}$$

with the standard error of $B = .06$, predictive power $= .56$, OLS $R^2 = .057$, indicating that the greater the preponderance, the less the probability of defeat, or, conversely, the greater the probability of victory. Due to an idiosyncrasy of the logit program, the results are given in terms of that value of the dependent variable that is coded as one; in our case this corresponds to defeat, or, more precisely, failure to win, for the stronger side, implying victory for the weaker side. The predictive power of this equation is rather substantial, indicating that 56% of the variance in "victory" is accounted for by the strength ratio. However, most of this is due to the constant term, which is based on the distribution of the dependent variable, as shown by the low estimate of the OLS R^2. As it turns out, the model's point estimates of the probability of victory indicate that the larger nation should have won in all 30 wars.

Relative Loss Ratio and Victory

The next bivariate relationship to investigate is the impact of the relative loss ratio on victory. The logit regression equation is

Log-odds defeat of the stronger = $-2.02 + 2.80$ Relative loss ratio

with the standard error of $B = 1.21$, predictive power = .62, OLS R^2 = .25, which clearly reflects the predicted relationship. The coefficient is in the predicted direction, indicating that the higher the relative loss ratio (the greater the stronger's loss rate relative to the weaker's), the higher the probability of defeat, or the lower the probability of victory, for the stronger nation. Further, although a large amount of our predictive power is from the given distribution, a goodly amount of the variance in victory *is* accounted for by the relative loss ratio.

Duration and Victory

The last bivariate link is from duration to victory, hypothesized to be negative: the longer the war, the lower the probability of victory for the larger nation. Given our logit program, the relationship between duration and defeat should be positive; the logit regression equation does confirm this:

Log-odds defeat of the larger = $-1.78 + .069$ duration,

with the standard error of $B = .033$, predictive power = .60, OLS R^2 = .20. We do not do as well here as we did when using the strength ratio or relative loss ratio as a predictor to victory, but the relationship is in the predicted direction, and duration seems to have some predictive power.

Summary

In all cases, the bivariate empirical results confirmed the hypotheses discussed under model specification. These can be summarized as:

1. The greater the initial numerical superiority one nation has, the less its relative losses.
2. The greater the initial numerical superiority, the shorter the war.
3. The greater the initial numerical superiority, the greater the probability of victory for the stronger nation.
4. The longer the war, the lower the probability of victory for the stronger nation.
5. The greater the relative losses suffered by the stronger nation, the less the probability of victory for that nation.

Relationships 1 and 2 were seen to be exponential. Such a finding seems to suggest that war is a dynamic and interactive process; thus, our use here of a static and linear model only captures a small portion of the "action." Further, the ability to predict the victor in dyadic wars seems to hinge on "threshold effects" that cannot be expressed fully in either a linear or an exponential model, although the logit regressions seem to do fairly well. Generally, the rout appears to be more manifest in history than the war of attrition, but this may change when we shift to the multivariate analyses and take the interaction among predictors of victory into account.

Multivariate Analysis of Victory

As the first step in this investigation of the combined effects of the predictor variables, let us examine the correlation matrix in Table 8-2.

These coefficients indicate that multicollinearity will not be too great a problem, because the predictor variables are generally more highly correlated with the dependent variable than with each other.

Table 8-2. Matrix of Simple Correlation Coefficient, $N = 30$

	Capability Ratio	Relative Loss Ratio	Duration	Victory
Capability ratio	xxxx	-.28	-.17	.17
Relative loss ratio		xxxx	.12	-.51
Duration			xxxx	-.45

This is important, because logit regression, as does OLS, assumes independent predictors.

Turning to the logit regression for a multivariate analysis of victory, Table 8-3 gives the appropriate summary statistics.

The first line of this table contains statistics for the constant term. The constant term in a logit regression essentially represents "history," reflecting the original distribution of victory. Technically, it is an intercept term, just as in OLS, and represents the best estimate for the log-odds defeat of the stronger nation if all independent variables are equal to zero. Thus, because -2.98 corresponds to a probability of defeat of roughly .05, the chances of victory for a larger nation are quite good when all predictor variables are zero (an admittedly impossible situation). The standard error of B is not particularly large, setting limits on the B which correspond to probabilities of .12 and .01. The coefficient is significantly different from zero at the .01 level and by itself accounts for 21% of the variance in the dependent variable, victory.

The second line gives corresponding statistics for the predictor capability ratio. A major shift is evident here, given our bivariate results. The coefficient of -.0047 is not significantly different from zero, and the strength ratio only accounts for .1% of the variance in

Table 8-3. Summary Statistics for Predicting Log-Odds Defeat of the Stronger Nation from the Capability Ratio, Relative Loss Ratio, and Duration

Predictor	B	Standard Error of B	Significance	Partial*
Constant	-2.98	1.026	.01	21.2%
Capability ratio	-.0047	.025	.42	.1
Relative loss ratio	2.73	1.27	.02	13.2
Duration	.067	.032	.02	12.5

Predictive power = .673 R^2 of OLS = .406 χ^2 = 12.94, df = 3 sig. = .01

*Percent error is reduced when variable is introduced.

victory. We can also note that this coefficient is not substantively significant. Similar to an OLS coefficient, the B represents the change in the log-odds defeat given a unit change in the independent variable. The effect, then, of a tenfold increase in the capability ratio would, *ceteris paribus*, be to decrease the constant term, -2.98, by .047, which is not even a .01 change in the probability of defeat of the larger nation. This suggests that initial numerical superiority has no *direct* effect on the probability of winning a war, but only an *indirect* effect through duration and relative loss ratio.

The influence of the relative loss ratio on victory is statistically and substantively significant, accounting for about 13% of the variance in the outcome of war. The coefficient indicates that a shift of 1.0 in the relative loss ratio, that is, the larger's casualty rate being twice that of the smaller rather than being equivalent, leads, *ceteris paribus*, to an increase in the log-odds defeat of the stronger nation of .27; the new prediction, -2.71, implies that the probability of defeat of the stronger nation has risen from .05 to .44. Thus, the impact of the relative loss ratio, in part depending on the capability ratio, on the outcome of a war is indeed substantial.

Duration is also a fairly good predictor of the outcome of war, accounting for approximately 12% of the variance. The coefficient of .067, being significantly different from zero, indicates that an increase of 10 months in the length of the war could change the predicted probability of defeat of the stronger nation from .05 to .09, and an increase of 20 months in the duration could change that probability to .16. We see, then, that duration is important to the outcome of a war, but apparently not as important as the relative loss ratio.

Overall, the logit equation is a rather good predictor of the outcome of war. The "predictive power" statistic which includes the effects of the constant term, indicates that two-thirds of the variance in victory is accounted for by the predictor variables. Using only the three predictors, and not the constant term, the OLS R^2 statistic indicates that the equation still accounts for 40% of the variance in war outcomes. Lastly, the χ^2 statistic is significant, indicating that the overall equation fits the data rather well. Further, we can note that the direction of influence of all variables upon victory remains the same in the multivariate mode; these are all in the hypothesized directions, thus lending credence to the original rout-attrition model.

Next, we turn to Table 8-4, which shows the calculated (predicted) probabilities of defeat for the stronger nation in each of the

Table 8-4. Predicted Probability of Defeat for the Numerically Stronger Nation, with Predicted and Observed Outcomes Noted

War (Year Begun)	Larger Armed Force	Smaller Armed Force	P (Defeat)	Outcome* Predicted	Outcome* Observed
Franco-Spanish (1823)	France	Spain	.241	V	V
Russo-Turkish (1828)	Russia	Turkey	.178	V	V
Mexican-American (1846)	United States	Mexico	.729	D	V
Austro-Sardinian (1848)	Austria-Hungary	Sardinia	.091	V	V
First Schleswig-Holstein (1848)	Prussia	Denmark	.112	V	V
La Plata (1851)	Brazil	Argentina	.115	V	V
Anglo-Persian (1856)	England	Persia	.061	V	V
Spanish-Moroccan (1859)	Spain	Morocco	.072	V	V
Italo-Roman (1860)	Italy	Papal States	.054	V	V
Italo-Sicilian (1860)	Italy	Two Sicilies	.329	V	V
Franco-Mexican (1862)	France	Mexico	.707	D	D
Ecuadorian-Colombian (1863)	Colombia	Ecuador	.020	V	V

War	Larger nation	Smaller nation	Probability	Outcome
Russo-Turkish (1877)	Russia	Turkey	.213	V
Sino-French (1884)	France	China	.133	V
Central American (1885)	Guatemala	Salvador	.666	D
Sino-Japanese (1894)	China	Japan	.235	V
Greco-Turkish (1897)	Turkey	Greece	.077	V
Spanish-American (1898)	United States	Spain	.281	V
Russo-Japanese (1904)	Russia	Japan	.191	V
Spanish-Moroccan (1906)	Spain	Morocco	.079	V
Italo-Turkish (1911)	Turkey	Italy	.934	D
Greco-Turkish (1919)	Turkey	Greece	.643	D
Manchurian (1931)	China	Japan	.781	D
Chaco (1932)	Bolivia	Paraguay	.783	D
Italo-Ethiopian (1935)	Italy	Ethiopia	.090	V
Sino-Japanese (1937)	China	Japan	.920	D
Russo-Finnish (1939)	Russia	Finland	.053	V
Russo-Hungarian (1956)	Russia	Hungary	.047	V
Sino-Indian (1962)	China	India	.090	V
Second Kashmir (1965)	India	Pakistan	.088	D

* V = larger nation victorious; D = larger nation defeated. If probability of defeat ≥ .50, the outcome is classed as a defeat.

30 dyadic wars, as well as showing the predicted and observed outcomes (Table 8-4). These results are rather encouraging. The logit regression not only correctly predicts 19 of the 21 observed victories by the stronger nation, but it also predicts 6 of the 9 observed defeats. Standard statistical tests on a two-by-two contingency table of observed and predicted outcomes indicate that we are rather close to reality: $\chi^2 = 8.27$, significance $= .01$; ϕ and $T_b = .56$; $\gamma = .90$. No single dimension seems to distinguish the five wars that were mispredicted by the model, but several variables can be suggested. First, one could argue that the United States won the Mexican-American War (1846) not only on the basis of numerical strength, but also on superior leadership and morale (Singletary, 1960), and the same might be said for the Turks in 1919 against the Greeks; neither of these variables is in the model. Second, for the two Japanese victories that were predicted as defeats, Japanese strategy, as well as industrial and technological advancements (again not in the model) are historically considered to have been of major importance in determining the outcome. Finally, for the second Kashmir War of 1965 between India and Pakistan, major power diplomatic intervention can be construed as a constraint on India's conduct of the war.

Before moving on to an analysis in which we examine intercentury differences, let us look in greater detail at the equation for predicting the log-odds defeat of the stronger nation by setting up some hypothetical examples. Table 8-5 presents eight different situations, involving different values of the strength ratio, relative loss ratio, and duration, and the calculated probabilities of defeat of the stronger nation in each situation. The values indicated in the table are substituted into the following equation (based on Table 8-3), which is then solved for the log-odds defeat, this figure being converted into the probabilities shown

Log-odds defeat of larger nation =
   $-2.98 - .0047$ (capability ratio) $+ 2.73$ (relative loss ratio)
       $+ .067$ (duration)

These results are consonant with the theoretical model. Row 1 represents the worst case for the larger nation, and defeat *is* predicted. Row 5 reveals that, even with a tenfold preponderance of strength, if a nation cannot pursue the war with low relative losses and is engaged in combat for a lengthy period of time, the odds of victory indeed favor the smaller nation. Further, from the probability column, we can see that the model predicts a high probability of victory (i.e., a low probability of defeat) for the stronger nation

Table 8-5. Hypothetical Situations with Predicted Probability of Defeat of the Stronger Nation

Capability Ratio	Relative Loss Ratio	Duration in Months	Predictions		Observed Outcome
			Logit	Probability	
2:1	.8	24	.80	.69	D
		6	-.74	.33	V
	.1	24	-1.11	.25	V
		6	-2.31	.09	V
10:1	.8	24	.77	.68	D
		6	-.44	.39	V
	.1	24	-1.15	.24	V
		6	-2.35	.09	V

when its loss rate is fairly low compared when compared the weaker nation's and the war is short, regardless of the margin of strength. These predictions show the low direct predictive power of the strength ratio. Interestingly, a short war *or,* more powerfully, low relative losses are enough to shift the advantage to the larger nation. However, the probability of victory is probably high enough for comfort only when the larger nation suffers fewer deaths/armed forces *and* the war is finished quickly.

Summary

Despite the problem noted of thresholds in predicting victory and the exponential nature of interrelationships among predictor variables, the model does relatively well when taken as a whole. The ability to predict duration is quite poor, but predictions of relative loss ratio are not too bad, and the model can correctly classify over 80% of the wars with regard to the victor. The direct impact of relative capabilities on the probability of victory for the initially stronger nation was seen to be less important than the bivariate results suggested, except in cases of extreme preponderance.

Controlling for Intercentury Differences

Because many prior empirical works on warfare have found some differences between the nineteenth and twentieth centuries, and, because World War I is often considered a "watershed" in the history of military strategy and tactics, we reexamine the two periods—1816-1913 and 1914-1965, separately. In the interests of brevity, though, only abbreviated tables of results are presented for the century-specific analyses. The bivariate results as shown in Table 8-6, are generally congruent across centuries, most coefficients being in the same direction.

Despite the overall similarity, we note that the relationship between relative loss ratio and duration changed from a slight negative in the nineteenth century to a moderate and positive one in the twentieth. Such a finding implies that heavy relative losses for the nation with the larger prewar standing army led to a shortened war in the nineteenth century but in the twentieth century served only to prolong the agony. This might suggest different strategies and cost tolerances operating in the two centuries.

With regard to the relationships of the three predictors to victory, we can see that relative capabilities is more important in predicting victory in the twentieth century; the impact is nil in the nineteenth, but, in the twentieth century, clearly, the greater the preponderance, the less the chance of defeat and the greater the chance for victory. Relative loss ratio also appears to be more important in the twentieth century, whereas duration seems to decline slightly in influence on victory.

The multivariate results, presented in Table 8-7, are a bit more complex.

In the nineteenth century, the impact of relative capabilities is negligible. The shift in sign is relatively unimportant, given the

Table 8-6. Century-Specific Results — Bivariate Correlations

	Capability Ratio	Relative Loss Ratio	Duration	Defeat of Stronger Nation
Capability ratio	xxx	−.30, −.45	−.13, −.41	−.01, −.23
Relative loss ratio		xxx	−.15, +.29	2.12, 7.28
Duration			xxx	.068, .053

NOTE: Entries in matrix are nineteenth century ($N = 18$), twentieth century ($N = 12$). For correlations between relative capabilities, relative loss ratio and duration the product-moment coefficient is given; for the correlations with "defeat" the regression coefficient from a bivariate logit regression is given.

Table 8-7. Multivariate Results for Predicting Log-Odds Defeat of the Stronger Nation in Each Century

	Nineteenth Century[1]			Twentieth Century[2]		
	B	Sig.	Partial	B	Sig.	Partial
Capability Ratio	.004	.46	0.10	−.103	.28	3.1
Relative Loss Ratio	3.54	.05	19.9	6.802	.12	10.8
Duration	.097	.03	21.3	−.024	.35	1.4
Predictive power			.75			.70
OLS R^2			.36			.51

[1] $N = 18$.
[2] $N = 20$.

sample size, whereas duration and relative loss ratio appear to be quite important in predicting the victor. For the twentieth century, the influence of duration is negligible, relative capabilities slightly important, with relative loss ratio being the most important predictor. The change in direction of duration is again not reliable due to the small sample size; this shift may also reflect the changed relationship between relative loss and duration between the centuries noted in the bivariate studies above.

Taking the equations as a whole, we see that, with the constant term taken into account, the equations are basically equivalent in predictive power. However, on the basis of the predictor variables alone, OLS R^2, the twentieth century model is a better fit. This implies that "rule of thumb" or other estimates based solely on aggregate historical trends were likely to be closer to reality in the nineteenth century than in the twentieth century. In other words, the predictive power of "history" alone is approximately 75% − 36% = 39% in the nineteenth century but only 70% − 51% = 19% in the twentieth century. Hence, to accurately predict the outcome of a twentieth century war, one needs to specifically take into account such factors as casualty rates and duration.

In terms of correct predictions, using only the multivariate results, we correctly predicted (or more properly, postdicted) the victor in 25/30 or approximately 83% of the two-nation wars between 1816 and 1965. The nineteenth century model correctly postdicts 16/18 = 89% of wars, and the twentieth century model correctly postdicts 10/12 = 83% of the wars. Together, this gives an overall rate of 26/30 = 86% correct, not much different from the total span results. Generally speaking, then, no need to separate the centuries is apparent for predicting victory, although century controls would need to be taken into consideration for predicting duration, given the changed relationship between the two centuries.

Conclusions

This paper reported an initial model of three basic costs of combat—duration, relative deaths per armed forces and defeat—and the empirical results based on 30 two-nation wars since 1816. The basic findings were:

1. The greater the initial numerical superiority one nation has, the less its relative losses.
2. The greater the initial numerical superiority, the shorter the war.
3. The greater the initial numerical superiority, the greater the probability of victory for the stronger nation.
4. The longer the war, the lower the probability of victory for the stronger nation.
5. The greater the relative losses suffered by the stronger nation, the less the probability of victory for that nation.

All these results are consistent with the postulated model of the duration, relative losses, and outcome of dyadic wars. Somewhat different results are obtained when the wars of the nineteenth and twentieth centuries are examined separately, but the differences are not, for the most part, statistically or substantively significant. Thus, this representation works fairly well and seems to be a promising start toward a more fully elaborated model of the dynamics of warfare.

Several inferences can be drawn from these analyses. First, the probable consequences for a state engaging in combat without a prewar preponderance of troops are high relative losses and, with a somewhat lower probability, a long war. The longer the war continues and/or the higher the relative losses of the larger state, the less likely that state is to be victorious. In other words, on the average, they need a large preponderance of military capability to ensure a rout or quick victory. If that rout cannot be achieved, and a war of attrition ensues, the advantage of power-in-being is lost; as the war continues and the losses climb, the chances of victory are diminished. "One last offensive" is not, apparently, the way to win a war. We might hope that models of the sort outlined and tested here will someday reduce—at the very least—the likelihood that governments will undertake wars that cannot be won, and whose political outcomes are dubious when weighed against the widespread destruction they produce.

9

Postwar Industrial Growth

Hugh Wheeler
Middlebury College

Most studies of war and other forms of social conflict focus on the causes and conditions of these phenomena. Whether quantitative or otherwise, such studies generally are based on the assumption that most if not all of the consequences of conflict are known and understood. Indeed, it is often *because* of the "known" consequences that such studies are conducted, primarily with the goal of finding ways to prevent, control, or otherwise mediate either the putative causal or conditional factors or the conflicts themselves.

We certainly know that wars often kill very large numbers of people. However, the study on which this chapter is based is founded on the belief that, beyond the killing in war, precious little in the way of systematic, reproducible, empirically based knowledge is available about the consequences of social conflict in general, and even less about war.

This chapter, then, reflects an overall concern about "filling the gaps" in our understanding of the consequences of war. As a study in world politics, however, it reflects an attempt to increase our understanding of the effects of war on a phenomenon that has long fascinated social scientists—national power. War represents an extreme test of national power. What are the effects on that power of using it in war?

To repeat a tiresome phrase, national power is a multidimensional concept. It is commonly agreed, however, that one of its most important dimensions is industrial output and growth. Determining the effects of war on these factors, therefore, represents an important step in our understanding of the consequences of war for national power.

In particular, this study deals with the problem of determining the consequences of interstate war between 1816 and 1965 in terms of two fundamental theoretical questions: (1) Does war affect the industrial growth of those countries involved in the fighting, and what, if any, are those effects?, and (2) Are the effects of war systematically associated with the characteristics of the war experiences and the attributes of the countries involved.

A Framework for Inquiry

It is important to ask how and why one might expect war to affect the industrial growth of nations. The following brief accounting of some of the factors making up the basic theoretical arguments found in the literature provides the context for this study. Although the body of literature dealing with the consequences of war is vast, ranging across many disciplines, it appears to be built around three basic theoretical arguments. Generally speaking, these arguments, or "models" if you prefer, support the positions that wars basically have positive effects, negative effects, or no effects on the industrial growth of countries.

The Traditional Arguments

Those supporting the positive effects position view war as leading to (1) increased efficiency in, and protection of, industrial activity, due in part to increased governmental power (Sombart, 1913; Foch, 1918; Schumpeter, 1939; Borton, 1941); (2) improved financial institutions and structures (Hansen, 1941; C. Wright, 1942); (3) technological advances which would not have occurred otherwise (Herring, 1941); (4) the discovery and exploitation of new resources

(Kaempffert, 1941); (5) better transportation and communications facilities (Fontaine, 1926); (6) superior managerial and organizational skills (Dorn, 1940; Dulles, 1942); and (7) an overall stimulation of the economic systems of states. These benefits are alleged to accrue to most if not all states, whether combatant or noncombatant, developed or developing, major or minor power, and winner or loser, for example, although there may be some variation within and between these groups, as discussed in the following paragraphs.

A statement by Kaempffert (1941) pretty well captures the positive effects position: "War may conceivably destroy civilization, but the greatest social, cultural, political, industrial, technological, and economic blossoming has occurred when belligerency was high."

The literature supporting the position that the effects of war on industrial growth are negative is based on an argument that concludes that there are few, if any, benefits to be gained by waging war and that there are certainly not enough benefits to offset the death and destruction of war. More authoritarian measures adopted by governments during war tend to be continued after war (Rothwell, 1941), whereas increased government spending to support the war effort seriously interferes with the normal functioning of the economy (Ogawa, 1926). The indiscriminant destruction of capital, both modern and obsolete (Boulding, 1945), the disinvestment and distortion of capital (Thorp, 1941), the increased debt (Hancock and Gowing, 1941), the maldistribution—sometimes permanent—of the work force along with manpower losses which often involve many of the healthiest, most able, and most creative citizens of the state (Thorp, 1941), the destruction of trade patterns, the disruption of communications, and the interference with transportation development needed for peaceful uses (Nicolai, 1918)—all are negative effects of war on industrial growth that cannot be offset by the putative benefits. As Nef (1950) puts it, "The more total the wars, the more they comprehend all nations of the earth, the more they have interfered with progress of every kind including mere abundance."

Turning to arguments that war has no effect on the industrial growth of countries, especially in the long run, one finds discussions of the recuperative powers of national economies (Clark, 1931) as well as simple assertions that most nations have seemed to grow and prosper over the long run, despite wars (Bryce, 1916). Knowledge is retained in the minds of war's survivors, the facilities to disseminate that knowledge may either survive or be quickly restored, and the sociopolitical organizations needed to utilize it can be readily reconstructed (Barbera, 1973).

According to this no-effects argument, then, the economic growth of nations is rarely permanently altered by war, either positively or negatively (Linton, 1940). Without "benefiting" from the observation of the world war experiences, Macauley (1913) makes this general argument with respect to the influence of wars in English history: "It can easily be proved that in our land, the national wealth has, during at least six centuries, been almost uninterruptedly increasing . . . in spite of maladministration, of extravagence, of public bankruptcy, of two costly and unsuccessful wars . . .".

Prior Quantitative Efforts

The literature surveyed so far offers little in the way of systematic, empirical evidence; it is supported largely by argument with a few historical examples called upon occasionally. But there are some quantitative studies of the consequences of war which have been completed. Among these are studies of the loss of life due to war, including the works of Bodart and Kellog (1916), Sorokin (1937), Q. Wright (1942), Richardson (1960), and Singer and Small (1972). The relationship between domestic conflict and international war, with causality flowing in both directions, has been investigated by Rummel (1964), Tanter (1966 and 1969), Rosecrance (1963), Huntington (1962), Wilkenfeld (1968), and Stohl (1973), among others. The five studies reviewed here represent efforts more closely related to the goals of this study.

Using growth rates of per capita GNP, Kuznets (1964) finds that prewar levels of development account for differences in the relative effects of World War II on nations, with higher levels of prewar development being associated with more positive consequences. He also suggests that the war experience may have led to technological innovations which in the long run will benefit all nations, although the "run" may be so long that the link to the war may be questionable.

Boulding and Gleason (1965), treating war as an investment, present a study of the effects of Japanese war experience from 1887 to 1960 on such factors as GNP, personal consumption, government purchases, and domestic and foreign investment. They conclude that, although war in the early part of the period may have "paid," the losses in the latter part explain why "It is little wonder that under these experiences Japan has become one of the least aggressive and least militaristic nations of the world."

A study by Dickenson (1940) analyzes the effects of World War I on industrial production in the United States. Using prewar levels and rates of growth in industrial output, as indicated by several derived measures which are similar to GNP, as his base of comparison, Dickenson examines postwar output in terms of what would be expected based on the prewar figures. Although many historians and economists have argued that World War I either had no significant impact on the industrial growth of the United States, or may have had a positive effect, Dickenson finds largely negative effects. That is, despite the apparent boom in the 1920s, production did not equal, much less exceed, the expected trends and levels.

Kugler (1973) and Barbera (1973) offer support for the position that war has no effect on the capabilities and development of nations. Kugler provides an operational test of some of the ideas articulated by Organski (1968), the most relevant of which is the notion that it is extremely difficult if not impossible to permanently alter the general course of development of countries, either positively or negatively, whether by war or any other means. Looking at the two world wars, Kugler analyzes the postwar fluctuations in GNP for various aggregations of developed states, grouped according to whether they were winners or losers, occupied or unoccupied, or neutral. He finds that, in general, as *groups* of countries, none experienced any permanent change in economic performance. That is, within 20 years after each war, each of the *groups* came very close to the level of economic performance expected, based on the prewar projections.

Barbera's work also supports the "no-effects" position via the analysis of changes in number of telephones per capita, used as an indicator of development. When controlling for degree of war involvement, military occupation, and prewar level of development, Barbera finds no systematic effects of the world wars, taken together or singly, either on national development or on the inequalities between rich nations and poor.

Concepts, Indicators, and Measures

Having indicated the general theoretical and research context for this study, it is now necessary to specify more precisely the key concepts, the indicators of those concepts, and how the indicators are measured in this examination of the effects of war on industrial growth.

The Referent Empirical World

As is the case with many of the other studies reported in this volume, only those interstate wars that began and ended between 1816 and 1965 are included in this study. One of the most important reasons for treating 1816 as a benchmark is directly related to the major concern of this study. What began in England about 1760 and came to be called the Industrial Revolution really began on the Continent of Europe after the Napoleonic wars were over. It was, therefore, at this time that industrial output and growth began to be such an important dimension of national capability, ostensibly changing both the causes and conduct as well as the consequences of war. Wars that ended by 1965 are the last to be included in this study because of the need to use, wherever possible, the decade after war to examine the war's effects.

The spatial realm of this study is only limited by the total number of interstate war experiences that satisfy the requirements for inclusion and for which data are presently available. Generally speaking, the inclusion criteria adopted by the *Correlates of War* project and articulated in Singer and Small (1972) are used here.

The spatial criteria are of two basic types, depending on (1) the political status of the belligerents and (2) the severity of the armed conflict in terms of battle-connected fatalities. Although the political status criterion is used here exactly as Singer and Small developed it, the severity criterion is modified slightly in this study. Singer and Small include all wars leading to at least 1,000 battle-connected fatalities among all the war participants who were interstate system members. But, where their thresholds used to determine whether any given system member qualifies as a war participant are (1) at least 100 battle deaths or (2) at least 1,000 troops in active combat, the criteria used for inclusion here are 1,000 battle deaths or .01% of the country's prewar population, if fewer than 1,000 were killed. Although this limit is admittedly quite arbitrary, as most such limits are, it does permit the examination of a wide range of war experiences, including the Sinai War experience of Israel, which suffered 200 (.01%) killed out of a population of 1,900,000, and the World War II experience of the Soviet Union, which suffered approximately

7,500,000 (4.4%) in battle-connected fatalities out of a population of 170,500,000. The national war experiences included in this study are listed in Table 9-1.[1]

The Outcome Variable

It is important to note how the outcome variable in this study, industrial growth, is used to tap the concept of national capability or power. It should not, for example, be confused with the more general phenomena of economic development, level of industrialization, or even economic productivity, which could be measured in terms of output per worker or output per capita. In other words, industrial *growth*, as used in this study, refers to *levels* and *rates* of change in industrial *output*.

The particular indicators of industrial growth selected for this study are iron production for the period prior to 1870 and energy consumption after that date. Hancock and Gowing (1949) and Rostow (1962) support the use of iron production as an overall indicator of industrial activity for the nineteenth century, and Cottrell (1955), Kuznets (1966), and Darmstadter (1971) argue that energy consumption is one of the best indicators of industrial activity in the modern era. The iron data used here represent annual measures of pig iron production, expressed in metric tons. Energy consumption is measured annually in metric coal ton equivalents of commercial consumption. It is a composite measure which includes coal during the period 1870–1975, petroleum from 1880–1975, natural gas and hydroelectricity from 1919–1975, and geothermal and nuclear electricity in the brief period 1966–1975. All industrial data were provided by the *Correlates of War* project (Thompson, 1973).

The Predictor Variables

Two classes of predictor variables are used in this study to account for the effects of war on the industrial growth of nations: characteristics of the national war experiences and prewar characteristics of the belligerent nations. The four variables used to measure the war a nation experiences are the intensity of the war, how long the nation fought in the war, whether the war was fought at home or abroad, and whether the nation won the war. Prewar characteristics

Table 9-1. National War Experiences and Industrial Consequences

		Predictor Variable Data					Industrial Growth Data			
Nation	War Experience	Battle Deaths/ Population[1]	Months	At Home?	Win?	F Test	Prewar Rate	Postwar Rate	Rate Diff. (* sig.)	% Change
Russia	Russo-Turkish	91.9	16.7	no	yes	.05	.03	.003	.027*	-18.0%
United States	Mexican-American	47.6	21.1	no	yes	NS	.037	.032	-.005	23.0
Austria-Hungary	Austro-Sardinian	16.3	4.7	yes	yes	.01	.053	.073	.02*	-3.2
Prussia	First Schleswig-Holstein	15.6	8.1	no	yes	.01	.026	.156	.13*	72.0
England	Crimean	76.7	23.1	no	yes	NS	.065	.039	-.026*	-22.0
Russia	Crimean	1,404.5	28.3	yes	no	.01	.016	-.002	-.018*	17.0
Austria-Hungary	Italian Unification	36.1	2.5	no	no	.01	.073	-.009	-.082*	-32.0
Austria-Hungary	Seven Weeks	56.2	1.4	yes	no	NS	-.009	.03	.039*	27.0
Prussia	Franco-Prussian	13.3	12.3	no	yes	.01	.077	.037	-.04*	18.0
Russia	Russo-Turkish	127.9	8.8	yes	yes	.10	.113	.081	-.032*	-4.0
France	Sino-French	5.5	11.8	no	yes	.01	.034	.026	-.008	-14.0
Japan	Sino-Japanese	12.5	8.0	no	yes	.05	.041	.119	.078*	91.0
China	Sino-Japanese	2.3	8.0	yes	no	NS	.082	.144	.062*	46.0
Turkey	Greco-Turkish	5.8	3.1	no	yes	NS	.083	.102	.019	-2.0
Greece	Greco-Turkish	25.0	3.1	yes	no	NS	.014	.016	.002	-8.0
United States	Spanish American	6.6	3.7	no	yes	.01	.039	.071	.032*	30.0
Spain	Spanish American	27.2	3.7	no	no	.05	.043	.030	-.013*	-2.0
Japan	Russo-Japanese	180.5	19.3	no	yes	.01	.119	.077	-.042*	-6.0
Russia	Russo-Japanese	32.0	19.3	no	no	NS	.090	.051	-.039*	-35.0
Spain	Spanish-Moroccan	102.6	8.5	no	yes	.05	.036	-.014	-.050	-6.0
United States	World War I	131.3	18.9	no	yes	NS	.048	.033	-.015	-21.0

Table 9-1. National War Experiences and Industrial Consequences (Cont)

		Predictor Variable Data					Industrial Growth Data			
Nation	War Experience	Battle Deaths/Population	Months	At Home?	Win?	F Test	Prewar Rate	Postwar Rate	Rate Diff. (* sig.)	% Change
England	World War I	1,965.4	51.2	yes	yes	NS	.010	-.009	-.001	-17.0
Belgium	World War I	1,151.3	51.3	yes	yes	.01	.024	.073	.049*	-20.0
France	World War I	3,292.7	51.3	yes	yes	.01	.025	.054	.029*	-8.0
Portugal	World War I	112.9	32.4	no	yes	.01	.042	.042	.000	-55.0
Italy	World War I	1,863.6	54.4	yes	yes	.01	.077	.058	-.019*	-35.0
Greece	World War I	463.0	23.6	yes	yes	NS	.074	.035	-.039	38.0
Rumania	World War I	4,781.7	19.7	yes	yes	.01	.130	.030	-1.00*	-68.0
Russia	World War I	1,049.4	40.2	yes	yes	.01	.051	.147	.096*	-72.0
Germany	World War I	2,686.6	51.4	yes	no	.01	.040	.036	-.004	-44.0
Turkey	World War I	2,210.8	109.1	yes	no	NS	.053	.041	-.012	-43.0
Bolivia	Chaco	3,200.0	35.9	yes	no	NS	.048	.093	.045	12.0
United States	World War II	314.1	44.3	no	yes	NS	.000	.018	.018	59.0
Canada	World War II	344.7	71.2	no	yes	.05	.009	.030	.021	79.0
Brazil	World War II	2.5	10.1	no	yes	.01	.021	.111	.090*	89.0
England	World War II	568.4	71.4	yes	yes	.10	.012	.025	.013*	-2.0
Holland	World War II	71.3	.2	yes	yes	.01	.004	.050	.046*	36.0

Country	War						
Belgium	World War II	114.3	.6	yes	yes	.10	-.015	.024	.039*	40.0
France	World War II	511.0	19.4	yes	yes	.01	-.012	.042	.054*	24.0
Poland	World War II	916.9	.9	yes	yes	.05	-.014	.081	.095*	188.0
Italy	World War II	186.9	64.7	yes	yes	.01	.007	.076	.069*	101.0
Yugoslavia	World War II	32.5	.4	yes	yes	.01	-.004	.123	.127*	136.0
Greece	World War II	140.9	5.9	yes	yes	.01	.039	.149	.110*	-27.0
Bulgaria	World War II	15.9	7.9	yes	yes	.01	.028	.106	.078*	114.0
Rumania	World War II	50.0	7.9	yes	yes	.01	.022	.159	.137*	-6.0
Russia	World War II	4,428.7	54.3	yes	yes	.01	.138	.085	-.053*	-71.0
Norway	World War II	69.0	2.0	yes	yes	.05	.013	.040	.027*	12.0
South Africa	World War II	87.0	71.3	no	yes	.01	.055	.018	-.037*	-4.0
Australia	World War II	432.4	71.4	no	yes	NS	.036	.055	.019	-6.0
New Zealand	World War II	1,081.3	71.4	yes	no	.10	.017	.010	-.007	26.0
Hungary	World War II	434.8	42.8	yes	no	.01	.009	.134	.125*	84.0
Finland	World War II	2,102.6	42.3	yes	no	.01	.084	.094	.010	-56.0
United States	Korean	34.8	37.0	no	NA	NS	.030	.029	-.001	-2.0
South Korea	Korean	1,995.2	37.1	yes	NA	NS	.148	.154	.006	-24.0
Russia	Russo-Hungarian	3.5	.8	no	yes	.01	.085	.058	-.027*	-8.0
Hungary	Russo-Hungarian	255.1	.8	yes	no	.01	.137	.069	-.068*	-46.0
Israel	Sinai	10.5	.3	no	yes	.05	.160	.086	-.074*	-45.0
U.A.R.	Sinai	12.9	.3	yes	no	.01	.025	.066	.041*	-24.0
Pakistan	Second Kashmir	3.3	1.6	yes	yes	.01	.078	.035	-.043*	-14.0
India	Second Kashmir	.6	1.6	no	no	.01	.083	.097	.014*	-13.0

[1] Expressed as per million population.
NA – Not available.
NS – Not significant.

of the nation include its industrial growth rate and whether the nation was a major power.

The view of Richardson (1960) and Singer and Small (1972) that the single best indicator of the "amount" of war experienced by a nation is its battle-connected fatalities is shared here. However, although suffering 10,000 casualties is a measure of "how much" war each of two countries, one very large and one very small, may have experienced, the effects of the war on industrial growth may be much more severe for the small nation. To control for the different size of nations, therefore, the battle-connected fatality figures for each one are normalized (divided) by its total prewar population, resulting in a measure of war *intensity* that is comparable across nations.

Turning to the second of the war measures, the length or amount of time that a nation is involved in a war, the concern here is for a measure of the amount of attention or resources a nation may have been devoting to the war effort during the war. A good indication of this is the rate at which fatalities were being sustained. For example, a nation that lost 2,000 soldiers in a six-month war would presumably have concentrated much more of its resources on that war effort than it would have in a ten-year war in which it lost 2,000 troops. By including the length of the war in the analysis along with the intensity variable, this important distinction is preserved.

The third predictor variable included here is the location of the war. Each war experience for each nation is coded yes or no, depending on whether at least one month of the war was fought on that nation's home territory. That is, were the military forces of the opposing nation(s) on a country's territory for 30 days or more during the time the war was going on.

The last of the characteristics of the wars to be considered here involves the determination of the outcome of the war. Was the nation on the winning or losing side of the war when it was terminated? The classification of nations as victorious or defeated in these war experiences is reported in Singer and Small (1972), and their classifications are used here.

Much of the debate about the effects of war on industrial growth involves the role that prewar characteristics of the nations themselves play. Kuznets (1966), for example, sees more highly developed states as being more mature, growing a little less rapidly than others, but possessing a greater reserve capacity for recovery after war. Prewar industrial growth rate, then, is the first national characteristic used as a predictor variable here. It is measured using the iron production and energy consumption data series; the prewar growth rate of these series is the rate of increase in each one, calculated over the ten-year period prior to the war.[2]

Some authors assert that the effects of war on national capabilities are different for major and minor powers, the second of the prewar characteristics used here. Usually having both size and development on their side, the major powers are alleged to be more able to do the following: to seize opportunities for expansion in territory and trade, to improve their capital positions, and to get a larger share of the spoils of war generally (Rostow, 1962). On the negative side, major powers may be more susceptible to territorial losses because of overexpansion in the process of empire building or may have to make larger reparations payments, relatively speaking, after losing a war (Lewis, 1955). As in the case with the winning or losing variable, the Singer and Small (1972) classification of states as major or minor powers is used here.

Detecting Change in Industrial Growth

Before an analysis of differences war may or may not make in the industrial growth of nations can be undertaken, a very critical question must be answered. What is meant by the term "difference," and how is the term operationalized?

The difference that war makes is determined in two steps in this study. First, we ask where the nation "would have been" or "should have been" in terms of industrial output had the war not occurred at all. The expectation of where the nation would or should have been is based on a projection procedure using prewar levels and rates of growth in output. That is, observed postwar economic output is compared with expected output, based on projections from prewar performance. Second, instead of just asking whether the nation is above, below, or just "gets even" with where it should have been, we also ask whether any gains or losses in foregone production are kept or made up. In other words, if the country comes out of a war producing less than it was producing when it went in, does it not only get back to where it should be but also *exceed* where it should be, at least temporarily, until any economic losses are made up? To whatever extent this does not happen is a measure of the "real" economic costs of war according to Boulding (1945).

Does Industrial Growth Change After War?

It is important to select a test for measuring change in growth that is appropriate for the particular definition of change used here. Having settled on a particular "model" for detecting such fluctuations that requires a comparison between observed and expected levels and rates of growth, a technique is called for that involves testing for what are otherwise referred to as parameter shifts (Campbell and Stanley, 1966). An appropriate test of parameter shifts in time series data, developed and used rather extensively in economics, is called Chow's F test (Chow, 1960). The test involves the use of regression to determine whether one overall line "fits" a time series as well as two separate lines. In this particular application, the overall line is the regression line calculated by regressing both the prewar and postwar observations of iron production or energy consumption on time as one single time series. This produces a measure of the change in the industrial indicators, with respect to time, for the entire series. The same procedures is then repeated for the prewar series and then for the postwar series, resulting in a measure of the change or growth in the indicators for each of those shorter series, respectively.

Chow's F test determines the statistical significance of any difference observed in the prewar and postwar series. How well, in other words, does the one regression line calculated over the total period (prewar and postwar, together) fit the observed data when compared to each of the separate lines. The F test provides the statistical significance of the improvement in "fit" when using the two separate lines by determining the significance of the reduction of the residuals when using the two lines.[3]

Turning now to the actual application of Chow's F test to the war experiences, we find that 44 (73%) of the 60 cases reveal statistically significant shifts in iron production or energy consumption after war.[4] The sixty cases include 52 single war experiences and 8 aggregate experiences (see note 1).

Table 9-1 indicates which of the 60 war experiences were indeed followed by significant changes in industrial growth, according to the F test. Given the fact that these war experiences involve many nations at different levels of development fighting throughout the past century and a half in large and small wars, it is difficult to avoid the conclusion that war does indeed very often affect the industrial growth of nations.

How Does Industrial Growth Change After War?

Having indicated that, in a sample of 60 national war experiences fought throughout the last century and a half, nearly 75% were followed by changes in industrial growth is important in itself. But, for a study of the consequences of war for national capabilities, an equally, and perhaps more, important set of questions remains to be answered. How does industrial growth change after war? Do *rates* of growth and *levels* of output change? Are the changes likely to endure? These questions are addressed next by examining more closely the 44 cases revealing statistically significant parameter shifts.

To respond to these questions about how growth changes, then, two different measures of change are needed—change in growth rate and change in amount of output. Using only the rate measure would not detect step-level increases or decreases in amount of output. Using only the amount of output measure would not distinguish between a country (1) that came out of a war with increased productivity due to increased government consumption during the war but reduced rates of growth due to the sudden reduction of government purchases and (2) a country that came out of war with drastically reduced production due to destruction, for example, but with a rapid rate of recovery—both countries could have the same total output for ten years after war and yet be going in opposite directions in terms of growth.

Changes in the rate of industrial growth may be calculated by using the regression coefficients obtained earlier when calculating the Chow's F test. That is, the coefficients for the separate prewar and postwar regressions of iron production or energy consumption on time indicate the rate of increase in those indicators. By subtracting the prewar from the postwar coefficients, therefore, a measure of the change in rate is obtained. Table 9-1 provides the respective prewar and postwar rates, the difference between the two rates, and the statistical significance of the difference between the two, for each of the national war experiences.

In the case of changes in the rate of growth, the expectation is that postwar rates will be the same as prewar, if the war is not associated with or does not affect rates of growth. In the case of level or amount of output, however, the expected postwar figures must be based on the prewar levels *plus* the prewar rates of growth. That is, how much iron was that nation producing or how much energy was it using, and how fast was that production or use increasing or decreasing?[5] Table 9-1 also presents the results of these calculations, expressed as a percentage deviation from the expected levels.

With these two different measures of change in postwar industrial growth in hand, we may address the questions of how growth changes and how lasting are the effects. These two variables are measured on ratio scales, however; that is, they have a meaningful zero point and the distances between any two values on the scale may be determined. Ordinarily, this scale of measurement is preferred because it conveys maximum information. In this case, however, some preliminary questions may be addressed more easily by collapsing the scales into ordinal ones. For example, how many war experiences were followed by amounts of iron produced or energy consumed that were above the expected amounts? Or how many war experiences were followed by rates of growth that accelerated, stayed the same, or actually decelerated?

To answer these questions, our two measures of change are collapsed, then, to gain initial insight into how growth changes after war. The amount of postwar output has two categories: above or below expected values. The rate of growth measure has three values: accelerated, no change, or decelerated. The determination of whether the rates changed significantly is accomplished by means of another F test designed to determine how well the assumption of equal rates or slopes actually fits the two categories, pre- and postwar in this case (Blalock, 1960).

After collapsing the two variables into ordered categories, they may be combined to form a matrix with two rows and three columns. Table 9-2 presents the matrix including all 44 cases for which there were the significant parameter shifts after war.

We note first that the amount of industrial output was above the expected amount in the ten years after for 18 (41%) of the 44 war experiences, whereas it was below the expected amount after 26 (59%) of the cases. Looking at the rates of growth, we see that in 23 (52%) of the 44 cases, the industrial growth accelerated after war, in 6 (14%) it did not change significantly, and in 15 (34%) of the cases it decelerated.

Turning to the particular cell entries for those nations which exceeded expected output after war, we see that in 14 (78%) of the 18 war experiences the nations were able to accelerate postwar growth rates as well as increase the amount of postwar output. These nations appear to have benefited from the war experience in both ways. Two (14%) of the 18 cases increased postwar output with no

Table 9-2. Change in Growth Rate and Amount of Output After Wars

	Rate Accelerate	No Change	Rate Decelerate
Amount Increase	Prussia, First Schleswig-Holstein Japan, Sino-Japanese (1894) China, Sino-Japanese (1894) United States, Spanish-American Brazil, World War II Holland, World War II Belgium, World War II France, World War II Poland, World War II Italy, World War II Yugoslavia, World War II Bulgaria, World War II Norway, World War II Hungary, World War II	Canada, World War II New Zealand, World War II	Russia, Crimean Prussia, Franco-Prussian
Amount Decrease	Austria-Hungary, Austro-Sardinian Belgium, World War I France, World War I Russia, World War I England, World War II Greece, World War II Rumania, World War II United Arab Republic, Sinai Pakistan, Second Kashmir	France, Sino-French Portugal, World War I Germany, World War I Finland, World War II	Russia, Russo-Turkish (1828) Austria-Hungary, Italian Unification Russia, Russo-Turkish (1877) Japan, Russo-Japanese (1904) Russia, Russo-Japanese (1904) Italy, World War I Rumania, World War I Russia, World War II S. Africa, World War II Russia, Russo-Hungarian Hungary, Russo-Hungarian Israel, Sinai India, Second Kashmir

significant change in the rate of industrial growth, thus experiencing a step-level increase in output. And 2 (14%) of these cases experienced an increase in the amount of output after war but also experienced decreases in rates of growth. These latter two cases exhibit an economic change after war which appears temporary; in other words, the slower rate of growth suggests a possible return to normal economic activity sometime after the war, or even an eventual or long-term decrease in industrial growth, possibly due to expedient measures taken during the war which would prove damaging in the long run (Prest, 1948).

Turning next to the 26 war experiences followed by reduced output after war, we see that 9 (35%) of the 26 accelerated their rates of growth, exhibiting possible "catch-up" characteristics after the war; 4 (15%) experienced no change in growth rate, or what can be considered a step-level decrease in output; and 13 (50%) of these 26 actually decelerated as well as declined in total output, suffering negative effects both ways and indicating possible retarding effects of the war experiences.

These findings strongly suggest that 33 (75%) of the 44 war experiences examined here led to enduring changes in industrial growth after war. That is, the 14 that accelerated and increased in amounts of output over expected figures, plus the two that increased in amount of output but had no change in rate, experienced postwar changes that are clearly positive; the 4 that decreased in amount of output with no change in rate, plus the 13 that both decreased in amount and decelerated in rate, experienced negative changes. The remaining 11 (25%) of the war experiences led to changes which could be only temporary.

In sum, then, treating the postwar growth *rates* as "pointers" or indicators of future industrial output relative to the postwar *amounts* of output observed here, one would conclude that war experiences do appear to often have enduring effects on the industrial growth of nations. However, the evidence as it has so far been examined indicates that the effects are as likely to be negative as positive. If we examine the *particular* war experiences in Table 9-2, on the hand, we note the tremendous impact of World War II for the number of cases experiencing enduring positive changes in growth. Of those 16 cases, 12 (75%) were World War II cases. Clearly, if World War II were removed from the analysis, the results of the analysis of *how* war affects growth would be clearly *negative*.

There are at least two plausible reasons why the World War II cases are generally so different. The first has to do with the particular analytical procedures used here. The reader will recall that expected postwar rates and amounts of output are projections of prewar rates and amount of output. In the case of World War II, of course, our projections are problematical because of the worldwide depression which preceded that war, leading most likely to unrealistically *low* projections of postwar economic growth. Perhaps, in other words, these particular postwar experiences would not be positive if they were compared with expected performance based on "normal" prewar activity. On the other hand, of course, we may recall the massive relief and reconstruction efforts undertaken after World War II, efforts which were really unprecedented. Perhaps the positive effects of World War II could be traced to those efforts. At any rate, it is in fact clear that the non-World War II experiences overwhelmingly led to changes in industrial growth which were clearly negative.

Accounting for the Effects of War on Industrial Growth

Having some knowledge, then, of how war affects postwar output and growth, we next examine how well the characteristics of the wars and of the nations themselves do in accounting for the observed changes or lack thereof. In the analyses which follow, all 44 cases revealing statistically significant fluctuations in growth via the tests employed earlier are examined. Both measures of change in growth—change in rate and change in amount of output—are used in this analysis.

The General Multivariate Analyses

As mentioned earlier, the major variables offered to account for the effects of war on the industrial growth of nations are generally assumed to act in a simultaneous fashion, calling for some form of multivariate analysis to determine the combined effects of the variables acting jointly as well as the separate effects of each one, controlling for all the others. For the multivariate analyses, the same general regression model is applied to each of the outcome variables. That is, the same six predictor variables—the intensity of the war, the length of the war, whether it was fought at home or abroad, whether the state won or lost, the prewar growth rate, and whether the state was a major power—are used to account for the changes in growth rate and then the changes in the amount of industrial output.

In Table 9-3, the results of the analysis of postwar changes in the *rates* of economic growth are presented, and the following statistics are included: the multiple correlation coefficient, R; the multiple coefficient of determination, R^2; the beta weights or standardized coefficients, b; the standard error of the coefficients, SE; the squared partial correlation coefficients, r^2; and the statistical significance of the overall regression as well as for each of the predictor variables. We find in Table 9-3 that the overall model accounts for 56% (R^2 = .56) of the fluctuations in postwar rates of industrial growth and is highly significant statistically ($p < .001$). Turning to the individual predictor variables making up the regression model, we find mixed support for the various arguments in the traditional literature. For

Table 9-3. Multiple Regression Analysis of Rate Change: General

	b	SE	r^2	p
Total Period[1]				
Battle deaths/population	-.24	.15	.07	.11
Months	.02	.13	.00	.89
Winning	.11	.11	.02	.34
At home	.27	.13	.10	.05
Prerate	-.55	.12	.35	.0001
Major	-.08	.12	.01	.51
Pre-World War I[2]				
Battle deaths/population	-.56	.68	.10	.45
Months	.19	.73	.01	.81
Winning	.16	.39	.03	.70
At home	.38	.42	.12	.40
Prerate	-.62	.39	.30	.16
Major	-.15	.53	.01	.77
Post-World War I[3]				
Battle deaths/population	-.26	.17	.09	.15
Months	.01	.14	.00	.97
Winning	.04	.13	.00	.77
At home	.28	.15	.13	.06
Prerate	-.58	.15	.37	.001
Major	-.03	.14	.00	.83

The significance test used for the regression is the f-test; the test used for each of the predictor variables is the t-statistic.
[1] $N = 44, R = .75, R^2 = .56, SE = .11, p < .001$.
[2] $N = 13, R = .65, R^2 = .42, SE = .31, p < .65$.
[3] $N = 31, R = .80, R^2 = .64, SE = .12, p < .001$.

the characteristics of the war variables, the independent contribution of the intensity measure (battle-connected fatalities divided by total population—battle deaths/population) is indeed negatively associated with postwar changes in growth rates, whereas the magnitude of the experiences (that is length, measured in months of participation—months) is virtually unrelated to the rate changes. Although winning the war has only a limited positive impact on rate change, the independent effect of fighting on the home territory of nations does have a moderate but positive impact. The minority view in the traditional literature to the effect that the destroyed sectors of the economy are replaced by more modern and efficient ones, and that fighting at home greatly stimulates those sectors which are not destroyed, seems to receive some support from these findings.

For the two variables measuring prewar characteristics of the nations incorporated here, the prewar rates of industrial growth (prerate) makes the largest independent contribution, among all six predictor variables, in accounting for changes in postwar growth rates. And the association is *negative*, clearly indicating that nations with lower relative prewar growth rates tend to fare better after war than those with relatively higher prewar rates. As suggested earlier, this finding can be interpreted to mean that nations with slower prewar rates may have their economies stimulated by war or, at the very least, that their economies suffer less damage as a result of war. This latter interpretation is consistent with the argument that nations growing more slowly may have a greater reserve capacity which can be used to recover from any destruction, disinvestment, or distortion of the economy due to war (Kuznets, 1964).

The independent effects of being a major power (major) are minimally negative. The large standard error relative to the size of the beta weight indicates that the sign could actually be positive.

Before examining the tables further, a brief word about the possible effects of the timing of wars is in order. Discussion of the significance of *when* wars occur are prevalent throughout the literature. Drawing on these arguments plus the growing body of empirical literature (Singer and Small, 1972; Singer, Bremer, and Stuckey, 1972; plus others), we examine the pre-World War I and then the post-World War I cases (including the World War I cases in this category) for possible differential relationships between the predictor and outcome variables. That is, are the arguments to the effect that wars in the modern era have very different consequences for nations valid in terms of industrial growth?

Looking at Table 9-3, we find the general model doing worse in the pre-World War I period and slightly better in the later period. Generally, the direction of the relationships between the predictor variables and postwar rate change are the same for the two separate periods as they were for the total period; the relative size of some of the coefficients does change somewhat. For the pre-World War I period, the overall model accounts for 42% ($R^2 = .42$) of the postwar fluctuations in industrial growth, although the regression is not statistically significant due to some extent to the small number of cases in this period. Among the characteristics of the war variables, the intensity of the war measure accounts for most of the variation in industrial growth rate changes after war, as it did in the entire period. The length of the war in months as well as winning may be minimally and positively associated with rate changes in this period, although the standard errors are so large that the coefficients could almost as easily be negative. Fighting at home is more likely to be a positive factor than winning, although once again the large standard errors indicate that both relationships could be negative.

The prewar characteristics of the states have the same role in this earlier period as in the total period. Prewar growth rate continues to be the most important of all the predictor variables in accounting for fluctuations in postwar growth rates, and it is negatively associated with those changes. Being a major power may be a liability in this period, but, as in the overall period, the independent effects of this variable are quite minimal.

In the post-World War I period, the overall model accounts for 64% of the fluctuations in growth rate, and is statistically significant. The intensity of the war experience continues to be negatively associated with changes in postwar growth rates, whereas the length of the war is basically unrelated to such changes when controlling for the other variables in the model. Being on the winning side in the post-World War I period makes a very little independent difference, as was true in the earlier period. Fighting on the home territory of states continues to be positively associated with changes in growth rates.

The roles of the prewar characteristics of the states in the later period also are similar to their roles in the earlier period. Prewar growth rates continue to be the most strongly associated with rate changes, and the relationship is still negative. Being a major or minor power makes very little difference in this later period, although the impact is negative.

Turning to the regression analyses of changes in the *amount* of postwar output, we see in Table 9-4 that the results are similar to those obtained in the analysis of changes in postwar growth rates. The model accounts for 46% of the fluctuations in level of output, whereas the figures are 28% and 55% for the pre- and post-World War I periods, indicated in Table 9-4; only the pre-World War I regression is not statistically significant. When examining the individual predictors, we see that the intensity of the war experience is negatively associated with postwar changes in level of output in the total period. This relationship is weaker and reversed in the two separate pre- and post-World War I periods, although the relationships are so weak and have such large standard errors that we cannot be that confident in the direction of the association in those separate periods.

The length of the war is weakly but positively associated with

Table 9-4. Multiple Regression Analysis of Amount Change: General

	b	SE	r^2	p
Total Period[1]				
Battle deaths/population	-.20	.16	.04	.22
Months	.08	.14	.01	.57
Winning	.10	.12	.02	.41
At home	-.05	.14	.00	.74
Prerate	-.53	.14	.29	.001
Major	-.18	.13	.05	.16
Pre-World War I[2]				
Battle deaths/population	.09	.76	.00	.70
Months	.05	.81	.00	.96
Winning	.34	.44	.09	.46
At home	.05	.46	.00	.92
Prerate	-.27	.44	.06	.56
Major	-.38	.59	.06	.55
Post-World War II[2]				
Battle deaths/population	-.07	.19	.01	.70
Months	.12	.16	.02	.44
Winning	.10	.14	.02	.49
At home	-.07	.16	.01	.67
Prerate	-.64	.17	.37	.001
Major	-.27	.15	.11	.09

[1] $N = 44, R = .68, R^2 = .46, SE = .12, p < .001$.
[2] $N = 13, R = .53, R^2 = .28, SE = .35, p < .86$.
[3] $N = 31, R = .74, R^2 = .55, SE = .14, p < .005$.

changes in level or amount of output for all three time periods, suggesting that the relatively longer war experiences were more often associated with positive changes in levels of output. Again, however, the associations are so weak that we can have little confidence in the signs.

Being on the winning side continues to be positively but very weakly associated with changes in level of output for all three time periods, as it was in the rate change analysis. The relationship between fighting at home or abroad and changes in level is also weak, but it is mixed for the three periods—negative in the total period, positive in the pre-World War I period, and negative in the latter period.

The prewar characteristics of the nations are both negatively associated with changes in level of output for all three time periods, as they were in the rate change analysis. Slower prewar growth rates are associated with higher levels of output after war and being a major power is more of a liability than an asset.

The Analysis of World and Non-World Wars

Much of the traditional literature suggests that the world wars were unique in history and should not be analyzed together with other more limited wars. Although the evidence is clear that the world wars involved more nations and led to more bloodshed overall than any other wars in history, it is not so clear that many of the particular experiences of individual nations were more severe than some other nations' in more limited wars. As Singer and Small (1972) point out, the Chaco War between Paraguay and Bolivia led to more battle-connected fatalities per capita than any other war between 1816 and 1965. The Russo-Hungarian War of 1956 led to more fatalities per month than either of the world wars.

Table 9-5 presents the results of the regression analysis of changes in postwar growth rates after world and nonworld war experiences. Generally speaking, the results differ very little from the previous analyses looking at all war experiences together for the total period and the two separate periods. The model accounts for 59% and 55% of the fluctuation in postwar rates for the world and nonworld war experiences, respectively. And both analyses are statistically significant.

Table 9-5. Multiple Regression Analysis of Rate Change: World War and Non-World War Experiences

	b	SE	r^2	p
World War[1]				
Battle deaths/population	-.60	.28	.20	.05
Months	-.12	.19	.02	.52
Winning	-.12	.16	.03	.45
At home	.34	.17	.17	.07
Prerate	-.14	.28	.01	.61
Major	-.03	.18	.00	.99
Non-World War[2]				
Battle deaths/population	-.37	.30	.11	.25
Months	.16	.36	.02	.67
Winning	.24	.23	.09	.31
At home	.31	.23	.13	.20
Prerate	-.67	.20	.48	.01
Major	-.17	.31	.02	.59

[1] $N = 25, R = .77, R^2 = .59, SE = .15, p < .01$.
[2] $N = 19, R = .74, R^2 = .55, SE = .19, p < .10$.

The intensity of the war experience is still negatively associated with growth rate changes in both categories of experiences here. The length of the experience is more weakly associated with such changes and may be different for the two classes of experiences. It is negatively associated in the world war cases and positively so in the others. But the larger standard errors generate less confidence in those relationships. Winning is very weakly and negatively associated with the rate changes after world wars and weakly but positively associated with the others. Fighting at home rather than abroad is still, perhaps surprisingly, an asset. Slower prewar growth rates are an asset overall, but more weakly so after the world wars. And being a major power is a liability, if anything, in terms of changes in postwar growth rates.

The results of the analyses of change in level or amount of output after world and nonworld war experiences are presented in Table 9-6, and some differences between the two classes of war are indicated. First, the model accounts for 63% and 37% of the changes in amount of output after world and nonworld wars, respectively, although the results for the latter war experiences are not statistically significant. The intensity of the war experiences is *positively* asso-

Table 9-6. Multiple Regression Analysis of Amount Changes: World War and Non-World War Experiences

	b	SE	r^2	p
World War[1]				
Battle deaths/population	.31	.27	.07	.27
Months	.27	.18	.12	.14
Winning	.07	.15	.01	.63
At home	-.07	.17	.01	.68
Prerate	-.97	.27	.43	.001
Major	-.38	.17	.22	.04
Non-World War[2]				
Battle deaths/population	-.05	.36	.00	.88
Months	.32	.43	.04	.47
Winning	.37	.27	.13	.20
At home	-.02	.28	.00	.94
Prerate	-.46	.24	.24	.07
Major	-.34	.37	.07	.37

[1] $N = 25, R = .79, R^2 = .63, SE = .14, p < .005$.
[2] $N = 19, R = .61, R^2 = .37, SE = .23, p < .39$.

ciated with output changes after world wars, whereas it is generally unrelated to such changes after more minor wars. And the length of the war experience is positively associated with such changes for both types of war. These two findings provide little support for those who argue that the world wars were more damaging for economic output because they were longer or more bloody.

Being on the winning side is basically unrelated to the changes in level of output after world wars, although it appears to be an asset in more minor wars. Fighting at home is basically unrelated to changes in levels for these two classes of war experiences. Prewar growth rate continues to be the most important factor in accounting for changes in output, when controlling for all the other variables, and being a major power continues to be a liability.

To sum this section on accounting for postwar growth, we note that the most important factors in accounting for fluctuation in growth after war over the last 150 years were, in general order of importance, prewar growth rates, intensity of the war, and fighting at home. Prewar growth rates and the intensity of the war experience were consistently and negatively associated with both changes in growth rates and levels of output, suggesting that states with slower growth rates having less intense war experiences fared better after war. Fighting at home was nearly always associated positively with changes in rate of growth of growth and was basically unrelated to changes in level of output.

Among the remaining three predictor variables, being a major power was nearly always a liability, whereas winning was usually an asset, although a weak one. The length of the war, to repeat, was usually either weakly and positively associated with both changes in rate and level of output, or not related at all.

Among the more important findings presented in this section, some result from the examination of the regression analysis of the separate pre- and post-World War I experiences and the analysis of the world war and nonworld war experiences. Generally speaking, the predictor variables are related to the industrial growth indicator—iron production and energy consumption—in the same ways, whether we look at war experiences before or after the beginning of World War I or whether we look at world war and nonworld war cases separately, with only a few exceptions. This does not mean that the effects of war are the same for these various categories—only that the same factors account for the observed changes.

Conclusion

This study addressed two related questions about the consequences of war for industrial growth: (1) Does war affect the industrial growth of those nations involved in the fighting, and what, if any, are those effects?, and (2) Are the effects of war systematically associated with the characteristics of the war experiences and the attributes of the nations involved? Generally speaking, the analysis presented here indicates that war has affected industrial growth, in the long and short run, and those effects can be accounted for to some extent by the characteristics of the wars and the nations.

In considering the three original arguments—that wars have positive, negative, or no effects on the industrial growth of countries the evidence is clearly mixed. Among all 60 cases examined, 44 were followed by significant changes in growth. Among those 44, 16 experienced clear *positive* effects, whereas 17 experienced clear *negative* effects. There are 11 cases of apparent temporary effects, 9 of which were negative and 2 positive. There were 16 cases where no significant fluctuation in growth was found after war. The cases are split just about as evenly as possible, and any decision could be determined by what one did with the 11 cases of temporary effects. But they could be claimed by any one of the arguments, depending on what was believed to be the long-term growth of those cases. Removing World War II from the findings would clearly tilt them toward the negative side. There is, in other words, no simple solution, when considering all the cases together.

What we can say, however, is that wars do very often affect the industrial growth of nations and often affect that growth negatively, especially in the case of more limited wars. Those who would take a mixed effects position seem to be supported more by the evidence presented here, however. That is, the effects of war on industrial growth depend on those factors used in this analysis to account for changes in growth. More often than not, war does affect growth, and, when it does, the effects are very likely to be negative, especially in the short run, and very often in the long run. It is significant that most of the cases of positive effects came from *one* war—World War II.

Very generally, the results of this study indicate that those who have believed in economic stimulation and growth through warfare have not considered all the evidence. There is a high probability that there will be either detrimental effects for industrial growth, both long and short term, or no enduring effects at all, making the bloodshed senseless as well as tragic, as it has so often been throughout the past century and a half. For those who would wage war for reasons other than economic gain, it should be kept in mind that the cost of doing so may very likely be the permanent setback or actual retardation of economic growth, national capability, and power.

V

The Findings and Their Implications

10

An Interim Summary and Evaluation

Karl W. Deutsch
Harvard University

For a variety of reasons, it is a pleasure to add this brief note to the second volume of the *Correlates of War* papers. Although the editor's generous dedication in the first volume may exaggerate my contribution to the work of Singer and his colleagues, I have had the opportunity of sitting with them eight or ten times a year for about a decade, participating in the Friday seminars, going over their working papers, and debating a range of substantive and methodological problems. It has not only been an opportunity to offer some modest guidance to a gifted and competent team, but also to observe the ways in which teaching and research can go hand in hand, leading to both an increase in our knowledge and in the critical mass of first-rate young scholars who will continue and accelerate the pace of serious investigations into the causes of war and the conditions of peace.

Turning to my assignment here, let me offer a brief overview of the project's work to date, and then turn to a summary and interpretation of some of the more interesting findings.

First, the *Correlates of War* project has created a new data base for research on war and peace, reaching back in time over more than the last 150 years and covering the entire international system of politically relevant states. In the same decade, Singer and his associates have identified a substantial number of variables relevant for the likelihood of war. They have made them operational for reproducible measurement, and they have explored many bivariate and multivariate relationships among these variables, so as to test familiar theories about the supposed causes of war and to begin the design of new and more clearly defined theories and models of the structures and processes by which wars are generated.

In the course of their work—which now includes 10 books and/or book-length Ph.D. theses and 61 articles and papers—they have already produced a large number of important findings. No serious theory textbook about international politics will henceforth be able to ignore them. Even though many more findings, more debate about them, and more and still deeper research will be needed, it can already be said that the field of war and peace studies will never again be the same.

A Valuable New Data Base

Thanks to the work of the Michigan group, we now have for the period 1816-1965 a standard list of international state-actors (Russett, Singer, and Small, 1968); a standard list of interstate, extra systemic, and civil wars, along with their magnitudes, duration, intensity and severity (Small and Singer, 1970; Singer and Small, 1972); a list of the initiators for each war and of the victors at the end of each (Singer and Small, 1972); a standard list of the diplomatic status of 144 states, in five-year intervals, 1816-1970 (Singer and Small, 1966; Small and Singer, 1974); a standard list of formal international alliances subdivided into defense agreements, ententes, or undertakings for mutual consultation and neutrality or nonagression pacts (Small and Singer, 1969); a standard list of international intergovernmental organizations (Wallace and Singer, 1970); standard indices of power potential and of power concentration (Ray and Singer, 1973); and measures of the structure and polarity of the international system (Bueno de Mesquita, 1975).

None of these nine standard lists and measures existed before the 1960s with explicit published coding rules, permitting their control by other scholars. Now that they do exist, any researcher can use them for his/her own studies and analysis, can check them for accuracy and realism, and, if desired, can change some one coding rule or several of them—indicating carefully, one hopes, exactly what he did—and study the sensitivity of the Michigan group's original findings to any such coding change.

Further standard lists are now in preparation, including notably a list of indicators of national energy consumption and industrial growth (Wheeler, 1975a and b), a list of civil wars, and a list of democratic national political regimes (Small and Singer, 1976).

If one uses only one time lag, of, say, five years, these 12 lists will generate 144 pairwise interactions on the level of the international system for the entire 150 years. Adding another lag would double the number of potential interactions to be considered, and so would a division of the time period, say, into the periods 1816-1899 and 1900-1965, respectively. A good many of these pair relationships, lags and time periods have been considered by Singer and Small and their collaborators. Other such studies by the same group will probably follow, and perhaps a fair number of studies of such pair relations among variables may be omitted or postponed. But, in any case, there remains a very large amount of further work to be done by many researchers at many places.

Comparing the interplay among pairs of variables or parameters has the purpose, of course, to gain information about questions of substance. What substantive knowledge about conditions favoring war or peace has the *Correlates of War* project produced so far?

The Distribution of War and Its Implications

During the 150 years, 1816-1965, the overall number of wars has remained about constant in the international system, averaging about one war beginning every 18 months (Small and Singer, *Wages of War*, 1970, Table 8.1 pp. 191-194). But, although the average number of wars per decade has not changed, the number of nations in the international system has grown more than fivefold, from 23 states in 1816 to 124 in 1965 (Singer and Small, *Wages* 1972, Table

2.2, pp. 27-30). Relative to the size of the system, wars thus have become about five times as rare as they were 150 years ago. And, if we think of the opportunities for war as proportional to the number of *pairs* of nations, analogous to opportunities for two-car collisions in a traffic system, which are given by the formula $n(n-1)/2$, then the number of such interaction opportunities has risen 30-fold from 253 in 1816 to 7,626 in 1965. From this viewpoint, too, there has been much *less* large-scale international war in the world than chance alone would lead us to expect, and it may be legitimate to ask of future research to discover what constraints, external and internal, have limited the number of outbreaks of war in recent decades.

The incidence of war has continued to be quite uneven. Many nations have a history of peace. More than one-half of all nations now in the international system have never participated in large-scale war under their own governments. Some of these nations, to be sure, have become independent so recently that they had little opportunity to enter wars, but some older, well-established nations, such as Sweden and Switzerland have never been at war during the entire 150-year period since 1816 (Singer and Small, 1972, Table 11.2, pp. 275-280). Some other nations have had a high propensity to become involved in war. Britain and France each have waged war 19 times during the period, Turkey 17 times, Russia 15 times, Italy/Sardinia 12 times, both Austria-Hungary and China 8 times, Japan 7 times, and Germany/Prussia and the United States 6 times each.

Something similar applies to regions. Of over 29 million battle deaths 1816-1965, Europe has contributed nearly 22 million, Asia 5-6 million. By contrast, the Western Hemisphere (0.9 million), the Near East (0.8 million) and Africa (0.03 million) show much less loss of life, thus far, from international warfare. Other indicators of war involvement show much the same picture. A few nations and regions account for a large part of war involvement, whereas many nations and some regions have only been involved in few wars or none.

Most of the highly war-prone countries are the major powers. Eight such powers—Britain, France, Russia, Italy, Austria-Hungary, China, Japan, Germany and the United States—constitute only 6.3% of the 144 nations that were at one time or another members of the international system between 1816 and 1965. Yet these 5.5% account for 101 war involvements, or 42% of the total 239 war involvements reported for the period. During these 150 years, then, major powers were on the average almost seven times more likely to become involved in war than were lesser ones (Singer and Small, 1972, Table 11.2, pp. 275-279; Small and Singer, 1970). A similar proportion holds for battle deaths. The same nine major powers comprised 46% of the world's population of 1965 but accounted for 25.5 million, or 87%, of all the 29.2 million battle deaths of the 1816-1965 period (Small and Singer, 1970, Table 11.3, pp. 282 and 67; Taylor and Hudson, 1972, Table 5.1, p. 295). From this point of view, we may say that the citizens of these nine major powers have had almost twice the likelihood of being killed in international war than had the rest of mankind.

But wars have become much more deadly. If we compare the world's population at some date with the total number of battle deaths during the preceding 30-year period, then we find that the number of such battle deaths per 100,000 population has risen from about 14 in 1850 to 33 in 1900 and to 460 by 1930, 1,110 in 1940, 733 in 1950, 612 in 1960, and perhaps over 800 in 1970. These figures at least indicate the average chance of a person anywhere in the world to be killed in an interstate war during a 30-year period, and this chance has increased by factors of 30 to 50 against the nineteenth century. Some particular wars, of course, have always been more deadly than the average of all wars during some longer period in which they were included. But this range of intensity, that is, of relative deadlines, has also increased. The deadliest war between 1816 and 1850 was the Russo-Turkish War of 1828-1829, which killed 166 persons in battle for every 100,000 of the population of the belligerent countries. The deadliest wars of the period since 1910, World Wars I and II, killed about 1,400 and 1,100, respectively, per 100,000 of the population of the belligerents—a six- to eightfold increase in the intensity of mass destruction (Singer and Small, 1972, Table 4.2, pp. 62-69).

In their distribution over time, wars show virtually no recognizable cycles, but there are several secular trends. In addition to the increase in the deadliness of wars, in both absolute terms and relative to the decrease in their frequency, when we control for the numbers of countries and of interaction opportunities, as reported, there is an increase in their variability. In the nineteenth century, the percentage of battle deaths in the population of belligerents stayed close to the regression line for the entire period. Wars, then, tended to be neither extremely bloody nor unusually mild. In the twentieth century, this distribution changes. Although its central tendency persists, the deviations from it now become much larger. Some wars now claim a smaller proportion of victims, others now show a vastly higher rate of killing (Singer and Small, 1972, pp. 198-201).

In sum, during the 150 years from 1816 through 1965, wars on the average have remained equally frequent across time but relatively more rare as compared with the numbers of nations and of conflict opportunities. In their totality, however, they have become *more severe*—that is, more deadly in the numbers of people killed—and *more intense*, in the sense of killing more people, relative both to the population of the belligerent countries and to the population of the world. They also have become much *more* varied in their severity and intensity. In the more recent half-century, there have been both more very small wars, killing relatively few, and more very large wars, killing many more. If there should be any future wars with a large-scale use of nuclear weapons or other means of mass destruction, this might well be a continuation of these trends, albeit to a new level with new consequences.

Throughout the period, the few major powers have shown a disproportionately high share of war involvements and war deaths, both absolutely and relative to population. This trend, too, may well continue. If so, and if there should be any major wars in the future, the populations of the major powers would be in the greatest danger.

Not only the variance among wars has increased but also their unpredictability. In the nineteenth century, and indeed until 1910, about 80% of all interstate wars were won by the states that had initiated them; in only 20% of the cases did the war-initiating power fail to win its major professed objective. In the wars from 1911 through 1965, however, only about 40% of the war initiators won; in about 60% of the post-1911 wars, governments and nations lost the wars they started, in the sense of failing to gain the professed main aims for which they initiated hostilities (Deutsch and Senghaas, 1975). In some cases, such wars ended with the destruction of the war-initiating state—such as Austria-Hungary—or of its regime—such as Tsarist Russia, Imperial Germany, Nazi Germany, Fascist Italy, and militarist Japan, and with the death or exile of their rulers. Twentieth century war policies thus seem to have become less adaptive or rulers less competent, or decision overloads more extreme, or—most likely—the international system may have become less predictable, and this 60% probability of failure may well apply to any decision to initiate war in the future.

Some Observed Correlates of War

Although one could go even further in analyzing and interpreting the basic war and dispute data that has been generated by the project, let me turn now to some of the more interesting relationships between the incidence of international war and certain factors that are seen as accounting for the variation in that incidence. And let me deal largely with the findings reported in this volume, for the sake of brevity, as well as because Singer and his colleagues are now at work on a book-length effort to integrate their own and others' results to date in a more theoretically ambitious enterprise.

As the editor's introduction makes clear, the project's research design embraces a number of interrelated questions, of which accounting for the war proneness of individual nations is one of the most direct. In Bremer's paper, we find strong evidence of a pattern more general than had hitherto been suspected. That is, the original compilations in *Wages of War* showed very clearly that a small fraction of the system's members fought, during the 1816-1965 period, a large fraction of its international wars. Here we can go a step further and note that the pattern holds not only for the select major power group of 8 or 10, but for whichever nations happen to be in the top 50 on the composite capability indicator. That is, their war proneness is less a function of the separate nation's idiosyncratic characteristics than of their mere position in the capabilities scale. Moreover, this strong correlation holds not only for the frequency of war entry, but also for war initiation and for the number of fatalities sustained in each war experienced. On the other hand, given the range in capability ratios among military adversaries, there is only a weak association between individual overall capabilities and the *duration* of the war experiences; as Bremer suggests, some additional analysis at the dyadic level is called for next.

Building on this preliminary investigation, as well as on the earlier efforts of project colleagues, Gochman next looks into the interactive effects of the capabilities and the diplomatic status of nations on their war proneness. Although Wallace (1973) found that the incidence of war in the international system was strongly associated with the incidence of status inconsistencies, Ray (1974) found little evidence that those nations experiencing some status inconsistency were the same ones to experience high frequencies or magnitudes of war. Following up these earlier studies, Gochman discovers some moderately strong but theoretically interesting empirical patterns. One is that the traditional major powers of Europe rarely resorted to war in response to periodic discrepancies between their material strength and the diplomatic prestige accorded them by the others; more often, they reacted to the opportunities provided by fluctuations in the system's polarity pattern, particularly vis-à-vis weaker adversaries. Moreover, he finds that the recency and severity of prior war has little effect on the subsequent war proneness of the classical majors unless that prior war was extremely costly.

Also in the first part of the volume is the Leng analysis, which attends as much to behavioral variables as to ecological ones in seeking to account for the incidence of military conflict. In this pioneering effort to sort out which influence strategies are most likely to produce defiance from the adversary, and to increase the likelihood of war, he finds that the more severe the threat, the greater the likelihood that the adversary will make concessions, but that the relative capabilities are quite critical. When the parties are more equally balanced, the tendency toward defiance of the threats goes up, as does the likelihood of war.

Following the editor's pattern, and shifting from the *incidence* of war itself to the *expansion* of war that is already underway, we find two suggestive but different analyses. In the first, Sabrosky finds that the historical likelihood of war expansion via the honoring of alliance commitments is less than the literature would lead us to expect, but tends to be higher in the nineteenth century, that defense pacts produce more frequent intervention, and that major powers are more likely to intervene on the side of other majors, but not on the side of minor-power allies. In the companion piece, Yamamoto and Bremer find that war expansion is not a function of independent national choices, but is highly conditional on the prior decisions of third and fourth actors to intervene or not. Moreover, the tendency of nth powers to intervene in an ongoing war as a function of prior interventions is not only greater in the twentieth century than in the nineteenth, but seems to be increasing with time.

In the concluding part, Cannizzo and Wheeler both examine the factors that bear less on the onset or expansion of war and more on the *outcomes* and costs of international war during the century and a half since the Congress of Vienna. Using for the moment the simple indicator of armed forces size, Cannizzo finds that the conventional wisdom is generally borne out. The greater the manpower edge of a belligerent, the fewer its fatalities, the shorter the war, and the greater its likelihood of victory. But there are some interesting exceptions, and these will, I trust, be examined in due course. She also finds in this connection that the longer the weaker side can hold out, and the greater the fatalities it can inflict, the lower the likelihood that the numerically superior side will emerge victorious. Following this paper, and in response to decades of speculation on the middle-range effects of war on a nation's economic and industrial growth, Wheeler discovers that the evidence is indeed mixed. He finds virtually no effects in 16 of the 60 cases examined, strong postwar industrial growth in another 16, strong negative effects in 17, and effects of an essentially temporary sort in the 11 remaining cases. But his is hardly a case for turning to war—or war preparedness—as a stimulus to industrial growth; that has occurred in only about one out of four historical cases, and it would be risky indeed to generalize from only the experiences of the defeated nations in two rather nonrepresentative wars (Organski and Kugler, 1977).

Summary

Although the temptation to offer one or more interpretive syntheses of these findings is strong indeed, the constraints of both space and time combine to still my pen. Rather, as noted, the members of the project are now putting more of their energy into precisely such an enterprise, even as they continue the less exciting but arduous and essential work of index construction, data generation, data analysis, and the other activities that mark a well-balanced and far-sighted research effort. I look forward to participating as fully in that phase of the *Correlates of War* project as I have in the earlier ones.

Notes

Chapter 1. The Trials of Nations: An Improbable Application of Probability Theory (pp. 3-35)

1. Dr. Zed seems to have been referring to J. David Singer and Melvin Small, *The Wages of War 1816-1965, A Statistical Handbook*, New York: Wiley, 1972.
2. It should be noted that Zed included both interstate and extrasystemic war involvements in his computations.

Chapter 5. Influence Strategies and Interstate Conflict (pp. 124-157)

1. Singer (1963) theorizes that the influence strategy chosen depends on the actor's preference for future target behavior, the perception of target's current behavior, and its prediction of future target behavior.
2. See Burton (1969) for some interesting evidence of the diversity of issues that different parties bring to conflicts. Each, it appears, is, in fact, involved in a different conflict (see pp. 14-19).

3. Schelling's definition of rationality will be employed in this paper. A different view has been taken by Boulding (1962, p. 9), who makes a distinction between rational and irrational behavior in the "content of the image either of the field or the value ordering." "Thus," he writes, "behavior is irrational if it is based on a false image of the world or a bad system of value order." The importance of perception in determining rationality is also recognized by Scott (1958), who argues that rational behavior means that "values or goals are explicit, mutually consistent, and objects or events are perceived or cathected according to their relation to these values" (p. 11). Again, the importance of perception of reality is stressed with a requirement for "empirical validity of the ends-means relationship." I mention this here because the absence of the role of perception in the model may be seen as one of its more serious missions.

4. The strategic game is not necessarily zero sum. Schelling defines winning as "gaining relative to one's own value system" (1960, p. 4). The model does not require the assumptions of a power drive, as expressed in Morgenthau's political realism, but is, however, fully compatible with it.

5. Morgenthau similarly argues that ". . . a diplomacy that ends in war has failed in its primary objective: the promotion of the national interest by peaceful means. This had always been so and is particularly so in view of the destructive potentialities of total war" (1973, p. 519). This definition, however, raises the question of whether Schelling's diplomacy of violence would be considered diplomacy by Morgenthau.

6. The prescriptive nature of the model, especially the works of Morgenthau and Schelling, should be evident. Some of Morgenthau's most noted work has dealt with criticism of those who would suggest that statesmen put other considerations above the demonstration, maintenance, and extension of power (see, for example, Morgenthau, 1951). The game theoretical model employed in Schelling's work is inherently prescriptive (see Schelling, 1969, p. 4; Rapoport, 1960).

7. An investigation is now underway employing the results of this study and the author's earlier exploratory analysis of the conflict process (Leng and Goodsell, 1975) in a prototype computer simulation.

8. The 1850-1919 time interval used here differs from other *Correlates of War* studies appearing in this volume, wherein the nineteenth century era is ended at 1900. The difference can be

explained largely by the systemic focus of those studies, as opposed to focus on internation behavior in the study at hand. It may well be that the systemic changes, which already had occurred by 1900, helped set in motion the upheaval of World War I which, in turn, ushered in the revolutionary changes in diplomacy at the end of the war.

9. Intercoder reliability tests are conducted at periodic intervals with scores ranging between .88 and .92 using Scott's pi. See Holsti (1969, pp. 140-141.)

10. In the course of conducting a pretest of the indicators, we found that the third logical possibility, a request that the target undertake action that would result in a tangible power *gain* also does occur, albeit rarely. In the Anschluss Crisis of 1938, Austrian Chancellor Schuschnigg was coerced into requesting that Germany undertake action which meant a considerable gain in power to Germany at Austria's expense. This sort of situation occurred too rarely for us to add this as a separate indicator and were coded simply as requiring no tangible power cost to the target.

11. This decision is made by the researcher after the material has been coded, not as part of the data generation process, to require as little inference by the coder as possible. See Leng and Singer (1970) for a full discussion of this.

12. The *Correlates of War* index is composed of six national capability measures: military expenditures, armed forces personnel, population, urban population, iron and steel production, and fuel consumption. See Singer, Bremer, and Stuckey (1972) for a summary, and the forthcoming *Strength of Nations* (Small and Bennett) for a more complete description. The emphasis on military strength in this definition is consistent with the realist notion that military force is the most crucial element of national power in a conflict situation (Morgenthau, 1973, p. 27).

13. If more than one request occurs on the same date, a decision must be made to determine which inducement belongs with which request. This is facilitated by the coding process which causes acts which are part of the same influence attempt to be clustered together.

14. Another approach would be to consider all of A's previous behavior toward B to form part of the "degree of inducement" for any particular influence attempt. Here one would score A's behavior toward B on a cumulative basis and use that score as the degree of inducement.

15. The longer the time interval between the influence attempt and response, the less certain the connection between the two because of the increasing opportunity for other influences to intervene. For an interesting effort to determine an appropriate time lag for action and response in the pre-World War I crisis (see Zinnes, 1968).
16. Because of the low number of observations appearing in some cells, response types have been collapsed into two categories: positive (*comply* and *placate*) and negative (*carrot* and *stick*, *ignore*, and *defy*) in computing χ^2 scores.
17. See Carr (1939) for one of the earliest of innumerable comments on the phenomenon.

Chapter 6. Interstate Alliances: Their Reliability and the Expansion of War (pp. 161-198)

1. This decision was made because of the problem of states that were forcibly annexed by one of their nominal allies but did not resist at a high enough level to warrant inclusion in the war list. Prominent among such cases are the German dismemberment of Czechoslovakia (1938-1939) and the Russian annexation of the Baltic states (1940). After considering the circumstances of those annexations, it was decided to include them both in the total number of war-performance opportunities *and* (as appropriate) in the cases in which alliances were violated during those war-performance opportunities.
2. "Major" powers and their tenure as such are Austria-Hungary, 1816-1918; Prussia-Germany, 1816-1918 and 1925-1945; Russia, 1816-1917 and 1922-present; France, 1816-1940 and 1945-present; England, 1816-present; Italy, 1860-1943; Japan, 1895-1945; the United States, 1899-present; and China, 1950-present. These states during the remaining years in the 1816-1965 period, and all other states throughout that 150-year period, are classified as "minor" states (Singer and Small, 1972, p. 1930).
3. It has been argued (Holsti, Hopmann and Sullivan, 1973; Sullivan, 1974) that 1919 is a more appropriate cutting point between the nineteenth and the twentieth centuries than 1899. Although their arguments have merit, we have not yet been persuaded to alter the decision to stay with the more conventional, chronological usage. For a detailed discussion of the

considerations involved in the original decision, see Singer and Small (1968, pp. 255-256).
4. For related discussions of this point, see Singer and Small, 1968, and Singer, Bremer, and Stuckey, 1972.
5. Parenthetically, the fact that many of the alliances that were active in the 1946-1965 subperiod did not encounter any war-performance opportunities may suggest an increase in their war-*deterring* properties. This will be explored in a later study.

Chapter 7. Wider Wars and Restless Nights: Major Power Intervention in Ongoing War (pp. 199-229)

1. If we designate the cell entries in a contingency table in the following way,

a	b	A
c	d	B
C	D	T

then the correlation ϕ is calculated by the formula

$$\phi = \frac{ad - bc}{\sqrt{ABCD}}$$

2. We used the table of binomial confidence limits provided by Beyer (1966, pp. 222-24).

Chapter 9 Postwar Industrial Growth (pp. 258-284)

1. It is clear from any examination of interstate war over the past century and a half that nations often become involved in different wars in rapid succession, if not at the same time. This clearly complicates the problem of determining the effects of any given war. To minimize such probable confounding influences, the war experiences of individual nations which occur in rapid succession—less than five years apart—are simply aggregated and treated as one experience. The following table presents a list of those war experiences which are aggregated; the asterisks indicate which experience is used to identify the aggregate experience in Table 9-1.

War Experiences Combined for Analysis

Nation	War Experiences
France	Crimean Italian Unification Franco-Mexican Franco-Prussian*
Prussia	Second Schleswig-Holstein Seven Weeks' Franco-Prussian*
Italy	Italo-Turkish World War I*
Greece	First Balkan Second Balkan World War I* Greco-Turkish
Turkey	Italo-Turkish First Balkan Second Balkan World War I* Greco-Turkish
Rumania	Second Balkan World War I* Hungarian Allies
Japan	Manchurian Sino-Japanese Russo-Japanese World War II*
China	Manchurian Sino-Japanese World War II*
Italy	Italo-Ethiopian World War II*
Russia	Russo-Japanese Russo-Finnish World War II*
Finland	Russo-Finnish World War II*

*Name used to identify the group of wars in subsequent references.

This particular aggregation procedure is least satisfactory when the country experiences several wars in rapid succession over a period of up to two decades, or more, as was the case for France from 1849 to 1871 and Japan from 1931 to 1945. Any projection of "expected" industrial growth over periods of this length is simply unrealistic (Kuznets, 1964). Therefore, these cases are regrettably dropped from the analysis.

2. The calculation is performed by first computing the natural logarithmic transformation of each ten-year series, followed by a simple linear regression of the logged series against time. The resulting regression coefficient, or slope as it is commonly called, is a measure of the rate of increase in the *unlogged* series. That is, because the logarithm of each year's energy consumption or iron production figure in the ten-year series is an exponent, the regression of these exponents on time results in a measure of the change in those exponents across time. If the log (or exponent) for any year (t) increases by .05 over the preceding year ($t-1$), then the rate of increase going from $t-1$ to t is precisely .05, or 5%. The regression results in the average rate of increase or decrease over the ten-year prewar period.

3. One might question the appropriateness of applying "straight line" or linear regression, which is necessary for the Chow's F test, to the *actual* energy consumption and iron production data. Because both these indicators increase at exponential rates for nearly all countries, any straight line will underestimate the realistically expected postwar figures (Darmstadter, 1971). Straight-line projection of the expected output would, in other words, be based on the assumption that the *rate* of increase in industrial growth should *decline* over time. Because the expected *amount* of increase would be the same each year, it would represent a decreasing percentage over the growing total. The actual exponential increase in industrial growth during "normal" times is due to a *rate* of increase that does not change very drastically for most economies (Kuznets, 1964). For the proper use of the significance test selected for this study, the natural logarithm of the energy consumption and iron production figures is calculated for each year. The increase in the logarithm for each year will be *linear* (see note 2) if the industrial output indicator is increasing at a constant *rate*. By applying the F test to the logged data, the assumption of linearity is met, and the F test will reveal the statistical significance of any change in the rate of increase in the indicator.

4. The statistical significance level used is .10 as opposed to the conventional .05 level because of the relative shortness of the 20-year overall prewar and postwar time period. Forty (67%) of the 60 cases actually revealed significant shifts at the .05 level or less. Using the .10 level means that there is still only a 10% chance that the F test would indicate a parameter shift when in fact none occurred.

5. To calculate postwar amounts of the industrial indicators produced or used, we go back to the prewar regressions of the

indicators on time and project or extrapolate the prewar figures into the postwar years. These regressions are calculated on the logged data. However, by calculating the antilogs of these figures, the expected values are again expressed in the same units as the actual untransformed data. Deviations from these expected values can be calculated by simply subtracting the expected values from the observed postwar values. The result will be negative if less iron were produced or energy consumed than would be expected. To normalize or control for the widely differing levels or amounts of these indicators for different nations, or the same nation across time, the deviations from the expected postwar values are then divided by the expected values for each year. The result is then a ratio comparable across time and nations. These ratios are then averaged for the ten years after the war, resulting in a mean deviation from expected postwar figures.

Combined References

Alger, Chadwick, and Steven J. Brams. "Patterns of Representation in National Capitals," *World Politics*, 19 (July 1967), 646–663.

Alker, Hayward, R., Jr., and Bruce Russett. *World Politics in the General Assembly.* New Haven, Conn.: Yale University Press, 1965.

Angell, Norman. *The Great Illusion.* New York: Putnam's, 1910.

Aron, Raymond. *Peace and War: A Theory of International Relations*, R. Howard and A. B. Fox, trans. New York: Praeger, 1968.

Azar, Edward E. "Conflict Escalation and Conflict Reduction in an International Crisis: Suez, 1956," *Journal of Conflict Resolution*, 16 (June 1972), 183–202.

Bailey, Norman T. J. *The Mathematical Approach to Biology and Medicine.* New York: Wiley, 1967.

Bakan, David. "The Test of Significance in Psychological Research," in Joseph Steger, ed., *Readings in Statistics for the Behavioral Scientist.* New York: Holt, Rinehart, and Winston, 1971, pp. 288–310.

Bandura, Albert. *Aggression: A Social Learning Analysis.* Englewood Cliffs, N.J.: Prentice-Hall, 1973.

Barber, Bernard. "Social Stratification," in David C. Sills, ed., *International Encyclopedia of the Social Sciences.* New York: Macmillan, 1968.

Barbera, Henry. *Rich Nations and Poor in Peace and War.* Lexington, Mass.: Heath, 1973.

Bell, Roderick, David V. Edwards, and R. Harrison Wagner. *Political Power: A Reader in Theory and Research.* New York: Free Press, 1969.

Berkowitz, Leonard. *Aggression: A Social Psychological Analysis.* New York: McGraw-Hill, 1962.

Beyer, William H., ed., *Handbook of Tables for Probability and Statistics,* 2nd ed. Cleveland: Chemical Rubber, 1966.

Bird, W. D. *The Direction of War: A Study of Strategy.* Cambridge, England: Cambridge University Press, 1920.

Bladen, Christopher. "Alliance and Integration," in Julian Friedman, Christopher Bladen, and Steven Rosen, eds., *Alliance in International Politics.* Boston: Allyn and Bacon, 1970, pp. 121-126.

Blainey, Geoffrey. *The Causes of War.* New York: Free Press, 1973.

Blalock, Hubert M., Jr. *Social Statistics.* New York: McGraw-Hill, 1960.

———. *Social Statistics,* 2nd ed. New York: McGraw-Hill, 1972.

Bloomfield, Lincoln C., and Amelia C. Leiss. *Controlling Small Wars: A Strategy for the 1970s.* New York: Knopf, 1969.

Bodart, Gaston. "Losses of Life in Modern Wars: Austria-Hungary and France," in Harald Westergaard, ed., *Losses of Life Caused by War.* Oxford: Clarendon Press, 1923, pp. 1-71.

———, and Vernon Lyman Kellog. *Losses of Life in Modern Wars.* Oxford: Clarendon Press, 1916.

Boulding, Kenneth E. *The Economics of Peace.* Englewood Cliffs, N.J.: Prentice-Hall, 1945.

———. "Towards a Pure Theory of Threat Systems," in David Edwards, ed., *International Political Analysis: Readings.* New York: Holt, Rinehart and Winston, 1970, pp. 100-111.

———, and Alan H. Gleason. "War as an Investment: The Strange Case of Japan," *Peace Research Society (International) Papers,* 3 (1965), 1-17.

Bremer, Stuart A. "Formal Alliance Clusters in the Interstate System: 1816-1965." Prepared for delivery at the Annual Meeting of the American Political Science Association, Washington, D.C., 1972.

Browning, Oscar. *Wars of the Century and the Development of Military Science.* Philadelphia: Linscott, 1903.

Bryce, James. "War and Human Progress," *International Conciliation* 108 (November 1916, entire issue).

Bueno de Mesquita, Bruce. "The Impact of Alliances on Industrial Development." East Lansing: Michigan State University, mimeo, 1973.

———. "Measuring Systemic Polarity," *Journal of Conflict Resolution*, 19 (June 1975), 187–216.

———, and J. David Singer. "Alliances, Capabilities, and War: A Review and Synthesis," in Cornelius P. Cotter, ed., *Political Science Annual: An International Review*, Vol. 4. Indianapolis and New York: Bobbs-Merrill, 1973, pp. 237–280.

Burton, John. *Conflict and Communication: The Use of Controlled Communication in International Relations*. New York: Free Press, 1969.

Butterworth, Robert L. *Managing Interstate Conflict, 1945–74: Data with Synopses*. Pittsburgh: Center for International Studies, 1976.

Calahan, H. A. *What Makes a War End?* New York: Vanguard Press, 1944.

Campbell, Donald T. "Common Fate, Similarity, and Other Indices of the Status of Aggregates of Persons as Social Entities," *Behavioral Science*, 3 (January 1958), 14–25.

———, and Julian C. Stanley. *Experimental and Quasi-Experimental Designs for Research*. Chicago: Rand McNally, 1969.

Caparaso, James A., and Alan L. Pelowski. "Economic and Political Integration in Europe: A Time Series Quasi-Experimental Analysis," *The American Political Science Review*, 65 (June 1971), 418–433.

Carr, Edward H. *The Twenty Years' Crisis*. London: Macmillan, 1939.

Carroll, Berenice A. "How Wars End: An Analysis of Some Current Hypotheses," *Journal of Peace Research*, 4 (1969), 295–323.

Cattell, Raymond B., and William Sullivan. "The Scientific Nature of Factors: A Demonstration by Cups of Coffee," *Behavioral Science*, 7 (April 1962), 184–193.

Choucri, Nazli, and Robert C. North. *Nations in Conflict: National Growth and International Violence*. San Francisco: Freeman, 1975.

Chow, Gregory C. "Tests of Equality Between Sets of Coefficients in Two Linear Regressions," *Econometrica*, 28 (July 1960), 591–605.

Clausewitz, Har Von. "On War," in Anatol Rapoport, ed., *On War*. Baltimore: Penquin Books, 1968, pp. 101–410.

Cline, Ray S. *World Power Assessment: A Calculus of Strategic Drift*.

Boulder, Colo: Westview Press, 1975.

Coleman, James S. *Introduction to Mathematical Sociology.* Glencoe, Ill.: Free Press, 1964.

Colson, Elizabeth. "Social Control and Vengeance in Plateau Tonga Society," *Africa,* 23 (July 1953), 199–212.

Corson, Walter H. "Conflict and Cooperation in East-West Relations: Measurement and Explanation." Paper presented at Annual Meeting of the American Political Science Association, Los Angeles, Calif., September 1970.

Coser, Lewis A. *The Functions of Social Conflict.* New York: Free Press, 1956.

———. "The Termination of Conflict," *Journal of Conflict Resolution,* 5 (1961), 347–353.

———. "Conflict: Social Aspects," in David L. Sills, ed., *International Encyclopedia of the Social Sciences,* Vol. 3. New York: Macmillan and Free Press, 1968, pp. 232–236.

Cottrell, Fred. *Energy and Society: The Relation Between Energy, Social Change, and Economic Development.* New York: McGraw-Hill, 1955.

Darmstadter, Joel. *Energy in the World Economy.* Baltimore: Johns Hopkins Press, 1971.

Davis, James. *Elementary Survey Analysis.* Englewood Cliffs, N.J.: Prentice-Hall, 1971.

Davis, Kingsley. "The Demographic Basis of National Power," in Monroe Berger et al., eds., *Freedom and Control in Modern Society.* New York: Van Nostrand, 1954, pp. 206–242.

Deutsch, Karl W. *The Analysis of International Relations.* Englewood Cliffs, N.J.: Prentice-Hall, 1968.

———, and J. David Singer. "Multipolar Power Systems and International Stability," *World Politics,* 16 (April 1964), 390–406.

Douhet, Guilio. *The Command of the Air,* Dino Ferrari, trans. New York: Coward-McCann, 1942.

Dumas, Samuel. "Losses of Life Caused by War, Part 1—Up to 1913," in Harald Westergaard, ed., *Losses of Life Caused by War.* Oxford: Clarendon Press, 1923.

Dumouchel, William H. "DREG Documentation," Ann Arbor, Mich.: Institute for Social Research, unpublished mimeo, n.d. (a).

———. "The Regression of a Dichotomous Variable." Ann Arbor, Mich.: Institute for Social Research, unpublished mimeo, n.d. (b).

East, Maurice A. "Status Discrepancy and Violence in the International System: An Empirical Analysis," in James N. Rosenau, Vincent Davis, and Maurice A. East, eds., *The Analysis of International Politics: Essays in Honor of Harold and Margaret Sprout.* New York: Free Press, 1972, pp. 299-319.

Enthoven, Alain C., and K. Wayne Smith. *How Much Is Enough? Shaping the Defense Program 1961-1969.* New York: Harper Colophon Books, 1972.

Ezekiel, Mordecai, and Karl A. Fox. *Methods of Correlation and Regression Analysis.* New York: Wiley, 1959.

Falls, Cyril. *The Art of War.* London: Oxford University Press, 1961.

Fedder, Edwin H. "The Concept of Alliance," *International Studies Quarterly*, 12 (1968), 65-86.

Feller, William. *An Introduction to Probability Theory and Its Application.* New York: Wiley, 1968.

Ferris, Wayne H. *The Power Capabilities of Nation-States.* Lexington, Mass.: Lexington Books, 1973.

Festinger, Leon. "The Analysis of Sociograms Using Matrix Algebra," *Human Relations*, 2 (April 1949), 153-158.

Foch, Ferdinand. *The Principles of War.* London: Chapman & Hall, 1918.

Forward, Nigel. *The Field of Nations: New Approaches to International Relations.* Glasgow: The University Press, 1971.

Fox, Daniel, and Kenneth Guire. *Michigan Interactive Data Analysis System (MIDAS).* Ann Arbor: Statistical Research Laboratory of the University of Michigan, 1972.

Friedman, Julian. "Alliance in International Politics," in J. Friedman, C. Bladen and S. Rosen, eds., *Alliance in International Politics.* Boston: Allyn and Bacon, 1970, pp. 3-32.

Fucks, W. *Formeln zur Macht.* Stuttgart: Deutsch Verlags-Anstalt, 1965.

Fuller, John F. C. *The Conduct of War, 1789-1961.* London: Eyre and Spottiswoods, 1961.

Galtung, Johan. "A Structural Theory of Aggression," *Journal of Peace Research*, 1 (1964), 95-119.

———. "East-West Interaction Patterns," *Journal of Peace Research*, 2 (1966) 146-177.

———. "Peace," in David L. Sills, ed., *International Encyclopedia of the Social Sciences*, Vol. 11. New York: Macmillan and Free Press, 1968, pp. 487-496.

German, F. Clifford. "A Tentative Evaluation of World Power," *Journal of Conflict Resolution*, 4 (1960), 138-144.

Gleditsch, Nils P. "Trends in World Airline Patterns," *Journal of Peace Research*, 4 (1967), 366–408.

Gochman, Charles S. *Status, Conflict and War: The Major Powers, 1820–1970*. Ann Arbor: University of Michigan, Ph.D. dissertation, 1975.

———. "Studies of International Violence: Five Easy Pieces?," *Journal of Conflict Resolution*, 20 (1976), 539–560.

Gordon, William I. "What Do We Mean by 'Win'?," *Military Review*, 46 (June 1966), 3–11.

Gulick, Edward V. *Europe's Classical Balance of Power*. New York: Norton, 1967.

Gurr, Ted. *Politimetrics*. Englewood Cliffs, N.J.: Prentice-Hall, 1972.

Guttman, Louis. "A General Nonmetric Technique for Finding the Smallest Coordinate Space for a Configuration of Points," *Psychometrika*, 33 (December 1968), 469–506.

Halperin, Morton. *Defense Strategies for the Seventies*. Boston: Little, Brown, 1971.

Hancock, W. K., and M. M. Gowing. *British War Economy*. London: Curwen Press, 1949.

Harbison, Frederick H., Joan Maruhnic, and Jane R. Resnick. *Quantitative Analysis of Modernization and Development*. Princeton, N.J.: Princeton University Press, 1970.

Hart, Hornell. "Logistic Social Trends," *American Journal of Sociology*, 50 (March 1945), 337–352.

Hays, William L. *Statistics*. New York: Holt, Rinehart and Winston, 1963.

———, and Robert L. Winkler. *Statistics: Probability, Inference, and Decision*. New York: Holt, Rinehart and Winston, 1971.

Healy, Brian, and Arthur Stein. "The Balance of Power in International History: Theory and Reality," *Journal of Conflict Resolution*, 17 (1973), 33–61.

Henderson, George F. R. *The Science of War: A Collection of Essays and Lectures, 1891–1903*, Neill Malcolm, D. S. O., ed. London: Longmans, Green, 1916.

Hobson, J. A. *Imperialism*. London: Allen and Unwin, 1938.

Holsti, Kal J. "Resolving International Conflicts: A Taxonomy of Behavior and Some Figures on Procedures," *Journal of Conflict Resolution*, 10 (September 1966), 272–296.

———. *International Politics: A Framework for Analysis*, 2nd ed. Englewood Cliffs, N.J.: Prentice-Hall, 1972.

Holsti, Ole R. *Content Analysis for the Social Sciences and Humanities.* Reading, Mass.: Addison-Wesley, 1969.

———, Richard Brody, and Robert North. "Measuring Affect and Action in International Reaction Models: Empirical Materials from the 1962 Cuban Missile Crisis," *Peace Research Society Papers*, 2 (1965), 170-190.

———, P. Terrence Hopmann, and John D. Sullivan. *Unity and Disintegration in International Alliances: Comparative Studies.* New York: Wiley-Interscience, 1973.

Hovland, Carl I. "Human Learning and Retention," in Stanley S. Stevens, ed., *Handbook of Experimental Psychology.* New York: Wiley, 1951, pp. 613-689.

Howard, Michael. *War and the Liberal Conscience.* New Brunswick, N.J.: Rutgers University Press, 1978.

Huntington, Samuel P. "Patterns of Violence in World Politics," in S. P. Huntington, ed., *Changing Patterns of Military Politics.* New York: Free Press, 1962, pp. 17-50.

Iklé, Fred C. *Every War Must End.* New York: Columbia University Press, 1971.

Ishii, G., and R. Hayakawa. "On the Compound Binomial Distribution," *Annals of the Institute of Statistical Mathematics*, 12 (1960), 69-80.

Jensen, W. G. *Energy and the Economy of Nations.* Cambridge, England: Cambridge University Press, 1970.

Johnson, Norman I., and Samuel Kotz. *Distributions in Statistics: Discrete Distributions.* New York: Houghton Mifflin, 1969.

Johnson, Stephen C. "Hierarchical Clustering Schemes," *Psychometrika*, 32 (September 1967), 241-254.

Jomini, Henri, Baron de. *The Art of War*, G. H. Mendell and W. P. Craighill, trans. Philadelphia: Lippincott, 1862.

Kahn, Herman. *On Thermonuclear War.* Princeton, N.J.: Princeton University Press, 1960.

———. *On Escalation.* Baltimore: Penguin Books, 1968.

Kaplowitz, Stan A. "An Experimental Test of a Rationalistic Theory of Deterrence," *Journal of Conflict Resolution*, 17 (September 1973), 535-572.

Kecsmeti, Paul. *Strategic Surrender: The Politics of Victory and Defeat.* Stanford, Calif.: Stanford University Press, 1958.

Keynes, John Maynard. *The Economic Consequences of the Peace.* New York: Harcourt, Brace, 1920.

Kissinger, Henry. *Nuclear Weapons and Foreign Policy.* New York: Harper, 1958.

Klingberg, Frank L. "Predicting the Termination of War," *Journal of Conflict Resolution,* 10 (June 1966), 129-171.

Knorr, Klaus. *Military Power and Potential.* Lexington, Mass.: Heath, 1970.

Kugler, Jacek. *The Consequences of War: Fluctuations in National Capability Following Major Wars, 1880-1970.* Ann Arbor: University of Michigan, unpublished Ph.D. dissertation, 1973.

Kuznets, Simon. *Postwar Economic Growth.* Cambridge, Mass.: Belknap, 1964.

———. *Modern Economic Growth.* New Haven, Conn.: Yale University Press, 1966.

———. *Toward A Theory of Economic Growth.* New York: Norton, 1968.

Lakatos, Imre. *Proofs and Refutations: The Logic of Mathematical Discovery.* Cambridge, England: Cambridge University Press, 1976.

Langer, William L. *An Encyclopedia of World History.* Boston: Houghton Mifflin, 1968.

Lankford, Philip M. "Comparative Analysis of Clique Identification Methods," *Sociometry,* 37 (June 1974), 287-305.

Larsen, Knud. "Aggression and Social Cost," *Peace Research Reviews,* 5. Oakville, Ont.: Canadian Peace Research Institute, 1973, pp. 1-76.

Leng, Russell J. "When Will They Ever Learn? A Study of Inter-Nation Behavior in Chronic Dyadic Conflict," American Political Science Association Chicago, August 1974.

———. *Coder's Manual for Identifying and Describing Internation Actions.* Middlebury, Vt.: Middlebury College, mimeographed, 1975a.

———. "The Diplomatic Historian vs. the Journalist: A Comparison of Two Event Data Sources," in D. Munton, ed., *Validity Problems with International Event Data.* 1975b.

———, and Robert Goodsell. "Behavioral Indicators of War Proneness in Bilateral Conflicts," in Patrick McGowan, ed., *International Yearbook of Foreign Policy Studies II,* Beverly Hills, Calif.: Sage, 1974, pp. 191-226.

———, and J. David Singer. "Toward a Multi-Theoretical Typology of International Behavior," in Mario Bunge et al. eds., *Mathematical Approaches to International Relations.* Bucharest: Academy of Social & Political Sciences, 1977, pp. 71-93.

Lenin, V. I. *Imperialism: The Highest Stage of Capitalism.* New York: International Publishers, 1939.

Lewis, W. Arthur. *The Theory of Economic Growth.* Homewood, Ill.: Irwin, 1955.

Liddell-Hart, Basil. *Deterrent or Defense.* New York: Praeger, 1960.

Lingoes, James C. "An IBM-7090 Program for Guttman-Lingoes Smallest Space Analysis," *Behavior Science*, 10 (April 1965), 183-184.

———. "Recent Computational Advances in Nonmetric Methodology for the Behavioral Sciences." International Symposium on Mathematical and Quantitative Methods in the Social Sciences, Rome, Italy, 1966.

———. "A General Survey of the Guttman-Lingoes Nonmetric Program Series," in Roger N. Shepard, A. Kimball Romney, and Sara Beth Nerlove, eds., *Multidimensional Scaling.* New York: Seminar Press, 1972, pp. 49-68.

Linton, Ralph. "The Prospect of Western Civilization," in Willard Walker, ed., *War in the Twentieth Century.* New York: Random House, 1940.

Liska, George. *Nations in Alliance: The Limits of Interdependence.* Baltimore: Johns Hopkins Press, 1962.

Lotka, Alfred J. *Elements of Mathematical Biology.* New York: Dover, 1956.

Mackinder, Sir Halford John. *Democratic Ideals and Reality.* New York: H. Holt, 1942.

MacRae, Duncan, Jr. "Direct Factor Analysis of Sociometric Data," *Sociometry*, 23 (December 1960), 360-371.

McClelland, Charles. *International Interaction Analysis: Basic Research and Some Practical Applications.* Technical Report #2, World Event/Interaction Survey, mimeo (November 1968a).

———. "Access to Berlin: The Quantity and Variety of Events," in J. David Singer, ed., *Quantitative International Politics.* New York: Free Press, 1968b, pp. 159-186.

McGowan, Patrick, and Howard Shapiro. *The Comparative Study of Foreign Policy.* Beverly Hills, Calif.: Sage, 1973.

McQuitty, Louis. "Elementary Linkage Analysis for Isolating Both Orthogonal Types and Typal Relevancies," *Educational and Psychological Measurement*, 17 (Summer 1957), 202-221.

Meadows, Donella et al. *The Limits to Growth.* New York: Universe Books, 1972.

Mesarovich, Mihajlo, and Eduard Pestel. *Mankind at the Turning Point.* New York: Dutton, 1974.

Midlarsky, Manus. "Status Inconsistency and the Onset of International Warfare." Evanston, Ill.: Northwestern University, unpublished Ph.D. dissertation, 1969.

———. *On War: Political Violence in the International System.* New York: Free Press, 1975.

Mihalka, Michael. "Discovering the Diplomatic Structure of the European State System," unpublished mimeo, 1974.

Miller, James G. *Living Systems.* New York: McGraw-Hill, 1978.

Modelski, George. "War and the Great Powers," *Peace Research Society (International) Papers,* 18 (1972), 45-59.

Morgan, James N., and Robert C. Messenger. *THAID: A Sequential Analysis Program for the Analysis of Nominal Scale Dependent Variables.* Ann Arbor: University of Michigan, Institute for Social Research, 1973.

Morgenstern, Oskar, and Klaus P. Heiss. *Long-Term Projection of Power: Political, Economic and Military Forecasting.* Cambridge, Mass.: Ballinger, 1973.

Morgenthau, Hans J. *Scientific Man versus Power Politics.* Chicago: University of Chicago Press, 1946.

———. *In Defense of the National Interest.* New York: Knopf, 1951.

———. *Politics Among Nations,* 5th ed. New York: Knopf, 1972.

Mowrer, O. Hobart. *Learning Theory and Behavior.* New York: Wiley, 1960.

Mumford, Lewis. *Technics and Civilization.* New York: Harcourt, Brace, 1934.

Nef, John U. *War and Human Progress.* Cambridge, Mass.: Harvard University Press, 1950.

Nicolson, Harold. *Diplomacy.* London: Galaxy Books, 1964.

North, Robert. "Perception and Action in the 1914 Crisis," *Journal of International Affairs,* 27 (1967), 16-39.

———, Richard Brody, and Ole Holsti. "Some Empirical Data on the Conflict Spiral," *Peace Research Society (International) Papers,* 1 (1964), 1-14.

———, and Richard P. Lagerstrom. *War and Domination: A Theory of Lateral Pressure.* New York: General Learning Press, 1971.

Northrop, F. S. C. *The Logic of the Sciences and the Humanities,* rev. ed. New York: World Publishing, 1971.

O'Connor, Raymond. "Victory in Modern War," *Journal of Peace Research,* 4 (1969) 367-385.

Ono, Giichi. *War and Armament Expenditures of Japan.* London: Oxford University Press, 1922.

Organski, A. F. K. *World Politics*, 2nd ed. New York: Knopf, 1968.
——, and Jacek Kugler. "The Costs of Major Wars," *American Political Science Review*, 71 (December 1977), 347-366.
Osgood, Robert E. *Alliances and American Foreign Policy*. Baltimore: John Hopkins Press, 1968.
Patterson, Ernest Minor. *The Economic Bases of Peace*. New York: McGraw-Hill, 1939.
Pfaltzgraff, Robert L., Jr. *The Atlantic Community: A Complex Imbalance*. New York: Van Nostrand, 1969.
Phillips, Warren R., Patrick Callahan, and Robert C. Crain. "Simulated Foreign Policy Exchanges: The Rationale Underlying a Theory of Foreign Policy Interaction," *International Interactions*, 1 (1974), 237-254.
Popper, Karl Raimond. *Conjecture and Refutations: The Growth of Scientific Knowledge*. New York: Basic Books, 1962.
Prest, A. P. *War Economics of Primary Producing Countries*. Cambridge: Cambridge University Press, 1948.
Rapoport, Anatol. *Fights, Games, and Debates*. Ann Arbor: University of Michigan Press, 1960.
Raser, John R. "Learning and Affect in International Politics," *Journal of Peace Research*, 2 (1965), 216-227.
Ray, James Lee. "Status Inconsistency and War Involvement Among European States, 1916-1970." Ann Arbor: University of Michigan, Ph.D. dissertation, 1974.
——. "Status Inconsistency and War Involvement in Europe, 1816-1970," *Peace Science Society (International) Papers*, 23 (1974), 69-80.
——. "System Structure and Global War." Paper presented to the Annual Meeting of the American Anthropological Association, Mexico City, 1974.
——, and J. David Singer. "Measuring the Concentration of Power in the International System." *Sociological Methods and Research*, 1 (May 1973), 403-437.
Richardson, Lewis F. *Arms and Insecurity: A Mathematical Study of the Causes and Origins of War*. Pittsburgh: Boxwood Press, 1960.
——. *Statistics of Deadly Quarrels*. Pittsburgh: Boxwood Press, 1960.
Ropp, Theodore. *War in The Modern World*, London: Collier Books, 1962.
Rosecrance, Richard. "Bipolarity, Multipolarity, and the Future," *Journal of Conflict Resolution*, 10 (September 1966), 314-327.

———. *International Relations: Peace or War?* New York: McGraw-Hill, 1973.

———, Alan Alexandroff, Brian Healy, and Arthur Stein. "Power, Balance of Power, and Status in Nineteenth Century International Relations." *Sage Professional Papers in International Studies.* Vol. 3, Beverly Hills, Calif.: Sage, 1974.

Rosen, Steven. "A Model of War and Alliance," in J. Friedman, C. Bladen and S. Rosen, eds., *Alliance in International Politics.* Boston: Allyn and Bacon, 1970, pp. 215–237.

———. "Tolerance of Human Life Costs for Foreign Policy Goals," *Peace Research Society (International) Papers,* 17 (1971), 61–73.

———. "War Power and the Willingness to Suffer," in Bruce M. Russett, ed., *Peace, War, and Numbers.* Beverly Hills, Calif.: Sage, 1972, pp. 167–183.

Rostow, Walt. *The Process of Economic Growth.* New York: Norton, 1962.

———. *Politics and the Stages of Growth.* Cambridge, Mass.: Harvard University Press, 1971.

Rothstein, Robert L. *Alliances and Small Powers.* New York: Columbia University Press, 1968.

Rule, Brendan G., and Elizabeth Percival. "The Effects of Frustration and Attack on Physical Aggression," *Journal of Experimental Research in Personality,* 5 (June 1971), 111–118.

Rummel, Rudolph J. "Testing Some Plausible Predictors of Conflict Behavior Within and Between Nations," *Peace Research Society (International) Papers,* 3 (1964), 79–111.

———. "The Relationship Between National Attributes and Foreign Conflict Behavior," in J. David Singer, ed., *Quantitative International Politics.* New York: Free Press, 1968, pp. 187–214.

———. *Applied Factor Analysis.* Evanston, Ill.: Northwestern University Press, 1970.

Russett, Bruce M. "The Calculus of Deterrence," *Journal of Conflict Resolution,* 7 (June 1963), 97–109.

———. "Components of an Operational Theory of International Alliance Formation," *Journal of Conflict Resolution,* 12 (1968), 285–301.

Rutherford, R. S. G. "On a Contagious Distribution," *Annals of Mathematical Statistics,* 25 (1954), 703–713.

Savage, I. Richard, and Karl Deutsch. "A Statistical Model of the Gross Analysis of Transaction Flows," *Econometrica,* 28 (July 1960), 551–572.

Schelling, Thomas C. *The Strategy of Conflict.* Cambridge, Mass.: Harvard University Press, 1960.

———. *Arms and Influence.* New Haven, Conn.: Yale University Press, 1966.

Scott, William A. "Rationality and Non-rationality of International Attitudes," *Journal of Conflict Resolution,* 1 (March 1958), 8-16.

Secerov, Slavko. *Economic Phenomena Before & After War.* London: George Routledge, 1919.

Shepard, Roger N. "Introduction to Volume I," in Roger N. Shepard, A. Kimball Romney, and Sara Beth Nerlove, eds., *Multidimensional Scaling.* Seminar Press, 1972, 1-20.

Shotwell, James T. *War as an Instrument of National Policy.* New York: Harcourt, Brace, 1929.

Shy, John. "The American Military Experience: History and Learning," *Journal of Interdisciplinary History,* 1 (Winter 1971), 205-228.

Singer, J. David. *Deterrence, Arms Control, and Disarmament: Toward a Synthesis in National Security Policy.* Columbus: Ohio State University Press, 1962.

———. "Inter-Nation Influence: A Formal Model," *American Political Science Review,* 57 (June 1963), 420-430.

———. "The Global System and Its Sub-systems," in James N. Rosenau, ed., *Linkage Politics.* New York: Free Press, 1969, pp. 21-43.

———. *A General Systems Taxonomy for Political Science.* New York: General Learning Press, 1971.

———. "The Peace Researcher and Foreign Policy Prediction," *Peace Science Society (International) Papers,* 21 (1973), 1-14.

———. "The Correlates of War Project: Continuity, Diversity and Convergence," in Francis W. Hoole and Dina A. Zinnes, eds., *Quantitative International Politics: An Appraisal.* New York: Praeger, 1976, pp. 21-42.

———. "System Stability and Transformation: A Global System Approach," *British Journal of International Studies,* 3 (1977), 219-232.

———, and Sandra Bouxsein. "Structural Clarity and International War: Some Tentative Findings," in Thomas Murray, ed., *Interdisciplinary Aspects of General Systems Theory.* Washington, D.C.: Society for General Systems Research, 1975, pp. 126-135.

———, Stuart Bremer, and John Stuckey. "Capability Distribution, Uncertainty, and Major Power War, 1816-1965," in Bruce Russett, ed., *Peace, War and Numbers.* Beverly Hills, Calif.: Sage, 1972, pp. 19-48.

———, and Melvin Small. "The Composition and Status Ordering of the International System: 1815-1940," *World Politics,* 18 (January 1966), 236-282.

———, and Melvin Small. "Formal Alliances, 1815-1939: A Quantitative Description," *Journal of Peace Research,* 3 (January 1966), 1-32.

———, and Melvin Small. "National Alliance Commitments and War Involvement, 1815-1945," *Peace Research Society (International)* Papers, 5 (1966), 109-140.

———, and Melvin Small. "Alliance Aggregation and the Onset of War, 1815-1945," in J. David Singer, ed., *Quantitative International Politics: Insights and Evidence.* New York: Free Press, 1968, pp. 247-286.

———, and Melvin Small. *The Wages of War, 1816-1965: A Statistical Handbook.* New York: Wiley, 1972.

———, and Melvin Small. "Foreign Policy Indicators: Predictors of War in History and in the State of the World Message," *Policy Sciences,* 5 (September 1974), 271-296.

Singer, Marshall R. *Weak States in a World Of Powers: The Dynamics of International Relationships.* New York: Free Press, 1972.

Singletary, Otis. *The Mexican War.* Chicago: University of Chicago Press, 1960.

Skinner, B. F. *About Behaviorism.* New York: Knopf, 1974.

Small, Melvin, and J. David Singer. "Formal Alliances, 1816-1965: An Extension of the Basic Data," *Journal of Peace Research,* 3 (1969), 257-282.

———, and J. David Singer. "Patterns in International Warfare, 1816-1965," *Annals of the American Academy of Political and Social Science,* 391 (1970), 145-155.

———, and J. David Singer. "Diplomatic Importance of States, 1816-1970: An Extension and Refinement of the Indicator," *World Politics,* 25 (July 1973), 577-599.

Smoker, Paul. "Analysis of Conflict Behaviors in an International Processes Simulation and an International System, 1955-1960," unpublished mimeo, 1968.

Snyder, Richard C., H. W. Bruck, and Burton Sapin. "Decision-Making as an Approach to the Study of International Politics," in

Richard C. Snyder, H. W. Bruck, and Burton Sapin, eds., *Foreign Policy Decision-Making: An Approach to the Study of International Politics*. New York: Free Press, 1962, pp. 14-185.

Sombart, Werner. *Krieg und Kapitalismus*. Leipzig: Duncher & Humbolt, 1913.

Sorokin, Pitirim A. *Social and Cultural Dynamics*, Vol. 3. New York: American Book, 1937.

Speier, Hans. *Social Order and the Risks of War*, New York: George W. Stewart, 1955.

Spykman, Nicholas John. *America's Strategy in World Politics*. New York: Harcourt, Brace, 1942.

———. *The Geography of Peace*. New York: Harcourt, Brace, 1944.

Starr, Harvey. *War Coalitions and the Distribution of Payoffs and Losses*. Lexington, Mass.: Lexington Books, 1972.

———. "An Appraisal of the Substantive Findings of the Correlates of War Project," in Francis W. Hoole and Dina A. Zinnes, eds., *Quantitative International Politics: An Appraisal*. New York: Praeger, 1976, pp. 99-127.

Stohl, Michael. "Linkages Between War and Domestic Political Violence in the United States, 1890-1923," in James A. Caparaso and Leslie L. Roos, Jr., eds., *Quasi-Experimental Approaches, Testing Theory and Evaluating Policy*. Evanston, Ill.: Northwestern University Press, 1973, pp. 156-179.

Sullivan, John. "International Alliances," in Michael Haas, ed., *International Systems: A Behavioral Approach*. New York: Chandler-Intext, 1974, pp. 99-122.

Taagepera, Rein. "Growth Curves of Empires," *General Systems Yearbook*, 13 (1968), 171-175.

Tanter, Raymond. "Dimensions of Conflict Behavior Within and Between Nations, 1958-1960," *Journal of Conflict Resolution*, 10 (March 1966), 41-64.

———. "International War and Domestic Turmoil: Some Contemporary Evidence," in Hugh Davis Graham and Ted Robert Gurr, eds., *The History of Violence in America*. New York: Praeger, 1969, pp. 550-569.

Taylor, A. J. P. *The First World War: An Illustrated History*. New York: Capricorn Books, 1972.

Torgerson, W. S. *Theory and Methods of Scaling*. New York: Wiley, 1958.

Vansant, Carl. *Strategic Energy Supply and National Security*. New York: Praeger, 1971.

Vedel-Pederson, Knud. "Losses of Life Caused by War—Part II, World War I," in Harald Westergaard, ed., *Losses of Life Caused by War.* Oxford: Clarendon Press, 1923, 132-182.

Voevodsky, John. "Quantitative Behavior of Warring Nations," *Journal of Psychology*, 72 (July 1969), 269-292.

von Riekhoff, Harald. "Status Inconsistency and the War Behaviour of Major Powers, 1815-1965." Conference on International Relations Theory, York University (Canada), 1973.

Wallace, Michael. *War and Rank Among Nations.* Lexington, Mass: Lexington Books, 1973.

———. "Status, Formal Organization and Arms Levels as Factors Leading to the Onset of War, 1820-1964," in Bruce M. Russett, ed., *Peace, War and Numbers.* Beverly Hills, Calif.: Sage, 1973, 49-69.

———. "Alliance Polarization, Cross-Cutting, and International War, 1815-1964: A Measurement Process and Some Preliminary Evidence," *Journal of Conflict Resolution*, 17 (1973), 575-604.

———, and **J. David Singer.** "Inter-Governmental Organization in the Global System, 1816-1964. A Quantitative Description," *International Organization*, 24 (Spring 1970), 239-287.

Waltz, Kenneth. *Man, The State, and War.* New York: Columbia University Press, 1959.

———. "The Stability of a Bipolar World," *Daedalus*, 93 (Summer 1964), 881-909.

———. "International Structure, National Force, and the Balance of World Power," *Journal of International Affairs*, 21 (1967), 215-231.

Whitman, J. E. A. *How Wars Are Fought: The Principles of Strategy and Tactics.* London: Oxford University Press, 1941.

Wickelgren, Wayne A. "Trace Resistance and the Decay of Long-Term Memory," *Journal of Mathematical Psychology*, 9 (November 1972), 418-455.

Wilkenfeld, Jonathan. "Domestic and Foreign Conflict Behavior of Nations," *Journal of Peace Research*, 1 (1968), 56-69.

Wood, David. *Conflict in the Twentieth Century.* (Adelphi Papers, no. 48). London: Institute for Strategic Studies, May 1968.

Worchel, Philip. "Displacement and the Summation of Frustration," *Journal of Experimental Research in Personality*, 1 (December 1966), 256-261.

Wright, Benjamin, and Mary Sue Evitts. "Direct Factor Analysis in Sociometry," *Sociometry*, 24 (March 1961), 82-98.

Wright, Quincy. *A Study of War*, 2nd ed. Chicago: University of Chicago Press, 1965a.

———. "The Escalation of International Conflicts," *Journal of Conflict Resolution*, 9 (December 1965b), 434–449.

Young, Leilyn M. " 'Win'–Its Meaning," *Military Review*, 46 (January 1966), 30–39.

Young, Oran R. *The Politics of Force: Bargaining in International Crises*. Princeton, N.J.: Princeton University Press, 1968.

Zinnes, Dina A. "The Expression and Perception of Hostility in a Prewar Crisis, 1914," in J. David Singer, ed., *Quantitative International Politics*, New York: Free Press, 1968, pp. 85–119.

Correlates of War Project Bibliography

I. Theoretical Orientation and Research Strategy

"Inter-Nation Influence: A Formal Model," *American Political Science Review*, 57 (June 1963) 420–430 [Singer]

"Multipolar Power Systems and International Stability," *World Politics*, 16 (April 1964) 390–406 [Deutsch and Singer]

"The Political Matrix of International Conflict," in McNeill, ed., *The Nature of Human Conflict*, 1965, 139–154 [Singer]

"Escalation and Control in International Conflict: A Simple Feedback Model," *General Systems*, 15 (1970) 163–173 [Singer]

"The Outcome of Arms Races: A Policy Problem and a Research Approach," *Proceedings of IPRA Third General Conference*, Oslo (1970) pp. 137–146 [Singer]

"Modern International War: From Conjecture to Explanation," in Lepawsky et al., eds., *The Search for World Order: Essays in Honor of Quincy Wright*, 1971, 47–71 [Singer]

"The Correlates of War Project: Interim Report and Rationale," *World Politics*, 24 (January 1972), 243–270 [Singer]

"Historiche Tatsachen u. Wissenschaftliche Daten am Beispiel der Erforschung von Kriegen," ("Historical Facts and Scientific Data in the Study of War") in Ludz, ed., *Soziologie und Sozialgeschichte: Aspekte und Probleme* (1973) 221- 241 [Small and Singer]

"The Future of Events Data Marriages: A Question of Compatibility," *International Interactions*, 2 (1975) 45- 62 [Leng]

"The Correlates of War Project: Continuity, Diversity, and Convergency," in Hoole and Zinnes, eds., *Quantitative International Politics: An Appraisal*, New York: Praeger (1976) 21- 66 [Singer]

"The Applicability of Quantitative International Politics to Diplomatic History," *The Historian*, 38 (February 1976) 281- 304 [Small]

"The Historical Experiment as a Research Strategy in the Study of World Politics," *Social Science History*, 2 (1977) 1- 22 [Singer]

"The Behavioral Approach to Diplomatic History," in de Conde, ed., *Dictionary of the History of American Foreign Policy*. New York: Scribner (1978) 66- 77 [Singer]

"Variables, Indicators, and Data in Macro-Political Research," in Deutsch, ed., *Methods of Political Behavior Research*. New York: Free Press (forthcoming) [Singer]

II. Constructing the Indicators and Generating the Data

"The Composition and Status Ordering of the International System: 1815- 1940," *World Politics*, 18 (January 1966) 236- 282 [Singer and Small]

"Formal Alliances, 1815- 1939: A Quantitative Description," *Journal of Peace Research*, 1 (1966) 1- 32 [Singer and Small]

"National Political Units in the Twentieth Century: A Standardized List," *American Political Science Review*, 62 (September 1968) 932- 951 [Russett, Singer, and Small]

"Formal Alliances, 1816- 1965: An Extension of the Basic Data," *Journal of Peace Research*, 3 (1969) 257- 282 [Small and Singer]

"Inter-Governmental Organization in the Global System, 1816- 1964: A Quantitative Description," *International Organization*, 24 (Spring 1970) 239- 287 [Wallace and Singer]

"Patterns in International Warfare, 1816- 1965," *Annals of American Academy of Political and Social Science*, 391 (September 1970) 145- 55 [Small and Singer]

"A Sociometric Analysis of Diplomatic Bonds, 1817-1940," East Lansing, Mich.: Events Data Conference, 1971 [Bremer]

"Formal Alliance Clusters in the Interstate System, 1816-1965," Washington, D.C.: APSA Meetings, 1972 [Bremer]

The Wages of War, 1816-1965: A Statistical Handbook, New York: Wiley, 1972 [Singer and Small]

"Measuring the Concentration of Power in the International System," *Sociological Methods and Research*, 1 (May 1973) 403-437 [Ray and Singer]

"Diplomatic Importance of States, 1816-1970: An Extension and Refinement of the Indicator," *World Politics*, 25 (July 1973) 577-599 [Small and Singer]

"Measuring Systemic Polarity," *Journal of Conflict Resolution*, 19 (June 1975) 187-216 [Bueno de Mesquita]

"Clusters of Nations in the Global System, 1865-1964," *International Studies Quarterly*, 19 (March 1975) 67-110 [Wallace]

"Toward a Multi-Theoretical Typology of International Behavior," in Bunge, Galtung, and Malitza, eds., *Mathematical Approaches to International Relations*, Bucharest: Romanian Academy (1977) 71-93 [Leng and Singer]

"Civil Wars, 1816-1976: A Typology and Tentative Population," Ann Arbor, Mich.: MHRI mimeo [Small et al.]

III. Testing Some Preliminary Models

"National Alliance Commitments and War Involvement, 1815-1945," *Peace Research Society (International) Papers*, 5 (1966) 109-140 [Singer and Small]

"Alliance Aggregation and the Onset of War, 1815-1945," in Singer, ed., *Quantitative International Politics: Insights and Evidence*, 1968, 247-286 [Singer and Small]

"Inter-Governmental Organization and the Preservation of Peace, 1816-1965: Some Bivariate Relationships," *International Organization*, 24 (Summer 1970) 520-547 [Singer and Wallace]

"Power, Status, and International War," *Journal of Peace Research*, 1 (1971) 23-35 [Wallace]

"Capability Distribution, Uncertainty, and Major Power War, 1820-1965," in Russett, ed., *Peace, War, and Numbers*, 1972, 19-48 [Singer, Bremer, and Stuckey]

"Status, Formal Organization, and Arms Levels as Factors Leading to the Onset of War, 1820-1964," in Russett, ed., *Peace, War, and*

Numbers, 1972, 49-69 [Wallace]

"Shared Memberships in Intergovernmental Organizations and Dyadic War, 1865-1964," in Fedder, ed., *The United Nations: Problems and Prospects*, 1972, 31-61 [Skjelsbaek]

Dimensions Historiques de Modeles Dynamiques de Conflict: Application aux Processus de Course aux Armements, 1900-1965, Geneva: Graduate Institute of International Studies, doctoral thesis, 1972 [Luterbacher]

"The Population Density and War Proneness of European Nations, 1816-1965," *Comparative Political Studies*, 6 (October 1973) 329-348 [Bremer, Singer, and Luterbacher]

"Alliances, Capabilities, and War: A Review and Synthesis," in Cotter, ed. *Political Science Annual*, 4 (1973) 237-280 [Bueno de Mesquita and Singer]

War and Rank Among Nations, Lexington, Mass.: Lexington Books, 1973 [Wallace]

"Alliance Polarization, Cross-Cutting, and International War, 1815-1964: A Measurement Procedure and Some Preliminary Evidence," *Journal of Conflict Resolution*, 17 (December 1973) 575-604 [Wallace]

Status Inconsistency and War Involvement among European States, 1816-1970, Ann Arbor: University of Michigan, doctoral thesis, 1974 [Ray]

"Status Inconsistency and War Involvement in Europe, 1816-1970," Peace Science Society (International) Papers, 23 (1974) 69-80 [Ray]

"Behavioral Indicators of War Proneness in Bilateral Conflicts," in McGowan, ed., *Sage International Yearbook of Foreign Policy Studies* II, 1974, 191-226 [Leng and Goodsell]

Probability Models of War Expansion and Peacetime Alliance Formation, Ann Arbor: University of Michigan, doctoral thesis, 1974 [Yamamoto]

"Structural Clarity and International War: Some Tentative Findings," in Murray, ed., *Interdisciplinary Aspects of General Systems Theory*, 1975, 126-135 [Singer and Bouxsein]

"Distance and International War 1816-1965," *Proceedings of the IPRA Fifth General Conference*, Oslo (1975) 481-506 [Gleditsch and Singer]

"The Incidence of Intervention in Interstate War, 1816-1965," Cambridge, Mass.: Peace Science Society (International) Meetings, 1975 [Cannizzo]

"From Bosnia to Sarajevo: A Comparative Discussion of Interstate

Crises," *Journal of Conflict Resolution*, 19 (March 1975) 3-24 [Sabrosky]

Status, Conflict, and War: The Major Powers, 1820-1970, Ann Arbor: University of Michigan, doctoral thesis, 1975 [Gochman]

"Effects of War on Industrial Growth," *Society*, 12 (May-June 1975) 48-52 [Wheeler]

The Effects of War on Industrial Growth, 1816-1965, Ann Arbor: University of Michigan, doctoral thesis, 1975 [Wheeler]

Capabilities, Commitments, and the Expansion of Interstate War, 1816-1965, Ann Arbor: University of Michigan, doctoral thesis, 1976 [Sabrosky]

"The War Proneness of Democratic Regimes," *Jerusalem Journal of International Relations*, 1 (Summer 1976) 49-69 [Small and Singer]

Costs of Combat: A Statistical Model for Predicting the Cost and Outcome of Interstate War, 1816-1965, Ann Arbor: University of Michigan, doctoral thesis, 1976 [Cannizzo]

"Hostilities in the European State System, 1816-1970," *Peace Science Society (International) Papers*, 1976 [Mihalka]

Interstate Conflict in the European State System, 1816-1970, Ann Arbor: University of Michigan, doctoral thesis, 1976 [Mihalka]

"Realpolitik, Arbitrations, and the Use of Force: The European Experience, 1816-1970." *Peace Science Society (International) Papers*, 27 (1977) 77-87 [Mihalka]

The Major Powers and the Pursuit of Security in the Nineteenth and Twentieth Centuries, Ann Arbor: University of Michigan, doctoral thesis, 1978 [Cusack]

"Systemic Polarization and the Occurrence and Duration of War," *Journal of Conflict Resolution*, 22 (June 1978) 241-267 [Bueno de Mesquita]

"Conflict in the International System, 1916-1977: Historical Trends and Policy Futures" in Kegley and McGowan, eds., *Challenges to America: United States Foreign Policy in the 1980s*. Beverly Hills, Calif.: Sage (1979) [Small and Singer]

"Periodicity, Inexorability, and Steersmanship in Major Power War," in Merritt and Russett, eds., *From National Development to Global Community* (forthcoming) [Singer].

"The Role of Arms Races in the Escalation of Disputes" *Journal of Conflict Resolution*, 23 (March 1979) 3-16 [Wallace]

"Capability Concentration, Alliance Bonding and Conflict among the Major Powers," in Sabrosky, ed., *Alliances and International Conflict* (forthcoming) [Champion and Stoll]

"Capability Distribution and Major Power War Experience," 1816-1965," *Orbis* (Winter 1978) 947-957 [Cannizzo]

IV. Practical Implications: Policy and Teaching

"Knowledge, Practice, and the Social Sciences in International Politics," in Palmer, ed., *A Design for International Relations Research*, Monograph 10, Philadelphia: American Academy of Political and Social Science (October 1970) 137-149 [Singer]

"Foreign Policy Indicators: Predictors of War in History and in the State of the World Message," *Policy Sciences*, 5 (September 1974) 271-296 [Singer and Small]

"The Peace Researcher and Foreign Policy Prediction," *Peace Science Society (International) Papers*, 21 (1974) 1-13 [Singer]

The Scientific Study of War, Learning Package Series, Number 14, New York: Consortium for International Studies Education of the ISA, 1975 [Bremer et al.]

"Early Warning Indicators from the Correlates of War Project," in Singer and Wallace, eds., *To Augur Well: Early Warning Indicators in World Politics*. Beverly Hills, Calif.: Sage (1979) 17-36 [Wallace]